P

'This book is a wonderful, funny, warm coming-of-age
memoir about finding your own path in life.
Long may she wobble'

*****

DAILY TELEGRAPH

'A very, very important book … I can't think of a work
that has so brilliantly expressed how a person disabled
from birth sees herself'

THE SUNDAY TIMES

'This illuminating, sharply-written page-turner is as
important as it is entertaining'

CHORTLE

'Very funny'

NEW STATESMAN

'Deeply personal … also a blistering critique of
the political and social forces that uphold this
damaging myth [of normality]'

MELBOUR

lot only funny but poigna

SYDNEY MORN

FRANCESCA MARTINEZ

WHAT THE **** IS NORMAL?!

1 3 5 7 9 10 8 6 4 2

Virgin Books, an imprint of Ebury Publishing,
20 Vauxhall Bridge Road,
London SW1V 2SA

Virgin Books is part of the Penguin Random House group of companies
whose addresses can be found at global.penguinrandomhouse.com

Penguin
Random House
UK

First published in the United Kingdom by Virgin Books in 2014
This edition first published in the United Kingdom by Virgin Books in 2015

www.eburypublishing.co.uk
A CIP catalogue record for this book is available from the British Library

ISBN: 9780753555354

Printed and bound by CPI Group (UK) Ltd, Croydon CR0 4YY

MIX
Paper from
responsible sources
FSC® C018179

To
Yaya and Yayo,
Mum and Dad,
Raoul
and
Kevin

I thank the universe every day
that I got to share my short time
on this bit of rock
with you.

CONTENTS

**** **** **

DISCLAIMER

* * * *

'Oh my God! You're disabled and you don't want to kill yourself? Inspire me now!'

Yep, most folk think that if a disabled person manages to achieve pretty much anything in their life beyond putting their own clothes on, taking a shower without the use of a pulley system, and undressing themself before bedtime at 7 p.m., then they are... An Inspiration. And if this plucky individual can combine one or more of these awe-inducing accomplishments (brushing their teeth, flushing the big loo handle, etc.) with a smile or – dare I say it – A Positive Attitude, then they're in imminent danger of being hailed as An Example To Us All.

With that in mind, it's always with some trepidation that I tell people that, as well as being disabled, I'm a comedian because then they really start to flip out. Okay, I go onstage and make strangers laugh. For a living. And I also happen to love life. Every single second of it. I don't want it to end.

Ever. I feel so incredibly lucky to inhabit a body and just be alive that, almost every day, I thank the universe that I am me and not, say, a sock. Or a pot of hummus.

Now, if we apply the popular equation:

Disability + Achievement + Positivity = Inspiration

then I might very well smash the Inspirometer, with a rating so huge not even a mathematician could write it down. This prediction is not based on arrogance but on the received wisdom that stand-up comedians are people of astounding courage. Add to that the idea of a disabled girl and – boom! – it's obscenely inspirational.

Alas, in my case, I have to admit from the outset that these results are highly misleading, so I advise you not to start thinking of me as motivational porn. Don't suddenly throw this book to the floor and – buoyed by the thought of my 'courage' as I wobble on to a stage to be greeted by a sea of hostile faces – go rushing off to arrange your first bungee jump. Because, the truth is, I'm small potatoes. And also because bungee jumping is stupid and dangerous! You see, that's how uninspiring I really am: bungee jumping terrifies me. Big time. The only way I'd consider dangling off a bridge with an elastic rope tied to my ankles is if someone I loved would be killed if I didn't. And I'd have to *really* love them. (And they couldn't be over eighty.)

I'm also terrified by thunder, lightning, big dogs (anything more than a poodle – and even they can be scary fuckers), bees, wasps, deep water, roller coasters, spiders, mice, rats, and dog poo.

Oh, and I sleep a lot. Which means that any 'inspiring' I might accidently pull off would have to take place during those few hours when I am not snoring or drooling. So, factor in twelve hours of sleep, plus time needed for washing, sitting on the loo, and using Facebook and Twitter, and that leaves about three and a half hours for activities that could potentially inspire. Which is pretty poor, frankly.

I once went to my GP to see if this devotion to sleep was linked to my wobbliness and if other people with the condition slept more than normal. 'There's no connection,' he said, 'you're just a lazy cow.' That's that mystery cleared up then.

I aim for twelve hours a night. Minimum. Anything less and I'm a zombie. I once heard that Margaret Thatcher slept for just four hours a night during her time as prime minister. Maybe that was why her politics were so inhumane – she was just cranky all the time. Perhaps right-wingers would be more empathetic if they spent more of their lives asleep. My politics are the opposite of Maggie's but, who knows, if I had to survive on four hours a night, maybe I'd want to destroy the unions too. Hey, maybe that's the alternative: get some bloody kip. It's possible that caring, humanist beliefs can only be held by people who sleep enough.

There'd certainly be fewer wars because everyone would be snugly tucked up in bed.

'Shall we invade Iraq?'

'Are you joking? I've only had eight hours!'

We'd also have destroyed a lot less of the planet because we wouldn't have been so active, and we wouldn't be facing runaway climate change because we'd have pumped far less carbon into the atmosphere. It's hard to generate tons of carbon dioxide from under a duvet. Who knew that such complex global problems could be resolved by a little more shut-eye?

Indeed, such is my commitment to sleep that not only do I indulge in it with reckless abandon, I encourage others to do so as well. Whenever I see someone under stress or unhappy, I advise them to sleep, to recharge, to rest. In short, I want everyone to do less and sleep more. So I am actually de-motivational. Sorry.

Right, that's that out of the way.

PROLOGUE

****

'**B**ut I'm not normal!' I looked at him defiantly, standing there in the middle of a pub in Soho.

'What do you mean?' His hair was the colour of dragonfly wings and his eyes, pale blue, stared at me and saw more than I wanted them to. I smiled to break the tension that was creeping slowly up the back of my neck. Tension that he seemed to embrace while waiting for me to speak, his eyes watching me with faint traces of amusement. I decided to go for it.

'I'm brain damaged.' The words shot out of my mouth, clumsy sounds that halted awkwardly in the air between us. After twenty years, they still made me jolt inside, and that annoyed me. Dylan's eyes didn't flicker.

'What do you mean?' His words sounded soft, calm, sensible, in stark contrast to the ugly ones I'd uttered that were still hanging, like dirty clothes, in front of me.

'I mean…' I meant what I said. I didn't want to say it again. Once should be enough. It wasn't.

'I mean… my brain was damaged. At birth… so…' The words couldn't even fall out awkwardly now. They just clogged up my throat like pieces of wet tissue. A few strands of the dragonfly hair fell in front of his eyes and a hand swept them away. I noticed then, suddenly, that he was beautiful. Astoundingly so. His beauty hit me in the stomach and I gulped.

'Who said your brain was damaged?'

'Er, the doctors?' Uncertainty had crept into my mind and was crouching there. An unwanted predator.

'The doctors.'

'Yes. They said I was… brain damaged.' I nodded as if to clarify the statement but I was unsure where this was going. 'And that caused my cerebral palsy.' I added this to try and sound as if it was no big deal, as if the rug was still firmly under my feet. Dylan took a sip of his beer. I looked at his lips. They were glistening.

'They're only words made up by other people. Sounds. Words that don't mean anything. You're not "brain damaged". You don't have "cerebral palsy". Those words are vague attempts to try and define you. Your brain is your brain and you are perfectly you.'

I let those ideas into my head one by one, each gingerly walking in with hesitant steps. All the people and the chatter and the grey smoke around me faded away and all I could see was Dylan. I fumbled for an answer in the new space I found myself in.

'But I'm… different.'

'Everyone's different.'

'I'm not normal.'

'Nobody's normal.'

'But people think I'm different.'

'How do you know what they think?'

'I don't. But I think they're thinking it.'

'But what you think they think is coloured by your own perception. Therefore, it's a pointless exercise. It will never lead anywhere.'

'But I want people to accept me.'

'Do you accept yourself?'

Silence.

'No.'

'Then you can't expect anyone else to.'

'So I shouldn't care what anyone else thinks?'

'The only opinion of you that matters, is yours.'

This hit me hard. In the gut, in my legs, in my arms, my feet. For the first time, I hated myself for hating myself.

'You mean, I can just… choose how to see myself? I don't have to be "disabled" or "brain damaged"? I can choose to be… me?'

Dylan drank more beer.

'If you want. The only power we have in life is the power to choose what to think.'

I laughed without wanting to, a bubble of joy escaping from me.

'So, I'm just… me.' I felt invigorated, as if I could see everything all at once.

'If anyone else wants to call you another label, that's up to them. But you choose how you see yourself. And that should be all that matters to you.'

I looked at his face, delicately marked by time, and glanced quickly at his eyes, which stared back at me calmly. He spoke once more.

'You are Francesca. Full stop.'

And that was the moment everything changed.

CHAPTER ONE

****

My first boyfriend was called Clint. I've always gone for the older man and he was nearly six. Scandalous, I know. Clint, as far as I could tell, was *hot*. There'd been several contenders for my heart but he'd won and we were now a proper couple. One of our favourite activities was playing with his He-Man Castle (not a euphemism), which impressed me greatly and which, I'm embarrassed to admit, was probably the main reason I chose him. When you're four, you don't need much more than a pair of sweet brown eyes and some way-cool action figures to knock you off your already shaky feet. Those He-Man sessions were great fun, always climaxing when we'd stop rattling our plastic figures at each other, rise on to our knees, lean over the top of Skeletor's lair, and kiss each other firmly on the lips, declaring 'I love you.' It took me many years to encounter that kind of romance again. But I'm getting way ahead of myself.

I'm wobbly. That's how I describe myself. Because the words 'cerebral' and 'palsy' are as attractive as an ingrowing toenail. With a fungal infection. The former evokes something cold, clinical, distant; the latter sounds like Shakespeare: *God's mercy! I have a palsy! The devil feasteth upon my face!* Or something like that. In short, 'cerebral palsy' is as far away from sexy as Rupert Murdoch is from a social conscience. (Okay, maybe not quite *that* far but you get my drift.) Does the medical world hold secret competitions to see who can concoct the label most likely to impede one's sexual relations forever? It's as if a party of highfalutin consultants take turns to pick words out of a tombola brimful of polysyllabic sibilants designed to induce pant-wetting dread at the very sound or sight of them. Disease, disorder, syndrome, dystrophy, sclerosis. (Not just one sclerosis: *multiple* sclerosis.) And I'm sure Mr Down was a really nice guy, but it's Sod's Law that he had such a bloody miserable name. Rainbow Syndrome would have been so much nicer.

So I'm not best pleased to have had this charming label stamped on me when I was just two years old. Athetoid Cerebral Palsy with Myotonia and Ataxia. I was a cute little girl with golden ringlets who had been branded a Doctor Who monster. Or a yoghurt drink '… NOW with added Myotonia and Ataxia!' I'm impressed that my parents, when gravely informed of my condition, didn't faint at the sheer awfulness of those words.

They were very much in love when my mother discovered she was pregnant. They were young students at university and, luckily for me, were delighted when I turned up one day in my mum's womb. I assume I was a happy foetus. I don't remember much about it. I guess that nine months of sleeping was pretty agreeable. My parents got married shortly before I was born, so as not to upset God. (Not true but it makes me laugh to think it.) On 6 August 1978, my mum went into a London hospital to give birth. She is a warrior woman (why didn't I get that gene?) and elected to have no drugs. Whatsoever. She was just nineteen and my dad was twenty-one, but they found themselves alone in a room with neither doctor nor nurse to be seen. It was a Sunday and the hospital was short-staffed because, as is well known, nobody is born on a Sunday. By this point I'd clearly had enough sleep and Mum went into labour while my poor panicking dad ran around the hospital to find someone – anyone – to help. (Perhaps the medics were busy coining new horror-names for disabilities.)

Eventually, he located a midwife and hurried her back to my mum who was trying desperately not to push. She immediately told Mum to start pushing, which she was more than happy to do and, miraculously, medical folk suddenly appeared everywhere. Within a few minutes, I was born. I'm sure my parents were very relieved to see me but the doctors looked nervous. I wasn't breathing and they whisked me away. I didn't take a breath for seven minutes. This is pretty impressive – now I can only hold it for about two minutes. Tops. The doctors got me breathing and I was handed back to my emotional parents who held me for the first time. Apparently, I looked just like my dad but bald, which, as a first image, is a tad disappointing. The only way is up, surely.

My mum was kept in overnight because they wanted to observe me. No specific reason was given and nothing out of the ordinary was said. Apparently, the only sign that something was up was when the doctor who tested the newborns' reflexes came back and did the test on me again. And again. And again. Clocking this but not knowing what to make of it, my mum pushed it to the back of her mind. A day later, the doctor handed me over and my parents could take me home, blissfully unaware of any 'complications'. Over the next few months, they noticed that their cute little girl (the 'bald geezer' look disappeared quickly, fortunately) was also, well, a bit floppy. I had trouble holding my head up and, as a one-year-old, I still couldn't sit up without being buttressed on either side by a mountain of pillows. At fourteen months, I was still crawling and shuffling around and nothing indicated that my nappy-clad bum would be leaving the floor any time soon.

Floppy or not, I was an incredibly happy baby. I was completely adored by my Spanish grandparents, Yaya and Yayo (the Catalan names we called them by), whose home in London we shared. For those unfamiliar with Spanish culture, *abuelas* and *abuelos* worship their grandchildren to the point of idolatry. If love was water I'd have drowned in an instant. If my mum had let them, they'd have whisked me off to Barcelona, had my ears pierced and paraded me around Las Ramblas like a floppy goddess. They hung on my every smile, gurgle and jerk.

I was so bloody loved, in fact, that I feel guilty now just thinking about it.

After the first eighteen months, in which they rarely left my side, my young parents were persuaded to have a romantic weekend in Paris. I waved them off, wedged happily in Yayo's solid arms. Apparently, I held court at a big party thrown in my honour and spent the evening surrounded by doting adults who hung on my every sound. While my mum cried all the way to Paris.

After months of assurances by various experts that I was fine, my parents were at last given a diagnosis in a bland hospital room when I was two. Apparently, my brain had been starved of oxygen at birth and part of it had died. The consultant not only walloped them with the Doctor Who moniker but also declared, with unshakeable certainty, that I was mentally retarded. This has proved not to be the case, as I have never watched *Top Gear*, read the *Sun*, or voted UKIP. But at the time, as you can imagine, it was a shock for my parents to hear their beloved only daughter diagnosed as physically and mentally disabled.

They left the hospital in a daze, trying to make sense of it all, while their little girl, ignorant of the verdict just pronounced on her, laughed and played all the way home. That evening my parents and grandparents decided that the doctor didn't know what he was talking about and that I was perfectly responsive and intelligent. The cloud that had loomed now lifted and my family were convinced that, while I might have the new name of a sci-fi monster, my intellect was intact. A return visit to the hospital for a second opinion confirmed their hunch. But this new doctor pronounced that I would still 'never lead a normal life'. Just what my young parents needed to hear.

I'm not quite sure what a normal life is. Surely everyone's life is normal to them? What I am sure of is my bemusement now at the ease with which these professionals make such weighty pronouncements. Words that take seconds to utter and decades to cast off. Unknown to me then, they disappeared into the ground around me and, over time, would emerge as the bars of a cage, hemming me in from the outside world. I would no longer be Francesca. I would be… different, faulty, an error, wrong, abnormal. A chain of negatives that would drag me down and make me flinch internally when I spoke them or even thought of them. I was also… wait for it, brain damaged! Yes, my brain, the most important part of me, is cock-arsed, crappy, mangled, blemished. If you'd received it from Amazon, you'd ask for a refund. Fab.

When I was old enough to understand it, I took an instant dislike to the word 'disabled'. It was a bodily thing, this resentment, a feeling somewhere deep in my bones that whoever I was and whatever I did would be overshadowed by this ugly tag that stuck to me like a label on a fruit, clumsily applied with thick stubborn glue. Eventually, I managed to peel it off, bit by bit, scratching at each piece until it was finally gone.

Of course, at the time, I wasn't aware of how terribly palsied my cerebrum was because I was too busy being a two-year-old, indulging in the joys of life, guzzling puréed apple and posing for the camera as I pooped in a potty. In fact, I felt anything but faulty, thanks to the shower of love that rained over me every day from my doting family. I don't want to blow my own trumpet but I was also devastatingly cute, with a killer combination of blonde ringlets, big smile and floppy limbs.

I didn't walk until I was three, which didn't bother me at all. Instead I filled the time reading books and doing jigsaw puzzles. I became so good at these that I could do them upside down, even without a picture to guide me. (We should have called Mensa.) Eventually, I struggled up off my behind and decided it was time to have a crack at this standing lark. I tottered across the living room to the delight of everyone in general and my mum in particular, whose back was relieved at the prospect of not having to lug me around any more. To this day, my relationship with gravity remains capricious, but those tottering steps opened up a new world to me and I felt indestructible. I thought I was capable of anything. My family had done such an incredible job of making me feel like the most cherished being on Earth that my self-confidence soared to ridiculous heights.

Striding (metaphorically, you understand) into infant school, aged four, I quickly won the admiration of the boys by marching across the playground to the forbidden bush, the one with the poisonous red berries, and plucking one as they looked on in awe.

'These can kill you if you eat them.' I paused, relishing the mix of fear and excitement in the wide eyes that peered back.

'Well, let's see about that!' And I popped the berry dramatically into my mouth, chewed it aggressively and swallowed it with a satisfied gulp. The boys stared intently, waiting for me to drop to the ground and writhe in agony. When it was clear that I had cheated death, they broke into cheers and I was their hero. I have since lost that strain of bravery/stupidity. In fact, if something in the fridge is a day over its best-before date, I have to call my mum, relay a detailed visual description of said product, and await her expert pronouncement. How times have changed.

The berry episode cemented my popularity with the guys and I became a tomboy. I promptly had my girly locks cut short and tried to adopt the swagger of a young lad. I must have been successful in my attempts because, once, in the local park, a man referred to me as 'sonny'. The grin didn't budge from my face for the rest of the day.

In my head, I was a tough, dungarees-wearing kid ready to climb any tree or perform any other scallywaggery. I know what you're thinking and you're right. Cerebral palsy and tree climbing are poor bedmates. Getting up was no problem but gravity seemed a lot more real when it was time to come back down. I had to be rescued more than once. The truth is, I forgot my physical limitations. As far as I was concerned, I was an intrepid explorer or a private detective or the survivor of a shipwreck. My imagination was far more real to me than the distant memory of some palsy or other. Really, I never considered it, mainly because there were better things to think about. Like boys. I started fancying boys probably about the same time I started eating solids. Boys were brilliant. They had no truck with annoyances like doing up buttons or tying shoelaces or any of that boring and unimportant stuff. And so I met Clint.

Clint was a great boyfriend. We were very committed to each other. So much so that, when he broke his ankle in PE one day and had to be taken off to hospital in an ambulance, I wept like a forlorn wife. I begged to be taken with him, pleading with the paramedics that I had a right to accompany him as I was His Girlfriend. My entreaties fell on deaf ears and, as the ambulance sped off, the tears flowed copiously while my teacher tried in vain to reassure me that a broken ankle was not life threatening. I can't remember why or how Clint and I broke up but it remains one of my less dysfunctional relationships and we remained friends, which, given that we were each barely half a decade old, is rather mature, I think.

For me, infant school had nothing to do with learning and everything to do with having fun. I had *no* desire whatsoever to sit down and be educated. I just wanted to play and I routinely made this abundantly clear to my despairing teachers. I discovered that flirting with the boys was a highly enjoyable pastime. I also wanted to put on plays and act. And that was it. Don't waste my time with maths and writing, teachers! I'm not interested. That was all too passive and boring and *rubbish*. Imagine my utter delight, then, when my teacher announced that the school play was to be Goldilocks and, thanks to the ringlets, I would be playing the lead! My joy quickly dissipated, however, when I found out that the eponymous character had only one line in the entire play. One line?! That changed everything. I marched up to my teacher and told him that I was not happy. Not Happy At All. With a sigh, he led me into an empty classroom where I sat on a table and crossed my arms defiantly.

'Why don't you want to be Goldilocks, Francesca?' His tone tried to mask his annoyance.

'Because she only has one line!' said I, as if it was the most obvious thing in the world.

'But it's a very important line.' He smiled to placate me. He failed.

'I don't care. I want more lines!' I looked him right in the eyes. No negotiating. He proceeded to offer me every other role apart from the two main ones. I turned them all down. Unequivocally.

'I want the main part.' He stared back at the wobbly diva sat in front of him.

'Francesca, we've already given those two parts to other people so we can't give them to you. That wouldn't be fair, would it?' Annoyingly, my sense of fairness made my head shake.

'The thing is, Goldilocks is still the star of the show. The whole play revolves around her.' My eyes flickered at the word 'star'.

'Really?' I said, not yet convinced.

'Yes, she's the heart of the play and you're the perfect person to play her.' The compliment was duly noted and accepted with a momentary smile.

'So, I'll be the star of the play?'

'Yes, Francesca, you'll be the star.'

'Okay, I'll do it.' I slid off the table and shook his hand. I think he shook his head. Where this barefaced ambition came from, I cannot say. (Such levels of self-belief are not supposed to be found among the palsied.)

I could hardly contain my excitement in the lead up to the week of performances. I was disappointed to discover that the costume consisted of a sparkly dress and some bright red ribbons in my hair but even this sartorial display of femininity didn't dampen my tomboyish spirits. The prospect of speaking in front of all those people made my heart beat faster and I couldn't wait to deliver my (one and only) line. On the night of the first performance, I counted down the minutes to my big entrance. A transformed school hall was packed with parents and siblings who sat on benches surrounding the centre, which was now a stage where dragons and monsters and fairies traipsed in and out. Finally the big moment arrived and I walked on, full of focus and having (like any actor worth their chops) worked out exactly what my motivation was. I savoured the electricity that the audience generated with their eyes before I delivered my line. *The* line.

'I…' – the pause was dramatic and I held it, knowing it would allow me to remain in the spotlight a little longer – '… ate all the tarts.' And then it was over. But I was hooked. I had not a single doubt that I was going to be an actor. I declared this to my parents shortly afterwards and, because they come from families of writers and artists, this was greeted with a wave of enthusiasm.

Once I'd made my decision, I became even less inclined to engage in academia, proclaiming to my teacher a loud 'oh, no!' whenever he announced that maths would follow lunch. I apologise to any mathematicians reading this but I had and still have no interest in numbers. None whatsoever. To this day, I am baffled by the five hours of maths a week that I had to endure. Beyond the simple arithmetic that I felt I'd clearly mastered by four and a half, I couldn't understand this numerical obsession. There were some (weird) kids who did seem to enjoy this ludicrous subject and I was more than happy for them to indulge in their peculiar fetish. They could do it all day and all night for all I cared. I just didn't want to be in the vicinity when they did it. I thought (and still do) that unless you want to be a mathematician or scientist, the amount of maths we are forced to endure is completely out of proportion to its usefulness in most people's lives. I doubt David Beckham is very familiar with Pythagoras or his blasted theorem but *he* seems to have done all right. It's not that I lacked interest in all learning, it's just that I was absorbed by people and nature and play and laughing and all those things which the doing of maths seemed to murder ruthlessly. I loved reading, no doubt because I'd had a lot of time to do it in my three years of not walking.

Once my career choice had fallen into place, it was patently clear that playtime was the sole logical reason to attend school. These golden breaks were opportunities to further my acting talents in hurriedly produced plays in which, by remarkable coincidence, I always had the main part. With my group of friends always willing to throw themselves into these epic productions, it was delightful to be able to scratch my performing itch every day. Once, I was so enthralled that I refused to go back to class at the end of playtime.

'I'm not going in!' I looked up at the teacher, who towered over me.

'Why not?' his eyes appealed to me.

'Because it's boring and I want to play.' My honesty could not be faulted. He looked unsure of what to say.

'But it's time for class. You have to come in.' I didn't move.

'Nah. I'm gonna stay here and play.' He stared at me.

'Okay.' And he walked away followed by my class. The empty playground stared back at me like a thrown gauntlet. I couldn't believe my luck. Wow, that was easy, I thought. Determined to make the most of my suddenly eerily silent situation, I tried to play on my own. It was a lot less enjoyable than I'd expected. I lasted ten minutes perhaps, before reluctantly admitting that a crucial aspect of play was having other people to do it with. Somewhat disheartened, I headed back to the classroom and opened the door. Everyone turned around and the teacher looked up with the vaguest intimation on his face of a smile of victory.

'Oh, you've decided to join us, have you?' I could sense a thin veil of disappointment descending over my classmates as it dawned on them that the maverick who had taken on authority and won had been beaten.

'Yeah, I got bored,' I answered, as nonchalantly as possible in an attempt to recover the shreds of my reputation.

In keeping with the tomboy outlook, I begged my parents to give me a brother. Not a baby, you understand. A brother. I was desperate for a partner in crime, a constant companion who wouldn't have to go home when it was time for bed. But I also wanted someone who would be a focus for my maternal feelings. Yes, despite framing myself as one of the boys, I was also ridiculously empathetic. This trait had revealed itself on a visit to London Zoo. Five hours after returning home, I was still crying my eyes out at the memory of all the animals locked up in their cages.

'What if I had to live in a cage? I'd be so sad!' I keened to my mum, the tears running down my face. Mum, a vegetarian, clearly felt my pain.

'Yes. I'd be sad too.' Her candour was appreciated but did little to ease the turbulent emotions racing around my body.

'I wish we could let them all out. I'd like them to be able to run free even if I never saw them. Especially the poor cheetahs...' And off I went again. The thought of those cheetahs being unable to run wild – which I'd been told they love to do – was too much to bear and I sobbed freely in my mother's arms. Needless to say, the zoo was off limits for years. It was from this highly emotional core that I yearned to have a baby brother to care for and, no doubt, to cry over when the time called for it. Happily, my parents wanted another child too. Indeed, they would have had one sooner had they not figured that a sibling would all-too-quickly overtake me in the walking, buttoning and shoelace-tying department. One day, my dad, just twenty-six at the time, stopped by the bathroom door.

'Guess what, Chessie? We have some news.' I stared at him, smiling. I loved surprises.

'What?' Excitement reared its head in my tummy.

'Mummy's pregnant.' I turned to look at my mum who, at twenty-four, was beaming and beautiful.

'YESSSSS!' The happiness pushed the word out before I'd even realised.

'Are you happy?' asked my mum, despite knowing the answer.

'YES! Will it be a boy?' I gazed up at them, hopefully.

'We won't know until it's born,' my dad answered. I pondered this for a moment.

'It will be a boy. I want a brother.' And that was that.

Understandably, given the experience that had attended my arrival, mum opted to have her second baby at home. Again, with no drugs. On 22 September 1983, I was given the choice between coming home after school and being there for the birth or going to play at my best friend Nancy's house. I opted for Nancy. Nancy lived up the road and I happily went off with her after school. That afternoon, my mind occasionally deigned to wander over to what was happening back home before I yanked it away and got back to the important business of play. When the doorbell rang, I rushed to the stairs and began to bump-bump down the steps on my bottom. I was halfway down when Nancy's mum opened the door to reveal my dad grinning widely. Beating me to it, she asked him if it was a boy or a girl. Catching my eye, he told us it was a boy. Nancy's mum started crying and I started laughing.

'I knew it!' I bumped the rest of the way down and rushed over to him.

'Do you want to meet your baby brother?' he offered, with a hug.

'Yes!' I squealed.

We left Nancy and her mum still in tears, jumped into the car and rushed home. I crept upstairs, aware of a new and delicate presence in the house. The bedroom door was open. I walked in slowly and saw my mum, tired but glowing, lying on the bed with a blue bundle in her arms. It was so peaceful. Suddenly feeling self-consciously big, I walked up to the bed and climbed carefully on to it.

'It's a boy!' I said, thankfully, as I peered at the little crumpled face that stuck out of the blanket. He was perfect.

'What's he called?' I asked my mum.

'Raoul,' she said with a smile.

'Raoul,' I said, for the first time, letting my mouth get used to the sound. 'Raoul.'

'You didn't call him Mickey after Mickey Mouse, then?' I enquired, somewhat disappointed. Mickey Martinez had quite the ring to it, I'd thought.

'No, we didn't,' said Mum, gently. 'Do you want to hold him?'

Nervously, I took Raoul in my arms and looked into his tiny blue eyes. That was all it took for me to adore him and, to this day, it remains one of the best moments of my life.

The arrival of my new brother had to be shared with anyone who would listen. I decided that it warranted a formal announcement during school assembly and waited with bated breath for the head teacher to introduce me, experiencing the same buzz of anticipation that I'd felt before my recent debut. I stood up and addressed the hall.

'I have a new baby brother and he's called Raoul.' The pride flowed out of me like rays of sunshine. The hall began to clap. I could get used to this, I thought. I went home and asked Mum to have another baby, possibly three or four more. She looked at me through sleep-starved eyes and told me that I should be happy with Raoul. Deflated, I realised I'd have to find other ways to take the spotlight and bask in applause. Ways that didn't include the creation of a human being. Back to the drawing board.

Hope glimmered when it was announced that there was to be a school concert given by those students who played the recorder. Despite the level of manual dexterity required to play this 'instrument' (a twig with notions, if you ask me), I had enthusiastically taken it up. By which I mean, I'd blow heavily into it as my fingers flailed about without rhyme or reason. Spare a thought for my poor parents, tortured daily by the cacophony of squawks and squeals. Discordance doesn't come near it. I was vaguely conscious that my fingers weren't up to the task but I did manage to bash out something not too far removed from Frère Jacques. And that was enough to satisfy me. I fricking loved that tune. So what if it was the only one I could 'play'? Who needs more than one tune? Especially when playing the recorder meant that you got out of class. That sealed the deal for me and I threw myself into concert practice with gusto. The new tunes were more complex but a small thing like piss-poor coordination wasn't going to get in the way of my confidence. I never thought about having to play in tune. No. All I saw was the being onstage bit. How cool! A month of intense practice followed in which we all played our little hearts out in a vain attempt not to emulate the strangling of a pack of cats. It paid off though, because, as I sat and listened to the group the day before the concert, I thought they sounded brilliant. That I wasn't joining in, had momentarily escaped my attention.

The following morning I turned up, sporting a special outfit for the musical extravaganza. Our teacher led us through the songs once more and finished with a stirring speech to inspire us and combat any nerves. Why would anyone be nervous, I thought. It's going to be amazing! I was the last in line as we filed out of the music room when, as I reached the door, the teacher put his hand on my arm.

'Francesca.' Something in his voice made me feel uneasy. I stopped.

'What?' I gripped my recorder tightly with both hands.

'Erm… the thing is, you can't be in the concert today.' His eyes flashed away from me.

'Why not?' I asked. My lower lip wanted to tremble but I stopped it. Just.

'Well, your fingers aren't fast enough to play the tunes properly.' He looked sad.

'But I can play Frère Jacques.' He looked unconvinced but let that go, which was magnanimous of him.

'We're not playing that today, though, are we?'

I thought this over and shook my head. I didn't want to say anything because I knew I would cry if I opened my mouth.

'Are you okay?' he asked quietly. I nodded.

'Would you prefer to stay here during the concert?' I nodded again, and sat down. The floor turned blurry and I blinked out a tear. Maybe I could persuade my mum to have another baby after all.

I quickly recovered from the devastation of Recorder-Gate and soon forgot that there was anything slow about my fingers. Aside from the ongoing battle to avoid maths (usually climaxing with an impassioned 'but that's what calculators are for!'), I couldn't have been happier. I'd decided that Raoul was objectively the most beautiful baby ever born. I decided also that it was my duty as his big sister to protect him from life's dangers by carrying out such brave acts as carefully diverting a woodlouse that had unwisely chosen to venture within thirty centimetres of him. Raoul was a constant source of delight to me and I could not understand my friends who were sometimes jealous of their new siblings.

'Why would I be jealous of him? I love him!' I would tell them.

'Because they get all the attention!' they would reply with serious faces. I didn't share their worries or resent Raoul's existence. Not the tiniest bit. I don't attribute this to any innate wisdom in me but to my Spanish grandparents who, despite now living a few streets away from us, were close enough to smother me with enough love and attention to stem any potential pangs of jealousy. In return for their unwavering devotion, I worshipped them back. I loved spending time with them. Yayo and Yaya left the discipline stuff to my parents and spoiled me rotten. I could eat chocolate any time of the day and I was even given something called Coke, which was brown, fizzy and disgusting. I loved it.

But even better than having sugar-loaded treats always at my disposal was that they made me feel not just normal but special. I still considered both myself and my life to be normal. Yes, I knew I was wobbly and struggled with certain annoyances like buttons but these were peripheral obstacles (and I soon discovered that Velcro sorted that problem out). In fact, I brushed aside any task that proved to be physically challenging, as if it were a momentarily bothersome insect. Once it was gone, it ceased to exist because I was too busy enjoying everything life had to offer. I didn't know that I was 'disabled', in the sense that I didn't feel it or want to feel it. That word was a bad word, something ominous and depressing, so I didn't think about it. At all. I just got on with doting on my new brother, and playing football. And Knock-down Ginger. That's the game where you ring someone's doorbell and run away. Yes. *Run* away. You'd think I might have wondered whether I was cut out for it. You'd think I could have accepted philosophically that it was not designed for the likes of me. You'd think I'd have figured out more appropriate methods by which to annoy my neighbours. Instead, without the merest whiff of a doubt in my mind, I decided it was my new favourite game. And, once again, I led my loyal group of local boy friends in this exciting adventure.

As the only girl in the gang, I occupied an exalted

position. Keen to retain their admiration, I volunteered to ring the first bell. I pressed it, turned around and, only then, realised that a quick escape might be beyond my competence. For a moment, reality collided with my iron-clad self-perception and I remembered that I wasn't as fast as I wanted to be. I felt a sharp prick of disappointment. But, by the time I'd slowly but safely staggered down the road, the reality of my abilities had quietly slipped away again, obliterated by the cheers of the boys whose faces were flushed with childish excitement at my act of daring. My luck held: I rang lots of bells and managed each time to 'scarper' before an irate grown-up could tell me off.

It couldn't last. When I was nine, the family visited an old friend called Herman on his estate in West London. (Estate as in council, not Lord and Lady's.) Herman had, as always, cooked an amazing dinner but Raoul and I were itching to play outside with the local kids. Leaving the grown-ups to their conversation, we scampered out.

'I know a game,' said I, with a glint in my eye. 'Let's ring on doorbells and run away!'

Raoul, still angelically perfect in my eyes, was in the middle of a naughty phase and immediately agreed. The other two kids concurred. The location was hardly conducive to the game as it was, essentially, a small courtyard with four doors opening on to it, offering, therefore, nowhere to hide. But, true to my signature short-termism, I didn't let that get in the way. Raoul (at four already faster than me) went first, picking a door, pressing the bell and then shooting back to Herman's flat where we all waited, giggling uncontrollably. This was *fun*. Next up, it was my turn and I picked the door right next to Herman's flat. A daring choice but that's how I rolled. I pressed the bell firmly, turned to step off the concrete doorstep and discovered with some annoyance that I was slower than expected. I even paused to wonder why my legs weren't moving faster. A second later, the door flew open and an arm grabbed me. My bravado melted and I screamed in shock. A hairy, tired-looking man stared at me.

'I'm a policeman and I work nights and YOU'VE just woken me up!' he growled.

I decided the best riposte to this was to pee in my pants. And down my leg. And on to my shoe. My parents came out to see what the hullabaloo was about and I apologised to the man. He also apologised to me, perhaps softened by the vista of the little girl standing in a pool of her own wee-wee. Game over.

I was led inside to Herman's spare room where my mum took off my wet trousers, knickers and socks. Not having anticipated a change of clothes for the dinner party, she went to look for possible options. A minute later, she returned with a pair of Herman's neatly pressed white Y-fronts. I reluctantly pulled them on. And there I forlornly stood. My mum probably realised that that was all the punishment I needed. I never played the game again.

There's nothing quite so effective as having to wear an old man's Y-fronts knotted at the waist to remind you that you that can't run fast, however much you want to.

CHAPTER TWO

* * * *

The nun looked angry.

'What have I told you about running round the school during lunchtime?'

I pretended to look scared.

'Sorry. We won't do it again,' I said, sheepishly. We did.

Shortly before I turned seven, I left Salusbury Road infant school and started at a bilingual Spanish and English junior school in Portobello. My parents hoped that it would facilitate my further learning of Spanish. They hadn't foreseen that it would also facilitate my terrorising of old nuns. The school had been a convent and I was intrigued by these fascinating creatures who stalked the school corridors like imperious ghosts. I grew up in a non-religious family, so the nuns seemed almost mythical figures to me. Not so mythical that I obeyed their commands, you understand, but in the sense that I could hardly believe they existed. Someone told me once that they weren't allowed to have boyfriends. I couldn't believe it. I looked on them with pity. Still prone to daydreaming about my afternoon trysts with Clint, I was sorry that they'd never know what it's like to be kissed by a boy. I wondered if they'd any idea what they were missing and if they cried into their nun-pillows at night. I'd already made a new group of boy pals and my two best friends were called Angel and Ramon. We quickly became an inseparable trio and I suspect I was in love with both of them at the same time and that they were in love with me. Sister Inmaculada would have been scandalised.

The school was old and huge. It was amazing: it went on for ever, stairs leading to rooms leading to corridors leadings to stairs. For three excitable seven-year-olds, it was virgin territory (no pun intended) crying out for exploration. However, for some important yet unspecified reason, it was Absolutely Forbidden to be in the building during lunchtime, so everybody was ushered outside into the grey, boring playground, and the big doors boomed shut behind us. No matter! Decreeing something as forbidden just fuelled the determination of me and my Spanish partners-in-crime to investigate. Just before the lunch bell, we'd sneak out of the classroom, run upstairs, then along a musty wooden corridor, and we were away. Every day we'd explore a new part of the building and pick a spot to sit down in and have our lunch. The rooms and halls and stairs were dark and woody, giving it a formal and intimidating air, which we loved. The eerie atmosphere hung like billowing sheets in the disused rooms. It made us giggle with that spicy delight that is tinged with a drop of terror. We tried to scare each other, finding dusty old cupboards to leap out from with a roar. It was the perfect way to pass the time and each morning I itched for it to come around, sharing conspiratorial glances with Angel and Ramon. One day, inevitably, we came tearing around a corner and crashed into our disapproving nun. The hardest part was trying not to giggle. We were summarily shooed out and the heavy door shut resolutely behind us. I bet Sister Inmaculada was just jealous that I got to hang out every day with my two hot amigos.

If it was possible, I felt even happier than I had at Salusbury School. With a double-dose of boy-candy and a whole new world to explore, my confidence rose like a high tide. My body served me well in these rambling escapades and long gone were any worries about the tricky realities of wooden instruments. Each day was a tantalising mix of adventure and laughter and mischief, all of which I was convinced were the prime ingredients of life. And in my tummy lay the giddy feeling of invincibility. I could do anything.

We were taught in Spanish one day and English the next. It was a great way to develop your language skills. My parents and I had lived with Yayo and Yaya until I was three, so we had spoken in Spanish at home and I'd soaked it up. Also, my mum had lived in Spain for eight years when she was young, so she was fluent too and it made sense that, although my understanding of Spanish was pretty good, I ought to improve my speaking skills beyond 'Quiero chocolate y Coca-Cola'.

What made less sense was the religious aspect of the school. Yayo's father had been tortured to death by

Franco's army in the Spanish Civil War and Yayo himself had fought against Franco before he spent three years in a prisoner of war 'rehabilitation' camp doing slave labour. Unsurprisingly, Yayo's attitude towards a Church that had backed Franco (not to mention various other repressive and violent regimes around the world) was less than enthusiastic. I think Yayo was amused by the reports he received of his little granddaughter having regular run-ins with agitated nuns. He may even have felt a spark of pride. My parents shared his suspicion of organised religion, so it was agreed that when the nuns gave their twice-weekly lessons on Jesus, I would be allowed to step out. This was welcome news to me and I couldn't believe my parents were behind it. Re-sult! I asked my mum why I was allowed to miss religion, and further suggested that they might consider removing me from maths too. Turned out, the Bible was a bunch of made-up stories that I didn't have to learn about but maths was 'important'. Damn! I asked my friends what they talked about in religion class and I wondered why the nuns were allowed to love Jesus. Wasn't he a man? (Years later, I would meet a very cool nun called Maeve. She was totally different from the nuns who frowned upon my daily antics.)

My other grandparents were quite fond of Jesus, and that Christmas they invited my mum, her four sisters, and their families to Spode, an old country house in Staffordshire that was run by an order of Christian brothers, where Catholic families could stay and do art-and-craft classes. I'm sure my dad was over the moon at the prospect of spending a whole week surrounded by his eccentric in-laws in the middle of nowhere. Actually, it turned out to be a lot more fun than it sounds.

The undisputed highlight of the trip for me was the present-giving ceremony. This took place in the grand entrance hall which was packed with excited families and kids eager to get their hands on those long-awaited pressies. I sat with my family, looking at an impressive Father Christmas standing halfway up the imposing marble staircase.

'Now, before we start,' boomed his deep voice across the hall, 'I need an assistant. Someone who can help me give out my presents. Who wants to be Santa's little helper?' I leapt out of my chair and stretched my hand up as far as it would go.

'Me! Me! Please!' I nearly dislocated my shoulder. Poor Santa had no choice but to invite the over-eager screamer on to the stage. I trembled with excitement as I carefully climbed up to him and stopped next to the tantalising gift-sack.

'And what's your name, little girl?' asked Santa, bending over to shake my hand.

'I'm Francesca and I'm seven,' I answered, remembering to project. 'How old are you?' The audience laughed.

'Eh, I'm sixty-six,' said Santa, taken aback at this impertinence.

'You look a lot older than that!' I said, with a grin. A wave of laughter swept around the room. This is amazing, I thought. I'm onstage and I can talk as much as I want! I

43

was starting to like this Jesus guy; here I was, performing to a hundred people, all because of him.

'Right, Francesca, let's get on with the presents, shall we?' Santa, it seemed, had had enough discussion about his age. He took the first present out of the bag, handed it to me and opened his mouth to speak but was beaten to it.

'Are we ready for the presents?' I asked. There was a polite murmur. 'Come on! You can be louder than that! I said, "Are we ready for the presents?"' The room clapped and cheered and whooped. And poor Father Christmas uttered not a single word more for the rest of the evening, demoted to the role of mute (and slightly grumpy) helper.

I thoroughly enjoyed my time onstage and came home with renewed determination to keep performing. What struck me most was that my cheekiness onstage had shattered the pity I'd felt from the audience as they'd watched me ascend the steps to Santa. I discovered that making people laugh was not only delightful in itself but stopped others feeling sorry for me. That, I decided, was a lesson worth remembering.

From an early age I dreaded a certain look I would detect in people's eyes, a particular tone of their voice. Before I found out what the word for it was, I already hated pity. Its lingering presence was like a mirror, reflecting back a reality I didn't want to see. I had started to do and say everything I could to make it disappear from people's faces and voices. My only desire was to smash that unwanted glass to pieces and prove that nobody had any reason to pity me. Because I was lucky. I was happy. I was fine. I wanted people to see Francesca. Not my wobbles or shakes or anything else.

Life at home continued to be wonderful, especially as Raoul was now old enough for me to play games with. He had big blonde curls and was going through a fat phase. He looked like a football with arms. We got on very well, even when he discovered, with evident glee, that he could push his big sister over with one finger. Just one finger! This became irresistible to him and, although he regularly deployed his new manoeuvre, I remained a very proud big sister who loved sharing a room with him and reading him stories in bed.

My parents chose not to have a TV in the house so I became an avid reader. I soon discovered the books of Enid Blyton and, blithely unaware of the casual old-world racism and sexism, they became my drug of choice. I devoured them. My cousin Aaron often (and very patiently) took part in the acting out of entire Famous Five adventures. (I, of course, always played George, the curly haired tomboy.) I remember declaring to him that I wanted to be buried in a glass coffin surrounded by all my Enid Blytons. They fed my imagination and were full of kids running, jumping, swimming, sailing, climbing and escaping – all the things I wanted to do but which were not generally viable. Being TV-less meant that I couldn't just plonk myself down on the sofa for a fix of escapism. I can't say I wasn't frustrated by this at times but I can see that my imagination grew more than it might have done had I been a passive viewer for hours on end. So I lived in my imagination and daydreams and books.

After a routine hospital visit, a new word entered my

consciousness and filled me with dread: exercises. My parents were told that certain physical exercises could improve my walking, talking, and coordination. It wasn't just moving around that was problematic: I struggled with anything that required fine control like cutting up food, lifting mugs, and carrying trays and plates. My speech was a bit slurred and I found certain sounds hard to master. 'Sn' was a bugger to say and, for years, I would excitedly announce 'It's nowing outside!' at Christmas and inform my friends that 'my dad nores loudly'. I wasn't too hot on lone 's's either. Let's just say 'soothsayer' has not surfaced often in my conversation.

Like any loving parents, they listened carefully to the physio and agreed with what sounded like a sensible idea. I was rather less enamoured of it. For starters, I couldn't see why I needed to do exercises at all. As far as I was concerned, I was normal. Where was the logic in practising certain words to improve my speech when I talked perfectly already? A fact clearly demonstrated by the clear voice I heard every time I spoke. Or in the suggestion that certain mouth exercises might help me not to dribble.

'I only dribble a little and only sometimes! It doesn't really matter, does it?'

'But it would be good if you learnt not to dribble at all, wouldn't it?' asked my dad, reasonably. I thought about this for a moment.

'But Yaya and Yayo don't mind me dribbling.'

And so the battles began. My poor dad would try to convince me to do an exercise or practise an activity and I'd refuse, appalled by the prospect of this boring, futile nonsense. I remember sitting on the bottom step at home, my feet in my shoes, as Dad stood patiently over me.

'Just try doing up your own laces for a change, Chess.' I stared up at him with a frown.

'It's too hard for my fingers. You do them!' Dad crouched down in front of me.

'If I keep doing them for you, you'll never learn to tie them yourself, will you?'

'I don't care! I just want to go and play,' I said, crossing my arms with dramatic finality. Dad sighed.

'No. You're going to do them yourself today. We're not going out until you do.' He sat down on the floor. He was in for the long haul. I could sense his resolve and decided that something spectacular was called for. Tears. Lots of them. With some stamping of feet thrown in for good measure. After a few minutes of this weeping and gnashing of teeth, I glanced at my dad. He wasn't buying it. I kept this up for thirty minutes until my throat was hoarse. Three-quarters of an hour later, my shoulders still heaved occasionally as my breathing slowly calmed down. I looked at my shoes and the laces, trailing miserably on the floor. Then I looked at Dad, as I sniffed up the puddle of snotty tears that had gathered on my top lip.

'Just try,' he said quietly. I sniffed again.

'Why can't I just have Velcro shoes?' I asked him. A last attempt. He remained silent. I sighed. A big, long, heavy one filled with frustration and self-pity. I bent down and grabbed the laces of the left shoe. I succeeded in tying the initial knot but the bow proved a lot more tricky and I soon dropped them in anger.

'See? I can't do it!' I glared at my dad, victoriously.

'Try again. You nearly did it.' His voice was firm. I jutted out my chin and cocked my head to the side, adopting my best put-upon face, hoping he'd relent. No such luck. I bent back down and, after a few abortive attempts, found myself staring at two messily tied bows.

'There you go. It wasn't that hard. See how independent you can be when you try?' Dad stood up, his shoulders rounded, looking weary. I didn't answer him and trudged moodily downstairs.

These arguments became common, often culminating in tears and shouting and my running to my mum who, naturally, was torn. It was the first taste of conflict with my parents and I hated it. But not enough to agree to do the exercises. I couldn't understand why my dad wouldn't just let me get on with my life. Why he was so intent on forcing me to do things I wasn't good at? And he couldn't understand my total disinterest in improving my physical abilities and becoming less dependent. I insisted that all I needed to be happy was food, family, boys and Enid Blyton. This did little to placate him and the next few years, though happy in many ways, were punctuated with intense rows replete with door-banging and the throwing of objects.

It's not that I wasn't interested in improving my abilities. It's just that I'd devised my own ways of outsmarting my disability. Ways that didn't require much expenditure of time or energy. That was solution enough for me. When I wanted to move around quickly at home, I would simply shuffle on my knees and build up enough speed to satisfy my impatient moods. I liked this because my usually constant battle with gravity disappeared when I was closer to the ground. I had thwarted my balance without exercises. Ha-haaa! Chuffed doesn't come close. I also learnt that I could attain more control when reaching for things if I steadied my right hand with my left one. Okay, it wasn't very gainly but what did I care? Ungainly trumped exercises any day.

To be honest, I don't think the primary problem was my natural laziness. It was the niggling feeling that doing these exercises would be an admission that there was something wrong with me. To agree would be to agree that I wasn't normal. And, although I would please my dad sometimes by having a go at the dreaded workouts, I never accepted that I *needed* to do them. Over time, these clashes chipped away at my confidence, and self-doubt began to leak in.

I remember watching my cousin, Tasha, spread butter on her toast one morning. I wondered if my dad would love me more if I could do that myself instead of needing someone else to do it. Another time, I was struck by the ease with which Raoul walked across the living room and realised how differently I moved, how much more effort it took. At mealtimes, I watched my friends pick up their glasses as I sucked on a straw. I was fascinated by the easy way they raised them carefully to their lips and placed them back down again without a sound. My dad had recently helped me practise picking up a mug. My hands had clenched it rigidly as I jerked it up towards my mouth, splashing my nose. I slurped a mouthful and then plonked it back down with a thump. Awkward, clunky and erratic. A far cry from the elegance of my friends. But I reasoned that nobody in their right mind would focus on what they couldn't do. So I just concentrated on what I was good at and forgot about the rest.

After nearly a year of nun-worrying, I moved to Malorees Junior School in the summer of 1986. Angel and Ramon were sorry to see me go, the Holy Sisters less so, I suspect. My new school was modern and idyllic, a low-rise building nestled between trees, lawns and a huge field. I settled in quickly, pleased at the many attractive boys I could survey. There was strong competition but I decided after a week (why rush such an important life choice?) that I loved a boy called Michael who had dark, wavy hair and delicate features. Alas, Michael was part of a gang that 'hated girls'. If a girl as much as brushed against him, he would blow on his arm as if to clear it of germs. A minor detail, I thought, and I was sure true love would prevail. I had just turned eight and my flirting technique was highly developed and sophisticated. If I liked a boy, I would start a fight with him. Impressive, eh? The idea was that fighting was a form of physical contact so it was a step in the right direction. I couldn't get near enough to Michael without him running away, blowing at his arms, so I turned my attention to Jake, the football star. Gathering my courage, I crossed the field and walked up to him. This, in the middle of a match! The ball was at his (beautiful) feet and

I deliberately hoofed it off into the distance before staring defiantly into his eyes (also beautiful).

'Hey! What did you do that for?' he said, with a mixture of confusion and annoyance.

'Because I wanted to!' I said, trying (and failing) to look menacing. I pushed him. He pushed me back. I fell on to the grass and he landed on top of me. We rolled around for a while as I tried to get a good look at his face. He was gorgeous. The scrum petered out and we got up. I smiled at him.

'Thanks!'

He looked baffled. I walked off, drunk with happiness. Adios, Clint, Angel and Ramon.

Malorees was run by good-hearted people who really cared about their students and this was apparent in the community atmosphere that abounded. Staff looked happy, students loved their teachers, and parents fought to enrol their children there. It was a charming school but it had a somewhat conservative streak. The first taste I got of it was in art class.

We were given an introductory painting lesson and, at the end of the day, I emerged covered from head to toe in primary colours. My mother sighed audibly when she saw me, clearly regretting her decision that morning to dress me in a new outfit. Her reaction disappeared when I showed her the paper covered in huge splodges, which, if studied acutely for a very long time, vaguely resembled a human form. Always encouraging of my exploits, she congratulated me on my fine painting and made me hugely proud of my artistic achievement. There is a reason why there is no limit to my list of ambitions: the overwhelming support and positivity of my mum. Thanks to her unwavering belief, I went through six months wondering if the English football team would actually consider changing their rules so that I could be the first girl to play for them.

My teacher Mrs Lack, who I adored, didn't share Mum's enthusiasm for my artwork. This was brought home to me when I saw where she had chosen to display it on the classroom wall. High up in a corner, partly obscured by a ceiling strip of neon light, there my painting languished. I gazed up at the distant recess and my heart sank. It could barely be seen. By anyone. Not even by Joe, who was really tall. But my faith in Mrs Lack won out and I told myself that the placement had been purely random. There were thirty paintings on the wall so someone's had to go in the corner and, this time, I drew the short straw. That was all there was to it.

When my second work disappeared behind the class plant, my suspicions grew. And when Opus Number Three was plastered just above the skirting board, to be masked by the bag rack, the game was up. Three rubbish placements in a row? I knew just enough maths to know that the probability of that occurring naturally was highly unlikely. That night, in the bath, I broke the scandal to my mum.

'My paintings are always hung in places where you can't see them properly.'

'What do you mean, darling?' she asked, as she scrubbed my back.

'I mean that my paintings are always hidden on

purpose. I think it's because they're messy.' I waited for her reaction.

'I'm sure everyone's paintings get hung in bad places sometimes,' she said, seemingly unflustered by my words.

'But every painting I do is put in a bad place. I've never had one in a good place! Isn't that a bit fishy?' I looked up, wanting her agreement.

'Well, maybe you're right. Maybe she's just not used to Chessie paintings. Don't worry too much about it. People have to deal with far worse problems than that! And we love your paintings!'

She was right. I could have been locked in a cage like those cheetahs in London Zoo. So I continued to enjoy the messy application of paint to paper, face, hands, clothes and shoes. And classmates. Mrs Lack soon kitted me out, and all the kids at my table, with full-length aprons. And she always wore one too, tightly tied, any time she cautiously approached the table to check our progress.

Like my art, my handwriting could also fairly be described as erratic. The quality varied greatly, depending on my state. When I was happy, relaxed and rested, the squiggles that left my pencil reasonably corresponded to our alphabet and numerals. Other days, when I was tired, stressed or unhappy, they looked like the scratchings of a lunatic. On crystal meth. I was slowly learning that this faraway condition of mine was affected by how I felt. (In fact, it's well known of the wobbly that the degree of success in carrying out various actions fluctuates substantially day-to-day and is affected by how they're feeling.) Annoyingly,

Mrs Lack was ignorant of this and simply 'could not understand' the huge disparity in the quality of my writing from one day to the next. She would be perplexed when I placed (dropped) my exercise book on her desk.

'Francesca! This is very hard to read.'

'I know. I can barely read it either,' I'd offer, hoping she would laugh. She didn't.

'But you wrote so beautifully yesterday. What happened?' Her eyes narrowed a bit. I should have said, 'Er, I don't know... d'you think it could be the brain damage?' Instead, I just sighed.

'I don't know what happened. I tried really hard.' This was true. I had forcibly willed my hand to make the correct shapes. But it hadn't listened. Mrs Lack handed me back my book and smiled.

'Why don't you have another go?'

I returned to my seat and slumped back down. My friends were all scribbling away – the neat, beautiful shapes falling gracefully on to their pages. I looked at my hand, which still ached from grasping the pencil so tightly, and told it off silently.

'Stupid hand. Why can't you just write properly? You're so crap. I hate you. And as for you, fingers, thanks a lot for being so rubbish!' I glared at them, hoping they would feel my anger and respond accordingly. I took a deep breath and picked up my pencil. My aching fingers clasped the stem as I focused on controlling my hand. The paper lay before me, almost threateningly perfect.

'Don't mess this up,' I told the pencil as I lowered it on

to the page and wrote the F of my name. It came out nicely. Phew! The muscles in my hand relaxed slightly. I started on the straight line of the R and my hand jerked roughly off the page. The meth dude had relapsed. The frustration sprang out of me like a frog's tongue.

'Bloody hell!' I shouted, and threw my pencil across the room. Everyone looked at me.

Mrs Lack got up, picked up my pencil and gave it to me. 'You can try again tomorrow.'

Contrary to her optimism (but in keeping with the laws of biology) my writing was still shit the following day. And the next. Mrs Lack began to see that the whole brain damage thing might be more of a mitigating factor than she had first surmised. A few months later, after talking with my parents, she proudly presented me with my very own typewriter.

'This is to help you write!' she said, excitedly. I looked at it.

'Wow. It's big!' And so it was. It was not so much a keyboard as a metre-long grey brick with an array of large holes, each containing a large button.

'Why's it so big?' I enquired. Yayo had a typewriter, as did my dad. And they didn't look like this.

Mrs Lack paused before she spoke. 'It's big because... it's made for children who can't use their hands, so they type with a stick attached to their head.'

'But I don't have a stick attached to my head.' I was eight, and fairly oblivious to the complex issues associated with councils and funding and specialist equipment.

'No you don't. But... this is the typewriter that was given to us.'

I took this in. 'Will I have to type with a stick on my head?'

'No. You won't, Francesca,' she assured me.

'Okay. Cool!' I was genuinely excited that the battle with my rebellious hands was over. And I was grateful that my teacher had taken note of my frustration and had helped me (while also protecting the school's limited supply of pencils from further abuse). Now I could forget all about my handwriting. And that's what I tried to do, reminding myself that I didn't need neat handwriting to be happy. The bulky machine was placed conspicuously in a corner and, as well as making my life a lot easier, was a much-talked-about addition to our class. I secretly hoped that Michael would be so impressed by this cutting-edge piece of technology that he would take an interest in me.

Unusually, most of my friends were now girls, including my best friend, Rachel. This hadn't been a conscious decision on my part; it had more to do with the mysterious and depressing fact that the boys in my class didn't seem to like girls. I couldn't understand their reluctance and I was sad not to have any trusty male companions. I liked, and missed, the direct way that boys communicated.

All my girlfriends knew of my crush on Michael and one of them, Julie, decided to facilitate the union. It took some convincing but I was eventually persuaded to let her ply her matchmaking skills. With me at her side, she walked over to Michael's table during break. The exchange went thus:

Julie: Hi, Michael.

Michael: What?

Julie: How's your day going?

Michael: Go away.

Julie: I have some important news.

Michael: What?

Julie: Okay. Francesca fancies you!

Michael: Oh.

Julie: What do you say to that?

Michael: I don't fancy her but she has very good taste.

Ouch! I stood next to Julie, my eyes searching out the smallest detail on my shoes. My cheeks felt warm and tingly and my lips felt dry. Julie tugged at my arm and we walked away. I silently vowed to stick to the pick-a-fight method of seduction.

Cringe-inducing romantic declarations apart, junior school was a lot of fun. It was true that the odd boy pushed me over in the playground sometimes, and a few kids in the neighbourhood occasionally ran up to me to enquire 'what was wrong' with me but, on the whole, life was sweet. The pressure on me to do exercises continued but my dad and I seemed to fight less frequently. Even so, I couldn't help feeling that I was a disappointment to him and this manifested itself in sharp pangs of regret. They were not pleasurable and I did my best to stifle them as much as possible, so I could carry on as normal, unbothered by my limitations and the trouble they caused.

Yayo and Yaya had seemed always to be there to brush

away any unwanted thoughts that appeared on my horizon. I loved them to bits and occasionally, when the thought of losing them crossed my mind, I felt sick. I was only eight but I knew that nobody else would ever love me quite as much as they did.

My grandparents were like a second set of parents to me. We lived with them until I was three because mum and dad were young students. And, although the flat was small, they had adored sharing their home with us. After two sons, Yaya was over the moon at having a girl to dress up in pretty clothes. She'd knit me one garment after another, many of them emblazoned with messages like 'I Love You' and 'Favourite Francesca', surrounded by a flurry of little red hearts. (When I started high school a few years later, I had to break it to her gently, following a rare flash of self-awareness, that it might be sensible for me to stop wearing her love-infused knitwear.)

Yayo, equally besotted by his granddaughter, chose to express his love in his own way. He was a man of few words but I knew how he felt about me by the way he carefully cut my food up, and his regular gifts of books, the covers of which he wrapped in brown paper, before writing the titles on them in elegant letters.

One November day, my parents couldn't pick me up from school, and I saw Yayo walking up the path towards me. His khaki jacket was zipped up to the top and his brown cap rested on his silver hair. My heart jumped.

'Yayo!' I called, picking up my bag and lurching towards him.

He took his hands out of his pockets and placed them on either side of my face. His leather gloves were warm and soft.

'Guapa!' He smiled at me as I hugged him. I remember the sheer delight that he had come to pick me up and that I had him all to myself.

He bent down on his knees in front of me.

'It's cold,' he said in his warm accent. He zipped up my coat and pulled up the collar so that it tickled my ears. I giggled.

'*Gracias!*'

'*De nada.*'

He stood up and put his hands back in his pockets, arching out his left elbow slightly for my right hand to hold. I took it and as my fingers clasped his jacket, he brought his arm close to his side so my hand couldn't slip out. Nobody else held my arm so snugly and I loved how safe and strong it made me feel. We began to walk.

'How was your day?'

'Good! I played football and did a painting of a robot.' My feet kicked the rusty leaves that had gathered in piles along the pavement.

'You must show me,' said Yayo.

'I will!' I looked up at him quickly.

'Are you going to Spain soon?' I said, squinting at the low autumn sun.

'Yes, in two weeks.' He looked straight ahead.

'Are you sad?' I said, watching his face.

'I don't like leaving you but…' His eyes looked straight ahead.

'I don't like you leaving either…'

He didn't need to tell me why he was going. Yaya and Yayo fought all the time, so they couldn't be together for long. I sighed. Yayo looked so sad sometimes and I wasn't quite sure why.

'Let's pick conkers in the park on the way home!' I pulled at his arm in excitement.

'Okay. Just a few, Chessie.' He smiled at my enthusiasm.

It was the best walk ever.

I still relished playing with Raoul who was the apple of my eye. As soon as he was old enough, we produced 'plays' for my parents, grandparents and their friends. To this day, the thought of them makes me wince. Back then, however, I hadn't a shred of self-consciousness. No inhibition darkened my horizon. And, when the auditions for the school choir came around, I made sure I was first in line. Not only did joining the choir mean getting a chance to sing in front of people, it also meant missing a class every week. So, it was with steely resolve that I stood in the school hall and waited impatiently to sing to Mr Rainbow (jolly and plump – a credit to his name). He positioned himself at the piano and called me over to him.

'Hello!' I beamed at him.

'Hi Francesca. Are you ready to sing?'

I nodded, and his small, pudgy fingers began to play the opening notes. I took a deep breath.

'Ha-ppy Birth-day to you. Ha-ppy Birth-day to you. Ha-ppy BIRTH…' Mr Rainbow stopped.

'Let's try again next year,' he said, kindly.

'But...'

I tried again the following year and made it to the second 'Ha-ppy' before the piano went silent. The third year, I didn't get past the first word. Mr Rainbow was polite but immovable. I'd have to find another way to miss classes.

A similar fate greeted my efforts to perform in the annual school production. These were performed by the oldest students in the school and took place just before they left for high school. Mr Rainbow's utmost dedication meant they were taken very seriously and were always highly polished pieces of musical theatre, delighting audiences of all ages. I had waited two and a half years for my turn to try out for this magnificent opportunity. The news was delivered to us in assembly one morning by an eager Mr Rainbow.

'It gives me great pleasure to announce that the Year Six production will be *Rodeo*, a take on the famous American musical, *Oklahoma!* Auditions will be held next week. All students are welcome to try out.' I started whispering excitedly to my friends and was told off immediately. That night, my parents got the full low-down.

'It's called *Rodeo* and it's based on a show called *Oklahoma!* and it's going to be brilliant. What is *Oklahoma!*?' My dad, a big fan of old American movies, told me that it was a musical with cowboys and Indians. I stopped eating.

'Are there any parts for girls in it?'

'Yes, there are cowgirls and bar ladies...'

'Oh, good! I'd love to be a cowgirl. They sound like

cowboys. I bet they're cool!' I started eating again. 'I can't wait for next week! And the rehearsals mean I'll miss loads of classes too!'

My parents, not the kind of people to rush their ten-year-old to a maths tutor at the first hint of disinterest in numbers, smiled at the exuberance. I'm fortunate that I just missed the era of 'education' where kids are bombarded with homework and SATS and Key Stage Tests, all designed to 'aid development' while, simultaneously, increasing the incidence of mental breakdown and high blood-pressure in the under-ten age group. I greatly appreciate that my parents were more than happy to let me play and read and joke around, without appearing the slightest bit perturbed at my lack of interest in algebra. They were content to let their ten-year-old be a ten-year-old.

I counted the days to the auditions and, when Mr Rainbow came into class to collect names, my hand shot up first. He wrote them down, about fourteen in all. I couldn't understand why some kids didn't volunteer but, then again, most of the kids who didn't put up their hand loved maths. The following day, fourteen of us piled into the hall and sat cross-legged on the floor as Mr Rainbow explained that he would be auditioning for the main speaking parts first. There were ten in total. I quickly did the sums (I admit it, maths has its uses) and worked out that there were probably thirty children across two classes competing for ten roles. My chances were one in three. Not bad, I reasoned, conveniently forgetting my past success rate. One of the cowgirl parts was up first, and I was called up in a group with Jemima, Polly and Meena. We were handed a script and had to read it opposite Mr Rainbow who, though he may have been playing an Indian, certainly didn't look or sound like one. I tried to imbue every line with wit, humour or any other emotion I judged to be suitable. At one point, I made everyone laugh which gave me a glow in my stomach. Surely he had to pick me now.

'Thanks so much, girls. You were all really good...' I couldn't help but feel his praise was directed mostly towards me.

'But the girl who got the part was...' I shut my eyes and made a quick wish. Not that I needed it. But it couldn't hurt.

'Jemima! Well done, Jemima!' Jemima smiled serenely, and tossed her long blonde hair away from her face.

'Thanks, Mr Rainbow,' she sang, as she skipped back daintily and sat down.

I couldn't believe it. Jemima was okay at acting but she was boring. By boring, I mean perfect. And she was. Everything about her, from her flawless white skin and rosy cheeks, to her wrinkle-free socks and immaculate fairy hair, was terrifyingly perfect. She won every class competition, played the violin in a devastatingly moving manner at every concert, had every girl craving for her approval (including me, much to my annoyance), and had every boy trying in vain to win her heart. Even Michael would have suspended his germ phobia, I reckoned, for a chance to kiss her poised pink lips. I moped back over to the group.

'It's just not fair! Some girls get everything!' I moaned that evening to Raoul who, at five, was more than capable of listening to my heartache.

'It's not her fault,' he pondered, characteristically philosophical and far too mature for his age.

'That's not the point! You're five. You shouldn't say stuff like that! You should be on my side,' I said, tantrum-like, as insecurity settled over me like an errant web.

'I am on your side,' insisted Raoul.

'Why do some people get everything? She sings in the choir. Her paintings are put up in the best places. She has the best handwriting in the class. I do everything so badly compared to her.' I felt the salty body of a tear begin to form in my eye. I wiped it away before Raoul could see it. But I wasn't fast enough because he lent over and put his chubby arms around me.

I wasn't used to talking like this to anyone. It felt weird. The saying of these words out loud felt like I was admitting defeat. That I was somehow acknowledging that things weren't always good. That I failed in so many ways next to Jemima. That for Jemima to be perfect, I had to be imperfect. It was strange to share the seeds of these awkward feelings and I was glad that nobody, apart from my little brother, had witnessed my tears.

With the main parts gone, auditions were held for the ensemble. These parts had no lines but featured in the crowd scenes and musical numbers. I had just enough self-awareness to know that singing and dancing weren't my strong points but I didn't have any options left so I turned up to the last audition, utterly determined to make my hands and feet move in an orderly and musical manner. Surely, my wobbliness could be buried for this short time.

The group of twenty hopefuls got up and faced the front. Mr Rainbow, although a large man, was surprisingly agile on his feet and danced his way merrily through the first number. I watched him intently. In groups of five, we attempted this dance. I was up second. Mr Rainbow's assistant eagerly played the piano while he led us through the steps. I fared well with the slow opening but, when the assistant began to speed up towards a crescendo, I had to admit defeat. My feet were moving as fast as they could yet I found myself five steps behind everybody else. I wanted to yell 'slow down' but thought it might compromise my chances.

When the dance was finished, Mr Rainbow, gasping heavily from the exertion, looked at us all. I wanted to ask him if he would take into consideration that, despite the effort required, I had remained vertical. That ought to count for something, right? Wrong. He picked three of our group. I was let go, together with a lanky boy, and we skulked off back to class, a couple of insults to the dance art form. That was it. Mr Rainbow had dashed my dreams AGAIN. Did he have a vendetta against me? My last chance to perform had passed. Six weeks of uninterrupted classes lay ahead, crowned by the prospect of watching Jemima act her little heart out as I sat, invisible, in the audience. Goldilocks was a distant memory and the irony that I tried to turn the part down because of the inadequate script made me smile sadly.

My parents must have sat through a number of impassioned and emphatic moaning sessions because my mum decided to pay a visit to the head teacher, Mrs Thomas. After relaying the huge joy that playing a cowgirl would bring to my life, Mum gently recounted the hanging-of-my-paintings-in-bad-places scandal to further illustrate a trend towards an unhealthy devotion to tradition. Perhaps shocked that such underhand tactics had been employed by her staff, and wanting to avoid the spotlight of the world's press on this major revelation, Mrs Thomas agreed that I should be given a part. I can only imagine Mr Rainbow's dismay at hearing that tone-deaf Chessie would be allowed to grace his cherished production. He had succeeded in sparing audiences my 'singing' for all these years and now his attempts to depict a jelly-free Wild West had been thwarted by my mum.

I was ecstatic and couldn't stop hugging her when she told me the amazing news. I hoped they'd give me at least one line. Just one line that I could anticipate every night. I'd be totally satisfied with that. A small speaking part made sense because it was the one thing I was good at. There was no way Mr Rainbow would make a girl who'd struggled to sing and dance just sing and dance. But Mr Rainbow thought differently. And so it happened that I was cast as Cowgirl #7, a lass with no lines but lots of ensemble singing and dancing. Yee-haw! I was baffled but I threw myself into the rehearsals, enjoying every minute of it. Cowgirl #7 was not only wobbly, she had a really cool outfit with tassels and boots and a hat. Learning the songs was great fun and I loved the energy created when we all sang together. Occasionally I caught Mr Rainbow wincing as I attempted a high note but, for the most part, I think he handled my destruction of his masterpiece with admirable fortitude.

The day of our first performance grew nearer and I could hardly sit still. Time seemed to crawl on its hands and knees making those last classes drag on interminably as I bashed my oversize typewriter. At last, the wait was over. I walked into school on a July evening, accompanied by my parents, Raoul, Yaya and Yayo. Being in school that late felt magical, special, more atmospheric. My parents dropped me off at my classroom and wished me luck. I changed into my outfit, drinking in the electricity that sparked around the room like fireworks. Mr Rainbow, dressed in a beautiful suit, presided over us like a proud mother hen.

'Just enjoy yourselves tonight. You've put the work in and you'll be fabulous!' His eyes settled on me.

'And, remember, Francesca will sit on the edge of the stage to save her walking on and off multiple times, so don't remark on it.'

In a desperate attempt to ensure that the musical numbers weren't quadrupled in length by my slower entrances and exits, it had been decided that I would remain sitting at the edge of the stage between the songs. I hadn't been entirely sure about the wisdom of this, pointing out that the presence of a lone, wobbly cowgirl sitting in every scene with head bowed and arms wrapped tightly around her knees could be, well, distracting...? Mr Rainbow nodded in agreement but thought that this option would ruin things the least. As a result, I had practised perching in various inconspicuous positions at home and was pretty confident that I could successfully pull off the role of Barely-There-Cowgirl #7.

Rodeo was a hit with the audience and the cast was exemplary. Even Jemima did an excellent job with the part she'd stolen from me. And my feet hadn't let me down during the dance routines, behaving in a surprisingly obedient manner. Only a handful of times had they misbehaved, but my balance held out and I remained upright. In your stinking face, gravity!

Despite the somewhat awkward intervals during which I radiated a strong 'DON'T LOOK AT ME CROUCHING AT THE SIDE OF THE STAGE' vibe, an intense joy pulsated through me the whole time I was onstage. As we took our bows, I smiled at Mr Rainbow, who beamed expansively. It had gone perfectly. I gazed into the audience who were on their feet, proudly clapping and cheering us. This is where I belong, I thought. If I'd needed any more convincing that I should pursue a life of performing, playing Cowgirl #7 did the trick.

Just before the school year was over, we went on a camping trip for a week. There were late nights in tents, scary stories and arm-wrestling competitions, which I'd been surprisingly good at, beating most of the boys in my class. The trip had flown by and I'd only been told off once. I'd been bitten in the groin area by a mosquito and, as a result, spent rather a lot of time with my hand down my trousers vigorously scratching the bite. This, to an outsider, looked very dubious and I was sternly told by a blushing

Mrs Lack to 'stop doing that!' I got the impression that, for some unknown reason, I shouldn't do it in the lunch queue or when I was lying in my tent alone.

It began to dawn on us that we'd soon be leaving Malorees for new pastures. We were very sad, especially as Mrs Lack had taught us for three years and we'd all fallen in love with her. As part of our farewell, the school threw a disco. This was a source of excited anticipation: for many of us, it would be our first ever. Rachel and I buzzed at the prospect of a night filled with music and dancing and boys. There were big decisions to be made, like what to wear. I'd had about as much interest in clothes as I'd had in clog dancing. To me, clothes were simply material you wore to stop being naked. That was my take on them. But even I could tell that the choosing of this outfit merited some serious thought. Ever the optimist, I still hoped that Michael would realise his mistake and ask me to dance. The right outfit could help him see the error of his ways. So, it was after a lot of careful contemplation that I finally and confidently settled on my choice – a white T-shirt and shorts bearing the grinning faces of Jason Donovan and Kylie Minogue. Because nothing wins a boy's heart like the sight of two gurning Aussie soap stars plastered across a girl's torso and thighs.

Before you question my mental health, please note that I was obsessed with *Neighbours*. It's hard to follow a daily soap when you don't have a TV but I gave it a bloody good try. Yaya and Yayo had one and Raoul and I would visit them after school. A maximum of ten words would be exchanged as we walked in the door and plonked ourselves in front of the box like a couple of junkies. This happened at least three times a week as Yayo and Yaya patiently waited on us hand and foot while we sat transfixed, determined to get our fill before our parents transported us back to the old-fashioned world of books and the art of conversation.

I couldn't get enough of *Neighbours* and I soon fell in love with the spunk that was Jason Donovan. I fantasised that I was Kylie and that we'd get married, while my friends gasped with envy that he was mine (Jemima may have featured prominently). Imagine my delight when Jason and Kylie released the pop sensation 'Especially For You'. It was my first ever record and I played it over and over. The lyrics were burnt into my brain and I regret to report that I can still recite them.

Anyway, Yaya, noting my loyal devotion to the Aussie sweethearts, sourced and bought this fetching top and shorts for me. I don't think I've been much happier than when I first donned them and looked in the mirror. God I'm cool, I thought, as I studied myself from multiple angles. The top had 'Especially For You' in twirly font written on it, and a big pink heart was printed underneath, from which Jason and Kylie beamed, their perfect white teeth enhanced by tiny glittering stars. What a brilliant piece of design, I thought. The shorts were just as beautiful and also bore their smiling faces, one placed artistically on each leg. I'd promised myself to keep this eye-catching combo until a special occasion warranted such glamour. And occasions don't get much more special than a girl's first disco. My mum, bless her, tried to talk me out of it. I didn't listen. But instead of forcing me to capitulate to her wiser opinion, she let me stick to my choice. Some parents just don't dominate their kids enough. Rachel was rather less supportive of my right to choose when I gave her a sneak preview of the killer outfit.

'Are you gonna wear that?' she asked, taken aback.

'Yes! It's so cool, isn't it?' Remarkably, Rachel did not share my love of *Neighbours* or of Jason but, never one for confrontation, remained silent.

'Don't you like it?' I said. She should have said 'No! It's a tacky piece of crap and if you wear it I will never speak to you again,' but she didn't.

'I wouldn't wear it but you should wear whatever you want to.' I felt her restraint and a crushing disappointment at her response to my awful taste. But my loyalty to Jason won out and I held my ground.

'Well, I will wear it, then!' I said, a little too defiantly.

I'd like to report that I came to my senses before the disco. Alas, fate hadn't the decency to save me from myself. I turned up proudly clad in the monstrosity. The hall was decked out with balloons and colourful lights. A huge 'Good Luck' banner was strung across the stage. Bowls of Hula Hoops and crisps and chocolate buttons were neatly arranged on tables along the sides. It was a slice of ten-year-old heaven. To their credit, nobody laughed or choked on their lemonade when they saw me. But a strange feeling came over me as I stood and watched the people dance and run and laugh. It was unfamiliar but I recognised it as the stirrings of self-consciousness. A dull pang that made me feel sidelined, different and alone, separate from everyone else. Perhaps my childish innocence had begun to release me slowly from its warm embrace, that soft cloud of protection that would gradually float away and leave me blinking at the starkness all around. I shuddered inside and wondered why I was feeling so lonely in such a busy place.

I pushed the feeling away and joined my friends. We hugged each other emotionally. The reality that we were leaving Malorees and all that that meant – the playing, the fun, the lovely teachers – hit us all there and then. We were aware in some small way that we would never be kids again. There was a collective sadness in the room, a tiny inkling that time was taking away something precious and was about to hand us something new and unknown. It was only a whisper in the mind but it was enough to hurt your stomach for a moment. I looked at the smiling faces around me and I suddenly felt so lucky to have been part of this school.

Michael failed to declare his undying love that night but he did smile at me. Perhaps my outfit sparked a flicker of sympathy in him. Once I had accepted that he was not to be my future husband, I got on with enjoying our great send-off and we all danced and played late into the night (10.30 p.m.). As the party drew to a close, the class gathered around an emotional Mrs Lack and, one by one, we clung to her and cried our eyes out. And that was how I left junior school: sweaty, emotional, and breathing fitfully between sobs, while splattering Jason and Kylie's twinkling smiles with multiple tears.

CHAPTER THREE

****

High school was shit.

CHAPTER FOUR

****

'll elaborate.

When I hit eleven, there was a lot of pressure on me to go to a special school. And I don't mean Eton. Oh no. Apparently most mainstream schools in my borough were not cut out to accommodate a wobbly girl and her huge typewriter. Actually, to my private relief, that monster would not be making the transition with me, partly because it wasn't mine and partly because it was hardly portable, unless you had access to a forklift. (I wonder how long it lingered in the corner of Mrs Lack's classroom, gathering dust like an ancient relic, to be peered at with curiosity by generations of perplexed kids.)

My parents and I had visited a few schools during summer term and they were, well, less than successful. In one contender the head teacher showed us around for an hour before blurting out that I shouldn't be sent there anyway because they didn't have the facilities to support me. I wondered what this mysterious 'support' might be. Another had a never-ending flow of teenage boys tearing around the hallways and stairwells, and my parents felt that this mightn't be the most harmonious environment for one such as me. The remaining schools were reminiscent of prisons, replete with warder-teachers locked in battle with hoards of uncontrollable angry inmates, or places where teenagers could get high, pregnant or arrested with equal ease.

None of these establishments quite satisfied my parents but they were still reluctant to send me to a special-needs school. I think they shared my discomfort at the idea. I had never been defined by my disability. The words 'cerebral palsy' were rarely mentioned at home. Of course, I was happy to play with other disabled children. I just didn't want us to be lumped together in some educational ghetto because of our conditions or because we had been written off as the kids who can't do things properly. It's a negative enrolment criteria – being there solely because of what you *can't* do. And, considering that I didn't give a shit about what I couldn't do, I didn't want to find myself in such a school precisely because I couldn't bloody do those things.

My parents looked at schools outside the borough and discovered Parliament Hill High School near Hampstead Heath. It was a girls' school and seemed quite nice, although I was disappointed there were no boys. It had a relaxed, liberal atmosphere that boded well for my artwork, and it had lots of drama. There was just one obstacle: no disabled child with a statement of needs had ever been sent to a school outside our borough before. This didn't deter my parents who were prepared to take on the local authorities. Because of this hiccup, I had no school to go to when September rolled around. Bliss! I duly prayed that they'd lose the fight so I'd be denied entry anywhere and could enjoy reading, playing, and acting at home instead. To my annoyance, my parents hired a couple of tutors to give me some lessons at home.

In between these bouts of unwanted tuition, I spent a lot of this precious not-at-school time with my group of local boys, playing football and performing dares. One involved me lying in the middle of our road for a full ten seconds. All of my mates were greatly impressed. Before I managed to get flattened, however, the news arrived that I could start high school in mid-October. In the end, it was the fact that they taught Spanish (curse you, Barcelona dad!) that made the authorities relent as they had a duty to provide me with classes in my heritage language. I was excited about meeting my new classmates. I hoped I'd make new friends quickly. I'd been reading lots of Enid Blyton's Malory Towers books and fantasised that we'd be skipping classes for picnics with ginger beer and other such derring-do. No such luck.

The first day arrived and I woke up feeling nervous. A photograph taken on the doorstep shows me in an orange-and-white striped top and skirt, with a green canvas string bag slung over my shoulder. (No gurning soap stars thankfully.) The council had arranged for a taxi to take me to school each morning. My parents wished me luck and I stepped into the waiting car to meet my escort Mrs Simon, a round Jamaican lady with glasses and a big afro hairdo. The driver, a friendly black guy, introduced himself as Desmond and we drove off as my parents waved goodbye. Mrs Simon took out a copy of the *Sun* and was soon poring over the pages, paying special attention to the dramatic pleas to 'Dear Deirdre' for help. Within fifteen minutes, I'd learnt that it was not a good idea to sleep with your husband's brother, especially when you were secretly in love with his father. And that the *Sun* would never be a publication to grace my lap, even if it was only 20p.

The journey took about thirty-five minutes and as we slowed down to drive through the wooden entrance gates, I shrunk back instinctively. The path was thronged with teenage girls as well as boys from William Ellis, the school next door. They all talked and shouted and flirted, schoolbags flung in haphazard piles, blocking the road. Desmond hooted. Everyone turned to look at the offending vehicle. I tried to disappear into the seat as the teenagers moodily stood aside, glowering at the window as we slowly rolled past them and snaked around to the back of the school. Not the best start.

The school had two buildings, imaginatively called Old and New, and were linked by a low-rise building of staff rooms and the canteen. My form class was in the New building and I stared at it as it loomed over me four stories high. By now, I was late and there was no one around. I took a deep breath, walked up the stairs, along the corridor, and stopped outside the second door on the right. The wooden floor smelt of sickly sweet polish. Muffled sounds could be heard from inside. I couldn't procrastinate any longer. My left hand gripped the rope drawstring of the bag and I pushed open the classroom door. Thirty girls who had been chatting and messing around suddenly went quiet and stared at me. I caught sight of Stacey, the girl who had shown us around when I'd first visited, and my eyes locked on hers.

'This is Francesca,' said Stacey, loudly. The girls continued to stare as the teacher, Ms Kitkat (I kid you not), got up to welcome me.

It appears that, prior to my arrival, Ms Kitkat had thought it a good idea to inform (i.e., scare the shit out of) the class by telling them that there would be a new girl with something called 'cerebral palsy'. This was a 'physical disability' and meant that she walked and talked 'differently'. Judging from the mixture of panic and horror that I could see dancing around the eyes gazing back at me, Ms Kitkat may as well have told them I was a tentacled alien from another galaxy. As the morning went on and the class realised that I belonged to the same species, their panic disappeared and they began to talk to me. Like a human being. I hoped Ms Kitkat would not try to help me again.

The first few months filled me with optimism as I found myself enjoying the new environment. My crushingly naïve approach to my new classmates was this – be nice to them and they'll be nice back. So I wobbled in every day and exuded niceness, to the popular girls, to the bullies, to the outcasts, to the nerds. I oozed niceness indiscriminately.

And it seemed to work. I started to make a group of pals. Granted, the popular girls barely spoke to me but I had just enough self-awareness to realise that wasn't ever going to happen. They were simply out of my league and I was never going to win them over. But I could live with that and something in my gut told me that I'd rather be out of their group than in it. Some days, as I walked between classes, girls would run up to me at random and shout 'You're a spastic!' and run away, laughing. I wondered if I should reply, 'Really? Shit! I hadn't realised!'

To my joy, I found out that drama was taught by a Mr Eady, who was lovely. Even better, he didn't share Mr Rainbow's obsession with perfection. He didn't mind giving main parts to an imperfect and wobbly girl. Alas, he wasn't one for mounting extravaganzas in front of large audiences but I promptly joined his after-school class anyway and fell in love with him. I cherished those afternoons where we put on plays in the basement studio. And, unbelievably, my artwork (generally, I'd say, of the abstract school) was hung up in places where it was visible to the human eye. To top it off, my Spanish classes were way behind my level so I did no work and chatted through each lesson but still managed to get an A* for every assignment. It was too good to be true and it couldn't last.

The cracks started to appear a few months in, almost imperceptibly at first. My teachers agreed that deciphering my handwriting was harder than cracking the Enigma code and decided that we'd all benefit from a writing aid.

Thankfully, I was not given another typewriter to rival me in size and weight. Instead, my parents bought me a small brown electronic typewriter, one designed to be used by actual fingers. It was all very exciting but it meant that I had a lot to carry, what with my schoolbag and packed lunch and all. So, once more, Ms Kitkat deployed her problem-solving skills and proposed that, each day, one of my classmates would be assigned the role of bag-carrier. I wasn't at all sure about this: I'd be getting help from girls who were less interested in me than in the gum they stuck underneath their tables. Ms Kitkat tried to persuade me that everyone would be delighted to help me, an assessment of teenage girls that I thought might not be entirely on the mark. But I gave in and she made her announcement the following day.

'Francesca needs help carrying her new typewriter around. I've designed a rota so that each of you will help her on a different day.' The girls looked at me. I cringed. I'd never forced anyone to help me.

'Today's helper is Jane.' I gulped. Jane was the prettiest and coolest girl in the class. I'd exchanged about two words with her. One of which had been 'Erm'. I was sure she had far more important things to do than carry my bag around. Her eyes caught mine and I smiled apologetically.

'Is that okay, Jane?' asked Ms Kitkat, as I looked down at the table.

'Fine,' replied Jane.

'Great. Okay. Off to Period One, girls.' Chairs scraped along the floor as everyone got up. Jane sauntered up to my table.

'Is this it?' she said, pointing at the typewriter case.

'Yes. Thanks a lot! I'm really sorry you have to carry it, it's just that I'm not very good at lugging it around! You should have seen my last typewriter, though, you're lucky you don't have to carry that, it was...' She had already coolly slipped out the door, the typewriter tucked under her arm like an awkward child. I followed, soon losing sight of her in the corridor. When I reached the next classroom, the typewriter had been left on a table. I sat down and looked over at Jane. She didn't look back. I hated the damn machine already.

The rota lasted about a month. I couldn't face the trauma of waiting each morning to see who I had to rely on, so my friends chipped in or I just carried it myself, reaching classes late as I inched my way up and down the stairs, determined to keep upright. I quietly promised myself that, if it was at all possible, I would not ask anyone for help again. Ever.

Well, with this vow of independence, you'd think I'd have been more open to doing those dreaded exercises but I wasn't. Back at home I was still an expert at ignoring the uncomfortable realities of my disability. Not content with burying just my head in the sand, I enthusiastically jammed my neck, torso and legs down there too, leaving only my toes wiggling in the air.

Ms Kitkat quickly forgot the rota and, much to my relief, I was no longer singled out. Apart from, that is, being dropped off by the taxi every morning. The girls teased me about this and seemed envious that I didn't have to endure the slog of a morning bus or train ride like the rest of them. The irony is I spent every journey wishing I could hop on and off public transport like everybody else. I dreaded driving through the school gates, scattering resentful teenagers, the embarrassment pushing its way on to my cheeks as I rode through them on this drive of shame. Trapped inside this bubble, the vibrant and exciting teenage world outside seemed so distant and I felt cut off from all that was happening, even though it was inches away. But, by the time I reached class, that daily dose of humiliation had usually drained away, and I could go back to being normal again.

At the beginning of the new year, I discovered that the school had arranged some 'support', which turned out to be a teaching assistant who would carry my bags, help draw graphs and diagrams, and take extra notes when I couldn't write or type fast enough. And what better assistant could there be for a fun-loving teen than a sixty-four-year-old ex-science teacher? Ms Kitkat introduced her to me one morning before class.

'Francesca, this is Ethel. She'll be helping you on Tuesdays and Thursdays.' Kitkat smiled graciously as if she'd done a Very Good Thing.

'Hi, Francesca. Pleased to meet you.' Ethel extended her thin hand. I shook it.

'Hi, Ethel. Nice to meet you.' I smiled. Ethel had short, cropped grey hair and a thin, pale face. A pair of glasses perched in front of her piercing blue eyes, and she wore a plain woollen jumper, grey trousers and 'comfortable' shoes. She looked older than my grandma and I wondered if, in fact, I ought to be carrying *her* bags. So much for my plans to blend in.

'Girls, I'd like you to meet Francesca's new helper, Ethel,' announced Ms Kitkat. The girls made some vaguely friendly noises. I felt a bit sorry for Ethel standing on her own and I recalled how awkward I'd felt when I'd entered this room on my first day.

'Come and sit next to me,' I said. Yes, she was old and would probably render me uncool for eternity but it wasn't her fault she was here. Also, to be honest, I liked old people because they were full of interesting stories and some of them gave really great hugs. And she might be really nice. She did look quite harmless.

She wasn't. The first inkling that Ethel might not be the sweetie I'd hoped she'd be came during maths. As usual, I was doing my best to make the time pass quicker by talking to my friends when Ethel cleared her throat loudly. I turned to her.

'Erm, Francesca, don't you think you should be working?' she said.

'I am. Look.' I pushed across my exercise book so she could see my paltry efforts.

'I mean. Don't you think you should be working… harder?' Her blue eyes were cold.

'The thing is, Ethel, I don't really like maths!' I said, conspiratorially, hoping my honesty would soften her tone.

'What kind of a person doesn't like maths?' she asked sternly.

'Well, me. I'm just not that interested in numbers.' My heart sank.

'Numbers are incredibly important, young lady. I taught maths and science for years. They are vital to your education.' I looked at her and saw what kind of teacher she must have been.

'But I really want to be an actress…' I said, trying to defend myself.

'I think you need to think of a more viable option, dear. One that could actually be attainable. Like working with a computer. What do your parents think?' She stared at me, the shadow of a smile forming on her lips. It wasn't nice.

'They think I should try and follow my dreams.'

Ethel snorted.

'Oh, do they really?'

Tuesdays and Thursdays were going to be rough.

One term in and high school wasn't looking great. It didn't help that I was a vegetarian. Who ate hummus and avocado sandwiches for lunch. From a Postman Pat lunch box. What. Was. I. Thinking?

My classmates were strangely neutral about Ethel but they could not comprehend how I functioned without a TV. There were two distinct types of student at Parliament Hill. One kind came from the wealthy, arty, families that populated the large houses surrounding Hampstead Heath. The other came from council estates in Camden, Archway, and Holloway. I came from neither. I lived in a maisonette in Queen's Park, so the rich girls thought I was riff-raff and the estate girls considered me a snob. But all of them, rich and poor alike, were united in their horror when they found out I was TV-less. The wobbles paled in comparison when that juicy titbit got out.

'My God, you're a freak!' shouted Lorna, whom I'd considered my best friend. Lorna came from a home that sported five TVs, three Gameboys, and two Nintendos, apparently.

'I mean, what do you do after school?'

'Er, well, I read and play with my brother, and talk, and…' I ran out of answers.

'That's like child abuse,' declared Winnie, one of the posh girls.

'It's not that bad. We watch it at my grandparents' house every week,' I said, trying to dispel the look of disbelief on Lorna's face.

'Nah, man. I'd go mental. I'd be so bored. You are well unlucky.' Lorna seemed genuinely disturbed by my plight and things between us were never quite the same again. My lunch gave rise to similar dramatics.

'Eurgh! What's that you're eating?' cried Emma, another friend, one day.

'Celery and brie,' I said.

'What's celery? And why can't you have fucking ham and cheese like us?' she said, with a surprising degree of aggression for a conversation about a sandwich.

'Because I'm a vegetarian,' I repeated, for the umpteenth time.

'But, why are you that?' she asked, in an irritated voice.

'I told you. I don't want to eat animals.' I put down the sandwich that my mum had made. It didn't taste good any more.

'But why? It's a natural cycle, innit,' said Emma, with a strength of conviction that suggested years of thinking had led to this conclusion.

'I just prefer not to eat them, that's all,' I said. This tiresome conversation was boring but I tried to stay nice.

'You're weird!' Emma shot back. Lorna nodded in agreement. That night I asked my mum if she could make me more normal sandwiches.

Unfortunately, my faux pas weren't restricted to sandwiches. I soon committed a fashion sin that would make the Jason and Kylie fiasco look like haute couture. My dad had instilled in my brother and me a love of Tottenham Hotspur early on – very early on – even before he taught us that hitting someone was wrong. Raoul and I loved them with a passion and our biggest dream was to be the proud owners of the full Tottenham kit. After much begging, this dream had come true at Christmas and we spent the holidays proudly sporting our fancy gear, pretending to be Gazza. I don't think that a polyester garment can ever be the source of such joy again.

You might think that, despite my elation at our wondrous new garb, I would have (and bloody well *should* have) thought twice about wearing it to school. Especially to a school where everyone supported Arsenal. Yes, you might think that but you would be wrong. Instead, I thought that what a wobbly girl with frizzy hair and in the peak stages of gawkiness needed, was to march into class decked out in a white T-shirt proudly advertising Holsten lager, a shiny pair of navy blue shorts and knee-high socks. I decided against finishing off this sartorial car-crash with footie boots (but only because I thought studs + polished wooden floors + cerebral palsy = hospital visit). I wore this nylon travesty with not a shred – not one scintilla – of embarrassment. In fact, I walked around school with the quiet confidence of the socialite who knows, irrefutably, that she has hit the Fashion Jackpot.

And I did it more than once.

Yep, I supported the wrong football team, continued to punch fashion repeatedly in the face, remained blissfully ignorant of the likes of make-up, hair-products and hair-removal, and was partial to a bit of Frank Sinatra. Let's face it: I was perfectly ripe for the ol' bullying. And not just by the girls.

Ms Bunt was my PE teacher. A short, stocky woman, she had curly red hair and thighs that looked chemically enhanced. Decked out in an array of shiny tracksuits, she strutted about school, whistle around her neck, with the pent-up energy of a bull elephant. Sport was her life. Alas, it wasn't mine. I'd finally let go of my playing-for-England fantasies and accepted that I wouldn't be competing in a professional sport in this lifetime. So, it was with a degree of calm that I sat, some distance away from Ethel, in the changing rooms and listened to Ms Bunt wax lyrical about basketball. As we traipsed into the hall, I caught her attention.

'Would it be okay if I did something else today, like the gym? It's just I can't really play basketball.'

Ms Bunt looked at me as if I had clicked at her in Swahili. 'What?' she snapped. Ethel smirked.

'I can't really play basketball…' I repeated.

'Why not?' said Ms Bunt, impatiently. I sighed. I'd have to say it.

'I've got… cerebral palsy.' My voice buckled under the weight of embarrassment.

'So?'

'Well, it means I'm not good at most sport…'

Ms Bunt shook her head. 'Rubbish! That's all in your head.' Technically, her diagnosis was correct.

'Yes, Francesca. Ms Bunt is right. You can't give up that easily,' smiled Ethel, angelically.

'Right. That's sorted. Come on.' And with that, the Bunt strode into the hall. I followed her while Ethel held the door open. I figured one lesson would be enough to demonstrate that it wasn't just all in my head and that there might be medical reasons why I wasn't a basketball sensation-in-waiting. By week four, I was still standing in the middle of the court as girls whizzed around me, my conviction in Ms Bunt's reasoning ability expiring rapidly. Couldn't she see me wobbling around like a newborn foal, trying – and failing – to keep up with the action? Or had she reached such a degree of enlightenment that all she could see was my inner soul? The piercing sound of a whistle cut through the air, followed by the high-pitch squeak of trainers halting on the shiny wooden floor. The girls stood still, their faces flushed and breathing intense.

The Bunt looked at me.

'Francesca doesn't seem to be getting involved. I think we need to address this. Stacey, throw her the ball.'

Stacey looked confused for a second, before throwing the ball towards me. I lurched for it and missed. The ball trickled miserably towards Ethel who was sitting on a bench at the side. She bent down, picked it up, walked over to me and placed it deliberately into my hands. I stood there.

'We've stopped the game for you to have a go. Come on,' said the Bunt, impatiently. The girls shifted uncomfortably. They had been enjoying their game and this was an unwelcome interruption. Their faces betrayed their annoyance.

'I don't want everyone to have to stop playing. I'm fine to watch,' I pleaded.

'Don't be silly! You have to join in. Don't take all day about it either!' barked the Bunt. My hands clasped the ball. I could feel the smooth ridges running across it. The smell of rubber wafted up my nostrils. A tide of humiliation began to rise in me. I wanted to throw back my head and scream. I closed my eyes and pushed that feeling down. My eyes opened and I threw the ball carefully towards Lorna who was standing nearby. It missed her by two metres and she turned round with a sigh to retrieve it.

'Okay. Lorna, now give the ball back to Francesca so she can try again,' instructed the Bunt. Lorna looked surprised. Waves of emotion began to move up my legs, this time threatening to overcome me. I looked at the Bunt in disbelief. Why was she doing this? Sensibly putting little faith in my catching skills, Lorna walked over to me and put the ball into my outstretched hands.

'Hurry up,' she growled quietly.

'Now how about you throw it to me? And focus this time. I know you can do better.' The Bunt walked towards me and stopped about five metres away. Frustration stared back at me as the girls rolled their eyes and looked at each other. Jane was nearest. Her beautiful face was cold. She looked past me as if I wasn't there. I fixed my gaze on the Bunt and threw the ball towards her. It bounced forlornly, well wide of the mark. She placed her hands on her hips and stared at me as if I was a child.

'I expect better next time, Francesca! Now go and get changed.' The girls sighed with relief that the pointless exercise was over and got ready to play again. Ethel looked at me, shaking her head in disappointment.

The Bunt was still singling me out in week six. Some of my classmates had stopped talking to me now. Even my precious friends, Lorna and Emma, had cooled down. They'd stopped saving me a seat on their tables in lessons, and they'd ratcheted up their regular impassioned critiques of my failure to own a TV several notches in intensity. I still hung out with them but couldn't help feeling that my presence was more tolerated than welcomed.

I had to do something fast. It was common among the girls to fake notes from their parents to get them out of PE. I considered this but, with my handwriting… (Unless I could convince my teacher that my mum had suffered a stoke. Or had broken several fingers.) The only option left was to ask

Mum to write the note herself. I could talk to my parents about anything but Dad and I were still at loggerheads over the exercises and I was worried that he might share some of the Bunt's enthusiasms. Because of this, I thought it best to raise it with my mum on her own but even this wasn't easy. Both of them had been blissfully unaware of my growing unhappiness and sense of isolation. Not because they were self-absorbed or insensitive, but because I didn't tell them. I'm sure they could tell I didn't enjoy going to school (what child does?) but they had no idea of the anxiety that had started to clamp down on my chest every time the taxi went through the gates, or of how alone I felt. It's not easy to explain why I didn't just come out with it. I guess I kept quiet because saying it out loud would have made it more real. If I could bury it inside me, I could convince myself – and everyone else – that everything was normal. And I wanted *that* more than anything. No fuss or pity or angst. Just normality. So I took all those difficult emotions that were swirling around me, forced them into a box, shut the lid, and locked it.

Mum was washing up when I walked into the kitchen. 'Mum…'

'Yes, honey?' Her yellow marigolds dipped in and out of the water.

'Would it be possible for you to write me a note for PE next week?'

'Saying what?' she asked, as she placed a glass on the draining board.

'Erm, just saying that you don't think I should play

basketball. That I should be allowed to do something else,' I offered, casually.

'Are you finding basketball too hard?' She looked at me over her shoulder briefly.

'Yes!' I said, trying to sound calm.

'Of course, I will. I'll suggest you do gym instead. That's good for you. Especially the exercise bike.'

I wanted to cry. But I walked out of the kitchen instead. The following week I presented the note just before basketball.

'What's this?' Ms Bunt looked at me and then at Ethel who turned to look at me too.

'It's a note from my mum,' I said, calmly. The Bunt read it out loud.

'Dear Ms Bunt,

Due to Francesca's cerebral palsy, she finds sports such as basketball very difficult and, as I'm sure you can imagine, does not get much benefit from attempting to play them. Would it be possible for her to go to the gym with Ethel instead? This would be a much more productive way for her to spend an hour, and would help her to improve her fitness.

Many thanks, C Martinez.'

She folded up the note.

'I do not accept, Francesca, your mother's reasons for you not playing basketball with the other girls. You're no different.' No shadow of doubt crossed her stubborn face. My ears started to burn.

'But I am different... I...' I paused. 'I have a disability.' I glanced down for a second as the word echoed around the space.

93

'I know what you have. And I don't believe you can't be included in our basketball games. What do you think, Ethel?' Ethel crossed her arms.

'Well, I happen to think it's good for Francesca not to be treated any differently. She should join in.' Her eyes didn't move from my face.

'But I can't play it. I can't run fast or catch the ball! I can't bloody do it!' The force of my words shocked me.

'Don't swear, Francesca,' said Ethel.

'Look, it's just so humiliating when you stop the game for me. The other girls hate it. I hate it. Can't you just let me go to the gym. Please?' My eyes begged her to relent. Mr Rainbow flashed across my mind. At least he'd had the decency to know what I was shit at.

'Not this week. No. You'll come and play like everybody else!' And with that, she turned to go.

'I'm fucking brain damaged!' My anger shoved out these words before I could stop them. The Bunt turned to me. Ethel stared at the floor.

'What did you say to me?' asked the Bunt, in a low and steady voice.

'I said I'm fucking brain damaged,' I repeated, surprised at my nerve.

The Bunt stared at me.

'Apologise now,' she said.

'No,' I said, quietly. Ethel breathed out noisily.

'You can't talk to me like that,' said the Bunt.

'You're treating me like shit because you can.' Tears

were pushing themselves up around my eyes. Angry ones that burned.

'You need to learn some manners, young lady. Now pull yourself together and stop this nonsense.' Ethel looked at her sympathetically at having to endure such rudeness.

'I'm not coming in,' I said, just managing to keep the hot tears from falling out of my eyes.

'What do you mean you're not coming in?'

'I'm not coming in. I'll do gym or I'll wait here but I'm not coming in.'

Perhaps sensing my resolve, the Bunt turned and marched into the hall.

Ethel sighed. 'That was unforgivable. Being so rude to poor Ms Bunt. She's only trying to help you.'

I stared into the distance.

The following week, a pair of keys were handed to Ethel, and I walked with her in silence to the gym. It was a momentary victory. The Bunt would resume her battle to turn me into a Paralympian before too long. My parents came in once to discuss the matter with the head, Ms Bax. A rather retiring older woman, she apologetically told my folks that she didn't have any control over her notoriously bolshie PE staff. So that was that. Over the years I took part in (i.e., watched) tennis, table tennis, rounders, cricket, netball and (no joke) sprinting. But since taking a stand a tinge of respect seemed to have crept into the way Bunt spoke to me. And, when I could be bothered to resist her, she handed over the gym keys without too much of a fight.

My relationship with Ethel, on the other hand, was over.

We no longer spoke to each other. She'd arrive, sit down, and follow me around all day, writing her shopping lists during class. I could no longer accept help from a woman whose sole aim, it appeared, was to rub my nose in my own uselessness whenever possible. I stubbornly refused to let her carry my typewriter or open any door for me. It may seem petty but it gave me great satisfaction to do everything myself. Ms Bax called me to an empty classroom one day and asked me what the problem with Ethel was. I replied that I'd just become more independent and that I was sure there were other kids who needed her help more than I did. (Not true of course: I thought that a kid with no arms or legs or head would still fare better without her.) Ms Bax told me how much all of the staff enjoyed Ethel's company and that they all wanted her to stay. I gently pointed out that Ethel hadn't been hired to entertain the staff. Bax had no answer to that. Finally, after six months, I was Ethel-free. Yes! I walked in the first Tuesday after she had left and heaved a big fat sigh of relief.

Boys became more and more absent in my life. The local group I'd hung out with had dispersed when we all went to different high schools, and the only male-shaped beings around were at the school next door. They seemed a different breed to any I was familiar with. Unapproachable and aloof, with their school ties hanging jauntily round their necks and their grubby white shirts trailing out from beneath their blazers, they did not seem the kind of boys that I could attack on the football field. I began to feel self-conscious in their presence. I didn't know what to say or do or even how to breathe properly. Some of my classmates were incredibly confident in their dealings with them, even laughing in a special way when they were near one. This unique boy-call sounded like the delicate chinking of glasses and would be accompanied by a slight tilting back of the head and a deliberate brushing of hair back from their face. I discovered that some girls were very 'experienced' and had done stuff that made me blush. The gamut of my experience extended to those afternoon kisses with Clint and the tumble with Jake. I began to feel horribly naïve. I was still very innocent and when my friends talked about sex, I would clam up and feel unable to join in. When Emma once mentioned oral sex, I thought it was a fancy term for dirty talk. And I only knew about that because of Mrs Simon's beloved *Sun*. The truth is, I was an old-fashioned, hopeless romantic. My daydreams about boys were laughably chaste. The hottest action they featured was a quick peck on the lips. Most of the time, my imaginary boyfriends were simply partners to play and joke with.

The summer holidays arrived and I was relieved to spend the time with Raoul and my cousin, Aaron, and lapping up the ceaseless adoration of my eternally loving grandparents. Yayo and Yaya were both in London and I made sure to make the most of having them around. We had yummy picnics in the garden and I would lie lazily in the ramshackle hammock as they pushed me back and forth. As always they made me feel safe and sheltered from the outside world, a world that I could almost forget if I tried hard enough.

I cherished each day. My home was a haven from all the complicated stuff of boys and name-calling and 'helpers' and friggin' basketball. The only source of sadness was the ongoing battle with my dad. I remained stubbornly unwilling to acquiesce and do those bloody exercises and this drove a wedge between us. I loved my dad madly and wanted to make him happy but I couldn't give in. I just couldn't. I knew, of course, that I was disabled but I only knew it in my head and, after twelve years, that still hadn't trickled down enough to make me *feel* disabled. Something inside me was still doggedly fighting to hang on to my self-worth. Despite my differences, I needed to feel right, healthy, able. And I needed my dad to see me as those things. To see me as someone who didn't need fixing because I wasn't broken. To make me feel that he loved me exactly as I was.

The biggest bone of contention was my walking. Dad was insistent that I try and improve my movements when we went out for walks. Unfortunately, this clashed head-on with my desire to *enjoy* my walks by daydreaming about exciting things like being a private detective or an international spy.

'Chess, remember to keep your head tall and bend your knees,' called Dad after me as I wandered in the park.

I tried to drown his words out by staring at the grass and counting the daisies that sprung up in random patches. I didn't want to think about my body, which I was discovering was a rather separate entity from me. One with a mind of its own. It was a strangely unsettling discovery so I marked it as something not to think about.

'Chess. Did you hear me?'

His tone was more strained this time, annoyance creeping in like grey fog. I stopped and turned around.

'I'm walking fine, okay! Stop telling me what to do! Can't I just enjoy myself?' The frustration made my hands clench as I looked up at Dad, now standing near me.

'The physio says that you should concentrate on walking tall and swinging your legs from your hips.'

'I don't care what the physio says. I can walk my own way.' My eyes shot up to the sky and its expanse seemed to press down on my shoulders.

'Well, you should care. Don't you want to improve?'

His words wounded me. I hated them.

'I just want to be happy! Why's walking so bloody important? There's more to life than how you walk!' I brought my eyes to his face, not understanding why he chose to hurt me with these words every time we went out.

'I can't believe you're so stubborn! If you put the effort in now, you could be more independent later. Don't you get that?' He raised his hand to his face and rubbed his chin.

I was making him sad and angry. But I didn't know what else to do. My face went hot. I could feel the tears swarming into my eyes like liquid ants.

'Just leave me alone! You make me feel like shit. Like whatever I do is wrong.'

'Why can't you stop acting like a baby and grow up for a change? It's ridiculous that you make such a big deal of this!' His arms gestured emphatically as he spoke and passers-by started to glance over awkwardly.

'YOU'RE the one making a big deal! I hate you.' The words flew out of me like knives.

I turned away from him and walked away as fast as I could. The anger and emotion that swirled inside me made my steps faltering and erratic and jumbled but I managed to keep myself upright. After a few minutes, I turned around and saw Dad, still standing in the distance, staring after me. My breath caught in my throat as I plonked myself down on the grass and shut my eyes to the world.

My mum was often stuck in the middle during these fights. She could see that Dad and I were locked in a war that obscured the genuine, deep love we felt for each other and which we struggled, increasingly, to express. But there was little she could do to stop the conflict. At some level, I felt guilty for forcing my family to endure these brawls and I feared that the grey hairs that had pushed their way on to my dad's head were my fault. He often spoke about my stubbornness and remarked that if I just applied that incredible willpower to my exercises, I'd make remarkable progress. I took some solace in that backhanded compliment and the implication that he didn't think I was a complete pain in the arse.

Sometimes, after one of these big stand-offs, I would go to my bedroom, lie on the bed and close my eyes. I'd daydream that I had two dads, my dad and another one, and that I was in the park playing on the swings. One stood behind me, one in front, and they pushed me, back and forth, higher and higher, until all I could hear was the sound of our laughter, as the wind rushed past my flushed cheeks.

School started again in September. My teachers, feeling that I could still benefit from some practical help, thought it a good idea to assign a staff member to help me on a more casual basis, as and when I needed it. The person they found was one of the admin staff, Prudence, who had a round chubby face surrounded by a short black bob, and a rather large frame which was often squeezed into a velour tracksuit. She possessed very strong feelings about a man called Jesus Christ. Such strong feelings that her four children were called Matthew, Mark, Luke and John.

I had spoken to Prudence a few times and she'd always seemed friendly. I figured anyone would be better than Ethel but, although Prudence was cheery in a way Ethel could never be, I soon discovered that she was devoted to rules and regulations.

'Don't say that, Francesca. Don't take the Lord's name in vain, Francesca. Don't do that, Francesca. Don't go there, Francesca,' she would reproach me, continuously, in her pious voice. She made me feel like a five-year-old. Why couldn't these 'helpers' just help instead of trying to crush my will to live?

Prudence was a constant reminder of what I couldn't do. The free spirit I'd always had inside that used to fly me to heady heights now seemed to have fluttered away, leaving me strangely hesitant and uncertain. I began to feel very judged, something I'd never encountered before. After just a year of high school, a growing feeling of unease and worry lay in my gut. For the first time, I dipped my toe into the murky waters of self-doubt.

One of the ways in which Prudence assisted me was during tests when I couldn't use the typewriter because the answers had to be written on the test papers. She'd sit beside me and I'd dictate my answers as she wrote them down. One morning, I had a biology test and Prudence, sporting a purple velvet number, sat next to me with pen in hand.

'You may start the test, girls,' said the science teacher. I turned to page one and promptly froze. *Label the male genitalia.* And beneath it a detailed diagram of the organ with three lines pointing to different parts. I coughed awkwardly. My eyes darted across to Prudence, who was massaging the golden cross that hung around her neck. I looked back to the paper and stared at the sketch which seemed to rise out of the page at me. How was I going to tell this Jesus-loving mother of four, that the answer to question 1(a) was scrotum? How on Earth could I utter that word to her? I cringed. My hands started to sweat. Prudence looked at me, waiting for me to speak. I weighed up the options. Which would be the best icebreaker? Penis, sperm, or scrotum? Penis? Sperm? Or scrotum? Penis was the least shocking because it was the most often used. But it's also quite a clinical word. I don't think I'd ever said it before. Sperm sounded softer, slightly warmer, and I could probably get away with mumbling it quietly. But it rhymed with germ, and so had dirty connotations. Not holy or pure or sacred. I rolled the sound of scrotum around in my head. Not too bad, I thought. Then I thought about what it was. A wrinkly sack of skin. A sperm purse. Hanging below a penis. Oh, God! Maybe sperm was the best choice after all...

'Come on, Francesca. Say something!' whispered Prudence loudly.

'Sorry. It's just, er, my mind's gone blank!' I smiled, unconvincingly.

'Well, you must know at least ONE of them. Think of your little brother. He's got one!' I died a little inside.

'Erm...' I stuttered. A bead of sweat rolled down my brow. 'Erm...'

'Come on. This is so easy. What's that?' Prudence tapped her pen on the drawing, harshly.

'Well, um...' The words dried up on my tongue.

'It's what a man puts in a woman's vagina to procreate,' she hissed. I flinched at the word.

'Oh, yeah...' I thought of how stupid I must have seemed to her.

'What does your brother have one of that you don't?' she said, slowly, as if I was an infant.

'He has a...' I couldn't say it.

'A what?' said Prudence, still stroking the image with her pen.

'He has a...' I wiped the sweat off my upper lip.

'What is it?' Prudence looked at me with raised eyebrows.

'It's a...'

'COME ON!' she growled.

'IT'S A WILLY,' I shouted.

The whole room turned around. Prudence stared at me as if I was barking mad. Then, in large capital letters, she slowly wrote 'WILLY' in the space provided.

I looked down at my hands and wished, more than anything, that I could write clearly. Or at least clearly enough to save me from having to discuss the finer details of the male sexual organ with a velour-suited, Bible-bashing, old hag, whose name started with Prude.

CHAPTER FIVE

****

Clearly I wasn't cut out for the medical profession. Not that I'd harboured any ambitions to become a doctor. I'd always had a strange relationship with medical folk. They were the only people in the world who made me really nervous. I had no problem performing in front of a packed assembly or dancing wildly to Frank Sinatra in drama classes. Or even having a crack at the old singing myself, delivering ear-obliterating renditions of Tina Turner to my parents and their long-suffering friends. Put me in a room with a doctor, however, and I turn into a gibbering wreck. One step through the doorway and it's clear that all they see is a medical condition. Without fail, doctors ignore me and speak only to whoever has come with me. I'm as invisible as a ghost. Here's a typical interaction:

Dr Bennet [*his eyes trained steadily on my mum*]: So Mrs Martinez, what seems to be the problem?

Mum: Well, Francesca says her ankle hurts.

Dr Bennet [*still looking at my mum*]: Hmm… can you tell me exactly how her ankle feels?

Mum [*calmly*]: Well, maybe you should ask her yourself.

Dr Bennet coughs and his eyes flicker over to me for a second, like a restless bird landing momentarily before fluttering away.

Dr Bennet: Erm… Okay… Right, then. So…

Dr Bennet gets up from his chair and walks cautiously around to me. He kneels down on the floor in front of me.

Dr Bennet [*to my mum*]: Can she take her shoes off by herself?

Mum [*with just a whisper of disbelief*]: I'm sure she'll tell you if you ask her.

Dr Bennet nods before directing his eyes towards my face. He manages to keep them there this time.

Dr Bennet [*slowly and loudly as if talking to a deaf ninety-nine-year-old*]: Can you take your shoes off?

Me [*with the same volume and pacing*]: Yes… I… can.

Dr Bennet looks confused for a moment, unsure whether the freak is being sarcastic or whether she is, as he suspects, intellectually deficient. I stare back at him.

Dr Bennet [*in the same manner*]: Will you take them off?

Me [*casually*]: Yeah, sure I will. My ankle hurts mostly on the outer side, near the back tendons.

Dr Bennet flinches. He flashes a vaguely apologetic look towards my mum, his mouth twisted into a 'smile' reminiscent of Arnie's robotic effort in Terminator 2.

I start to untie my shoes and he watches as my hands tug at the knots in an ungainly way. My struggle with the laces is too much for him to bear and his face turns white. I don't want the poor creature to expire in front of me – he is still young and has so much more patronising still to do – so I smile at him reassuringly.

Me: Don't worry, it's not catching!

Dr Bennet [*tugging at his tie and forcing a smile*]: No, I know. It's just that... I... er...

At that moment my shoe falls off and I lift my foot up to him.

Me: Here we are.

Curtain.

I had no idea I could reduce a grown man to such a state. Talk about power.

It was disconcerting having adults behaving so nervously around me. I began to feel acutely aware of the negative ways in which others viewed me. I grew frustrated at my lack of power in influencing how they saw me. I wanted to yell at them, 'I'm normal, really! Don't look at the way I do things. Look at who I am!' But whenever these awkward situations occurred I shrank a little inside.

Raoul, on the other hand, just saw me as Chessie. And I loved him deeply for that. He didn't see me as wobbly or shaky. And, unlike my friends, he didn't have an issue with me being different or uncool or kitted out in full footie gear. At some level I knew how wonderful his unconditional acceptance of me was and I cherished our relationship more and more.

I think he thought of me as his pretty awesome big sister. And, largely, I tried hard to fulfil this role. However, I have a horrible feeling that something I did when he was seven scarred him for life. As we were telly-less, we spent a lot of time at home doing old-fashioned things such as writing, reading, drawing and actually talking to each other. For the most part, this was great until Raoul decided, over the Christmas holidays, that he really, really, wanted a Gameboy. By today's standards, it's a clunky prehistoric brick of a thing but back then it was the cutting edge of technology. He begged my parents to buy him one but they wouldn't, encouraging him, instead, to draw. (Today he's an accomplished portrait painter but he could have been a computer game junkie… nice one, Mum and Dad.) When he realised that the Gameboy wasn't going to happen, Raoul gave up on the pestering and set about making his own one. Out of paper. A few hours later, he was the proud owner of a, erm, tissue box-sized object with a 'screen' and buttons drawn on to it in felt-tip pen. I'm not sure why he derived such pleasure from holding and staring at this Sellotape-covered oblong, but he loved that piece of crap, and spent hours 'playing' on it. I have to thank my parents for their refusal to have a TV or computer in the house because nothing develops your imagination more than utter boredom.

The 'Gameboy' became Raoul's treasured possession and he carried it everywhere. A few weeks into the new year, we had a row and I committed a terrible crime. I knew it was terrible but I did it anyway. I grabbed my brother's precious creation, looked him straight in the eye, crumpled it up and threw it on the floor. He gazed up at me in shock and disbelief and then burst out crying, his angelic face contorted in misery. Twenty-four years later, I still feel guilty about it.

In the spring and summer of 1991, I grew taller. That fact, in itself, is not remarkable. This particular spurt was significant because it signalled the end of my moderately successful attempts to walk on my own. My balance summarily decided it was time to jump ship and fuck off. It didn't give me any warning about its departure either, selfish git. One day, I was charging around school (erratically but with pace), the next, I was shuffling about like an ancient and pathologically shy three-legged tortoise. I stepped out of class, with rucksack on back, typewriter in one hand and lunch in the other, and started down the hall to find, to my annoyance, that my legs simply would not move fast enough. Stopping, I composed myself for a second, marshalled my resources and told my body to behave itself. I tried again. I put my right foot forward and placed it on the floor, then my left foot. It all happened far too slowly. I sighed. Maybe I was just tired. More and more, my walking reflected how tired or stressed or nervous I was. When my mum used to pick me up from sleepovers at Aaron's house, she could tell immediately how little sleep I'd had. I'd walk out of the front door and she'd say 'You were up late, weren't you?'

'No!' I'd lie, having had two hours' sleep in between chatting, laughing and playing.

'I can see how shaky you are, Chessie!' she'd reply. It seemed so unfair. My cousins and brother could stay up all night and no one would be any the wiser. I cursed my body for being so damn transparent.

Anyway, slightly shaken by the sudden slowness, I went home and decided that a weekend of vigorous sleep was in order. I slept like a bloody baby but, come Monday morning, my steps were still slow and laborious. It was a complete mystery. What the hell was my stupid body playing at? I pumped the accelerator and got nothing for my efforts but a lousy crawl. Then I thought it had happened because I hadn't done those damn exercises. My dad had wanted me to do them for so long and I hadn't tried hard enough and this was my punishment. It was karma, yes, and I was staring right into its smug and punchable face. It never occurred to me that this fluctuation might be a natural part of my condition. I chose, there and then, to blame myself for not trying hard enough. It was all my fault and I just had to try harder. Because, as I was determined to prove to the world, I didn't have cerebral palsy.

Unlike my balance, alas, Prudence hadn't fucked off. I'd learnt to minimise her presence in my life by doing most things myself. The summer term was coming to an end and I was looking forward to six weeks of freedom. Most of the girls had turned thirteen and when you put teenage girls together, they become… bitches! Slowly, the girls either stopped talking to me altogether or decided that

I had to work to win their approval, over and over again.

Reluctantly, I had to admit to myself that I was now largely friendless. I had lost touch with my old best friend, Rachel, who had gone to a different school, and Emma and Lorna had officially cast me aside having concluded that I was a loser – and an odd one at that. They often rolled their eyes when I spoke up in class and I felt they'd rather listen to fingernails scraping down a blackboard. Their dropping of me had been cemented by the fact that I wasn't invited to their highly publicised joint birthday sleepover party. In my twelve-year-old mind, it was the ultimate rejection. I went to bed that night and cried into my pillow at the thought of not snuggling up in sleeping bags, drinking Lucozade and watching *Lost Boys*. *Quelle tragédie*!

The difference between my home life and school was almost comical. By day, I was The Undesirable One, by night and weekends I was The Beloved. I was living two very separate lives and I made sure they were kept well away from each other. My family remained mostly unaware of my dejected schoolgirl alter-ego and that was the way I liked it. As long as I could keep this sorry character from them, I could pretend she didn't exist when I was at home.

As we neared the last day of school (time had never passed slower), I sat and waited for the English lesson to end. Ms Kitkat was banging on about something or other while I stared out of the window, fantasising that I'd landed a part in a Hollywood movie opposite Kevin Costner, that embodiment of gorgeousness. (Actually, I'd like to thank Mr Costner for helping me make it through most of high school without having to jab a fork into my leg.) Those daydreams were now well worn and, inevitably, featured me starring in a glorious movie role opposite Kevin, whose real-life marriage breaks up, and he professes his undying love for me. Needless to say, I would soon sit in the cinema, transfixed and wooed by Kevin in the cinematic masterpiece *The Bodyguard* on more than one occasion. As I indulged in my latest whimsy, a fire alarm rang through the air. Ms KitKat ran out to see what was happening and I prayed that the school was burning down. The look on her face when she returned put paid to that. The alarm shrieked on for another five minutes and then stopped.

'Someone in the school set the alarm off for a joke,' she said, sternly. 'Does anyone know who did it? It's been happening rather a lot lately!' She looked around the room. A few girls smirked but nobody said a word. We all stared back at her.

'Right, well nobody leaves until somebody owns up.' The girls sighed. 'So, if you've got anything you want to say, now is the time to say it.' She sat on the edge of her desk and folded her arms.

'But it's not fair that we all get punished, Ms!' moaned Emma, voicing the consensus in the room.

'Well, that's the only way that we're going to get to the bottom of this,' shot back Ms Kitkat. The clocked ticked on and soon we'd been there a whole fifteen minutes after the end of school. Agony. A car horn beeped outside and Ms Kitkat peered out the window.

'Francesca, your taxi's here. I think you shouldn't keep them waiting. You can go.' My heart jumped for joy as I gathered up the mass of bags and slowly (and rather conspicuously) made my way out. I could feel the eyes burning into my back. Another reason for them to hate me! But this time, I didn't care and bumbled off, smiling, to Mrs Simon.

The next day, I was snailing my way along the corridor as everyone else glided effortlessly past me. Walking shouldn't be this hard, I reasoned. It's just a way of moving from one place to another, right? I'm spending far too much time thinking about this mundane act, hours analysing my walking and then studying how other people do it. I watched Jane walk down the corridor and was mesmerised by the smooth, elegant way her legs bent from the hips and swung forwards. No juddering, just fluidity and attractiveness and ease. That, I told myself, is how I should be walking. I want the same grace and elegance as Jane. Obsession gripped me, vice-like and unyielding. My ruminations were suddenly interrupted by Ms Wilson, the year head.

'Can I have a word, Francesca?' An awkward look flashed across her face.

'Er, yes, sure.'

'Yesterday, you left detention ten minutes early.' She looked at the floor as she spoke.

'Ms Kitkat told me to,' I said, my eyes on her lowered ones.

'I know. But… the other girls stayed ten minutes longer than you, so we think it's only fair that you make up those extra ten minutes of detention in my office at lunchtime.' For the first time, she met my eyes.

'Are you serious?' I said, quietly.

'Yes. It's only fair.' She pursed her lips.

'Fair? Why?' I asked, politely.

'Because the girls waited ten minutes more than you.' I looked at her as she placed her thin hands on her hips.

'Well, on the one hand, the girls had to stay ten minutes longer but, on the other, they can walk properly. I think they win.' I smiled at her, picked up my bags and shuffled off. Wilson stood still for a moment and then walked away. I never sat the detention.

Finally the last day ended and I sunk into my taxi, smiling from ear to ear as we passed through the gates. Six weeks of holiday sprawled out enticingly ahead of me and I felt my body relax as we drove off. I was especially excited because I was going to Barcelona with my grandparents for three whole weeks.

My dad opened the front door.

'Hi, Dad!' I said, beaming with happiness.

'Hi, Chess.' He sounded a little subdued. I walked up the stairs to our flat and dumped the school things on the floor.

'I'm on holiday!' I shouted at the house. Dad walked into the kitchen. I followed.

'We got a letter from Mrs Jaffa today, Chessie.' He held up a piece of paper. Mrs Jaffa was the Deputy Head. I wondered why she was writing.

'What does it say?' I asked. He handed it to me.

```
Dear Mr and Mrs Martinez,
I thought it necessary to write to you
because there has been a noticeable
decline in Francesca's walking lately.
It seemed sensible for me to pass this
on to you in the hope that something can
be done about it.
Yours sincerely,
Mrs Jaffa.
```

I read it again. My head felt heavy as I lifted it to look at my dad. He looked sad.

'Has your walking got worse?' he asked, quietly. I gulped.

'Yes… just one day… it got a lot slower. I don't know why…' I stopped and looked at my feet. The happiness that had been racing around my tummy had gone.

Dad sighed. 'Chess, this is why I've been trying to get you to do exercises. So this wouldn't happen.' His voice made me want to cry.

I just wanted him to hug me. We stood there in silence. The shame burned out of my skin. I couldn't look at him.

'I know. I'm sorry… I'll try harder. Promise.' My throat tightened with emotion and strangled my words.

'I hope so,' I heard him say, softly. The tears fell silently on to my scuffed shoes as I trudged slowly out of the kitchen.

I flopped down on my bed. The joy had been sucked out of me. Bloody Mrs Jaffa. Why did she have to stick her nose in? What did it have to do with her? No other girl's mobility was being scrutinised. I stared at the ceiling, focusing on a tiny crack that snaked into the corner. My body lay eerily still and I suddenly felt utterly disconnected from it, as if it didn't belong to me, as if I was an alien inhabiting it. This body isn't me, I thought. It's broken and stupid and lets me down all the time. *I'm* free and capable and together. That's what defines *me*. Not this thing.

For a moment, I felt trapped in this faulty shell. I wished the inner me could sit up, climb out and walk away, leaving my body discarded on the bed like a crumpled mess of clothes. But that wasn't going to happen. I'd just have to put up with this annoying unwanted appendage.

On the day I flew to Spain, my nose decided that Heathrow departure lounge would be the perfect place to shed some blood. The emotions I felt at leaving my parents and brother behind decided to express themselves in the form of a giant nosebleed. I'd adopted this extreme form of expression quite often and was used to the eerie sensation of blood rushing down my nose. Once, my mum scalded herself with hot coffee and screamed. Hey presto, a nosebleed! My uncle Francisco had recently argued that I was tough enough to attempt a second visit to London Zoo. It wasn't long before I was painting the viewers' area outside the penguin enclosure a rich claret as my Uncle sighed with frustration. The latest nasal explosion, therefore, was not a huge shock to Yaya or me. We were quickly surrounded by the concerned, offering tissues and eager not to see a fellow passenger bleed to death. Thankfully for all, the flow eventually stopped and I waited, relieved and a little bit shaken, to board the plane. I could feel Yaya's excitement at having me all to herself on this holiday and she hugged and fussed over me throughout the flight.

Yaya was a true Spanish grandma. Larger than life, her capacity to love and infuriate were equal in measure. Strong and hard-working, she was at her happiest when bestowing huge amounts of love on her family by serving up never-ending dishes of amazing food. Raoul and I still couldn't believe it when she served us a whole stick of garlic bread each. We didn't have to share it with anyone! Yaya had been a very beautiful woman with dark curls, high cheekbones, film-star nose and perfect beauty spot just above her mouth, and she still prided herself on her looks, flirting with any man who had a pulse.

Yayo, too, could have passed for a Hollywood heart-throb. They looked like the perfect couple. They weren't. Had they been from a later generation, they would have cut their losses and separated long before. Instead, they stayed together and argued. Daily. Big, passionate rows that saw them shouting and screaming and banging doors. Realising that these conflicts were neither pleasant nor productive, they had taken to spending the year largely apart. One would live in their London flat while the other would go to their small Barcelona apartment for five months at a time. This way, they were spared the sadness of a life of constant fighting. I loved them both deeply but was slightly apprehensive about how three weeks with them under the same roof would pan out. Very likely I'd have to be a peacemaker, a role at which I'd grown quite adept over the years.

Anyone with eyes could see they weren't made for each other. Yayo was quiet, thoughtful and creative, with a mind that never rested. Yaya was loud, dramatic and practical, with a mind that often slept. She had manic depression, and swung between extreme lows and highs. Yayo left school at fourteen to fight in the civil war, discovered he had a natural talent with words, and developed into a powerful writer. He was highly intelligent and questioning, with a healthy suspicion of authority. When one of his anti-Franco novels was published in Mexico in the fifties, he became worried about his young family's safety in Barcelona and sought political asylum in London. He was granted this on condition that he would publish another book within a year. He did. So Yaya and her two small sons moved over to start a new life in the capital.

One of the biggest sources of conflict between them was the huge gulf in intellect. While Yayo read constantly, wrote novels and scripts, and debated life's big questions with his group of creative friends, Yaya enjoyed a good gossip over her sewing machine, the music of Tom Jones, and that literary gem known as *Hello!* magazine. For Yaya, a deep discussion usually involved a detailed deconstruction of why someone's outfit was wrong. Her only comments, made repeatedly, on an extended interview with Jeremy Irons, concerned his red socks. 'I don't know why such good-looking man wear awful socks. So silly,' she lamented, as if the world's pain rested on her shoulders.

Yayo and Yaya did, however, share a few things in common. They were both brave, incredibly generous, loved throwing dinner parties, weren't interested in material things like power or money, and took great pride in their appearance. They were unfamiliar with the concept of modesty and enjoyed being beautiful. Their London flat had a mirror in every room so a quick sidewards glance of appreciation was always possible. For a couple who didn't have much money, they always looked immaculate, with perfectly ironed clothes, glowing olive skin and carefully combed hair. As you'll have gathered from my earlier adventures, this gene has passed me by.

The heat that assaulted me when I opened the taxi door was heavy and intense. We were in Besos Mar, a tatty suburb of Barcelona. A large block of flats stood to my right, overlooking a dusty patch of ground where a few trees struggled admirably against the glaring sun. Yaya, decked out in a glamorous outfit, big earrings and impressive hair, looked out of place in this run-down area. Picking up our bags with her strong arms, she began striding towards the entrance doors. A few kids were playing football outside and stopped to stare at us. I kept my head down and followed Yaya as quickly as I could. The entrance hall was refreshingly cool and, in contrast to the outside, was spotless. It smelt of bleach. We climbed four flights of stairs and stopped at a dark wooden door on the left. Yaya knocked on it, the sound of her gold rings on the wood echoing around the stairwell. Yayo opened it. I ran towards him and flung my arms around him, burying my face in his shirt. It had been months since I'd seen him and I had missed him. I looked up at his face with a trace of self-consciousness, the kind that grips you when you haven't seen a loved one for a while. His eyes were happy to see me and he held me tight for another minute before I walked into the apartment. Behind me, my grandparents exchanged a formal kiss on the cheek. The apartment was small and an impressive number of ornaments filled every shelf and surface available. I stood in the middle of the room as my clothes stuck to me with ferocious tenacity and my grandparents looked at me with palpable pride. It was nice to be here.

The homesickness quickly left and I began to relish the holiday. Every morning I'd wake up to the comforting sound of Yaya in the kitchen and I'd emerge to find freshly bought pastries piled high on a plate and a mug of hot chocolate that was so thick you could stand a spoon upright in it. None of that pathetic cocoa powder for Yaya's precious grand-daughter. Oh, no. She'd melt a whole bar of chocolate every morning. The grin on my face as I consumed this calorific wonder was matched by Yaya's as she stood over me, watching me slurp the goo through a straw until nothing was left. She adored doing things for me. I suspect she was bloody delighted when she found out I was wobbly, for it meant she could do more for me. And she always wanted to do more for me. For her, this extra dependence was a dream come true. She cherished not just cooking feasts for me every day, but even being the one to cut up my food, carry my plate and wash my dishes. All this, despite the fact that I'd just turned thirteen. I made her feel useful and I still remember her sadness when, aged twenty-five, I gently declined her offers to help me have a shower.

It was a treat to have my own telly and I gorged myself on it, even though I understood barely a word of it (Spanish TV people fire off words at the speed of a machine gun). Nevertheless, I watched endless hours of shite, concluding that Spain consisted of a lot of very pretty young women and a lot of ugly old men. Looks seemed very important in Spain, especially if you were female, and I felt faintly self-conscious as I watched these women with their perfect faces. But I loved these unrestricted TV marathons and made the most of them. I was allowed to stay up as late as I liked and often fell asleep strewn across Yaya as she sat glued to one of numerous shows that slavishly followed groups of attractive, young, semi-naked people gyrating about as they held cocktails and smoked cigarettes. For five hours straight! Appalled by this cultural black hole, Yayo would sit and read, occasionally glancing at the mindless drivel that passed as entertainment before looking despairingly at his wife, shaking his head silently, and returning to his book.

Most days we didn't go out until after five because the sun's fervour was too much. The apartment had been built before the prevalence of air-con, which meant that it was like an oven inside. Not used to the searing heat, I would sprawl on the sofa, my two feet dangling in a bowl of cold water and a wet flannel placed across my forehead. Contrary to my predictions, I did not melt. Some days we would take a trip to the beach and I'd amuse my grandparents with my 'swimming'. I also loved writing poetry and Yayo would often assign me a subject and say 'write me one about that'. The first topic he picked was bull fighting. I sat down on the tiny balcony and the words tumbled out as I imbued the poem with a sense of intense tragedy – as only a staunch vegetarian could.

I was dutifully paraded around all of Yaya's friends over long lunches. I desperately tried to make sense of their fast-spoken Catalan before giving up and begging them to speak in plain old Spanish. The arguments between my grandparents that I feared happened only infrequently, often arising from some highly controversial topic such as the price of olive oil. I would sit quietly as voices increased in volume and blood pressures rose, and just before I felt objects were in danger of being thrown, I'd step in and remind them that the topic, although clearly important, didn't merit such a furore.

We would visit Las Ramblas, the broad promenade that ambles through the city centre and I would try not to drop the chocolate ice cream that was rapidly melting in my hands. Barcelona was preparing to host the Olympics the following year and the city was being spruced up for the world stage. We'd sit and watch cranes lurch about like huge dinosaurs in the sky. Some days, when the heat threatened to cook us in the apartment, Yaya and I would trudge out to the bus stop and hop on to the first bus that came along, stepping eagerly into the delicious air-conditioning. We would just ride the bus to wherever it was going, gratefully basking in the frosty air. Sometimes we'd find ourselves outside El Corte Inglés, a huge shopping store, and I would spend hours carefully choosing presents for my family with the twenty pounds pocket money I'd been given. It was more money than I'd ever seen and it seemed to last for ever. Other days, we'd just stroll around Besos, stopping to sit on the shaded benches that line the walks, and chat with a never-ending flow of inquisitive neighbours. Everyone, it turned out, knew my grandma and I could see her eyes light up as she became the centre of attention, laughing and flirting with men, young and old.

As I watched my grandma bathe in the glow of male adoration on these local outings, I realised something that I hadn't wanted to. I was no longer cute. I was awkwardly gangly. Boys didn't like to look at me, not in that way anyway. And they probably never would, no matter how nice my brown curls were or how lovely my dress was. I had known this for a while but only now, on that Barcelona street, did I allow my thirteen-year-old self to feel it for the first time.

After months alone in the small flat, Yayo was pleased to have someone to talk to. When Yaya went out, we would sit together on the tiny balcony and he would tell me about his time in the civil war, about when he met Yaya, about his continuing heartache at losing his beloved mother when he was only thirteen, and about how unhappy he was in his marriage. I felt out of my depth engaging in these huge matters. But, I pulled my legs up to my chest and listened patiently. Yayo would talk and then go silent, before starting up again. He would stare into the distance, remembering his past. Sometimes his voice quivered with deeply buried emotion. He told me that he loved Yaya but that she had never been in love with him, only marrying him because she fell pregnant. Her love had never grown and he'd spent his life in a loveless and chaotic marriage. It broke my heart to hear him voice these truths out loud. I knew that he'd been sad, of course, but kept it hidden, along with other painful things, in a place that I chose not to visit. I was too young to realise that he'd been young too, once, that he'd had all my hopes and desires about the future, that I might be his age one day. But I felt privileged that he shared so much and I hoped that, as he confided in me, my love would in some small way help to ease the pain that fell across his eyes like heavy curtains. I didn't have the words but I made sure to give him extra hugs.

I didn't know why but I was certain that Yayo was the kind of human being the world needed more of. Strong, fair and brave, his presence filled me with admiration. I knew he had suffered hardships way beyond my comprehension and had experienced the ugly reality of war, poverty and repression, but he embodied so totally a sense of morality and justice and kindness and courage that I was in awe of him. All the struggles he had been through had not dimmed his commitment to live by his principles. He was the kind of person I hoped I could be.

Because of nosy Mrs Jaffa, my dad had urged me to focus on my walking in Barcelona. This weighed on me heavily any time we stepped out. I'd promised him that I wouldn't link arms and would practise walking unaided, but it was becoming increasingly difficult to do so and the lure of Yaya's and Yayo's sturdy arms was hard to resist. Besides, I was on holiday and wanted to enjoy myself. I was torn. Sometimes, I struggled along on my own, out of loyalty to Dad, but my steps were tentative and unsure, reflecting a growing uncertainty with myself. I slowed down even more when I felt people were looking at me, and I'd bend my head and look at the ground, trying to disappear. The fragmented attitude that I'd recently adopted towards my body was creating a real split in me. I felt increasingly distant from my limbs that wouldn't do as they were told, and my inner voice regularly ticked them off for being so troublesome. My grandparents, always keen to see me happy, encouraged me to stop beating myself up about taking their arms but I couldn't help it. I felt like a traitor to my dad.

I cried my eyes out when it was time to leave Yayo and return to London. After the turbulence of school, the last three weeks had reminded me how it felt to be loved so much, to be accepted just as I was. I would miss being in such a place. I sat on the sofa next to Yayo and begged him not to die. He assured me that he had no plans to do so any time soon. I made him promise me he wouldn't. I looked at his strong, beautiful face and thought of all the sadness that it contained. I didn't want to leave him in this hot, cramped, sticky apartment on his own with nobody to talk to. I took his hand in mine.

'I'll only go if you promise to come to London soon.' I held his hand tightly.

'Of course, Guapa,' he laughed.

'No, I'm serious.' I looked up at him with wet eyes.

'Chessie, I will come back very soon,' he said, not laughing this time.

'Good. Because I love you. A lot.' He pulled me close to him.

'I love you too. Mucho.' His accent made the words sound more beautiful than they normally did. My head lay on his chest and, for a minute, I wondered if I could just miss our plane and stay. I didn't want to go back to school where people didn't care if I was there or not. Why waste time somewhere you didn't want to be when there were people in the world who loved you and needed you? My grandfather needed me. And I needed him.

'Don't be lonely,' I told him, and myself, quietly. He held me tighter.

'I won't,' he said, with a sad voice.

'Okay. I better go.' I didn't move.

'I will be happy if you are,' he whispered in my ear.

'I'll try to be,' I replied, as a large red drop left my nose and landed with dramatic contrast on Yayo's crisp white shirt.

CHAPTER SIX

★★★★

Yayo kept his word. He returned to London a few weeks later where I subjected him to a cuddle-onslaught, pleased that he had escaped from the demons that loneliness can bring. I was far less pleased about returning to school. My body stiffened as I pushed open the classroom door and walked in. About twenty girls were lethargically draped across desks and chairs, their bodies weighed down by the harsh reality that the holidays were well and truly over. Heads slowly turned to see the latest arrival. Multiple pairs of eyes hovered lazily on me for a moment before turning away.

At lunch, Lorna broke the silence.

'No one will ever go out with you. Well, apart from someone like… Jesus!' She laughed as she finished, as did Emma and Stacey. Well, at least it was communication.

'What do you mean by that?'

'I mean the only kind of guy that would go out with

you would wear sandals and be a vegetarian,' said Lorna, smirking.

'I don't think it's been established that Jesus was a vegetarian,' I riposted with the panache of an accidental fart.

Lorna scowled.

'That's not the fucking point, is it? I'm saying the only guy who would fancy you is a yoghurt-eating, carrot-munching hippy!' She spat the words out.

'Thanks for your considered opinion. I'll bear that in mind when I'm looking for potential partners.' I smiled.

'You think you're so fucking clever don't you? Well, just because you eat frigging celery and don't have no TV, you ain't better than us!' (She pronounced 'celery' with a hard 'c' – I let it go.) Emma and Stacey nodded in agreement.

'I never said I was better than you,' I replied.

'Yeah, but you think it. With your taxi and your fancy typewriter and fucking slaves like Prudence doing everything for you!' She seemed genuinely angry.

'If it makes you feel any better, I wish I didn't need any of those things. I'd love to be normal like you guys.' The words jumped out of me before I'd had a chance to think about the consequences of sharing them.

'Whatever. You're a freak. And, fuck it, no man will ever fancy you. Not even Jesus!' She turned away from me and stuck the gold cross of her necklace in her mouth. Conversation over.

The girl had a mass of frizzy hair, big features, and a gap between her two rather prominent front teeth. Her limbs were lanky and her skinny legs – covered in light fair hair – were stuck like toothpicks in a pair of giant purple Doc Martens. I looked in the mirror and sighed. Not, I had to admit, a vision of beauty. Staring back at me was that awkward teenager, with a nose that didn't fit her face, and eyes that were clouded with self-doubt. I'd never really been bothered by what I looked like or what I wore or how I walked, talked or moved. Lately these things had become overwhelmingly important to everyone else. Lots of other people appeared to think these things were fundamental. This is stupid, I thought. I didn't pick the way I look or walk or talk so why does it matter? I always believed people would judge me by what I said or did or how funny I was. I've gotten it all wrong. It's what I look like that matters. The shoes and clothes I wear. This was not good news – when it came to sartorial calamities, my fashion sense was the gift that kept on giving.

Even worse was the dawning realisation that people seemed to form their opinion of me on the one aspect of me that didn't work properly – my body. Like judging a present on its crummy wrapping paper!

The thing is, I didn't feel like a proper teenager. I still quite liked Lego. But a strange, hormonal shift had taken place in my classmates. Many of them started wearing make-up and sporting tighter trousers and lower-cut tops to emphasise their newly hatched breasts. It scared me. Nothing seemed to have sprouted in my bra.

I was also concerned by a stark change in my peer's choice of footwear. Styles varied greatly from boots to sandals to slip-ons, but there was one consistent factor. They all had very high heels. I had enough trouble staying vertical in my flat, clumpy Doc Martens – trying to totter around on skyscraper heels would probably result in a broken neck. It was with deep regret that I had to admit those elusive feminine foot slippers breathlessly screamed 'sexy young minx' while my boots growled 'good in mud and rain'.

And I was missing boys. The only guys I encountered were the male teachers, who were uniformly lovely, far – FAR – nicer than the female staff. I developed a crush on Mr Gurman, my history teacher, and looked forward to his lessons where I could gaze at him for a WHOLE hour! Some of the pretty girls, like Jane and Stacey, had made friends with boys from the school next door but I was petrified of these creatures with floppy hair and grown-up bodies. I'd peer at them shyly from the window of the taxi as they pushed each other around and joked loudly. A nagging feeling told me they wanted something else in a girl. They wanted her to be aloof and pretty and flirty. And I was none of those things.

A cute boy called Ben caught my eye one day, as he chatted to Jane. His long yellow hair fell in front of blue eyes and he kept brushing it off his face as he laughed and kicked a foot restlessly against the kerb. Each morning, I looked for him as we drove through the gates. I wasn't the only one. Lots of girls stole glances at him and He Knew It. One day, I was making my way carefully down the battered stone steps that led into the Old building. Just before I reached the bottom, a shock of blonde hair filled my eyes. Ben stood just below me, blocking my path, the strap of his shoulder bag tight across his un-ironed white shirt, his hands in his pockets. I froze. Ben grinned, two dimples digging into his cheek.

'Allo!' he said, cheerfully. He didn't move.

'Hello...' I said, surprised.

'I got something to ask you.' He tilted his head a little as I towered over him. My knees shook and I tried to lock them straight.

'What?' He took his hands out of his pockets and dropped on to one knee, his right hand on his chest.

'Will you go out with me?' he said, as a lock of hair fell over his eyes.

'What?' The blood rushed into my face.

'Will you go out with me?' he repeated, louder this time. I looked into his eyes staring up at me. Then I heard laughter from somewhere behind him. Looking up, I saw a group of boys doubled-up with laughter. Ben stood up. He was laughing too. He turned and jaunted over to his buddies who high-fived him as they laughed. He looked over at me.

'Oh, you're sooo sexy!' Another guy pretended to hug himself and made loud slurping noises, sending the group into fits of laughter again.

I was strangely unaffected by this mock proposal. It felt as if it was natural, as if it was meant to be. *I* wouldn't ask me out, so why would he? Instead of being hurt and angry, I accepted it as more evidence of my ugly, unappealing self. That night, as I lay in bed, I decided I was over boys. Perhaps, one day, I'd meet someone so wonderful, he'd win my heart with scintillating conversation, red roses and lots of poetry. But I wasn't going to make it easy. I would be a hopeless romantic who never went out with anyone. That, I concluded, was the answer.

I soon discovered the only thing worse than high school is a high-school trip. The thought of having to sleep, wash, dress and eat with the girls and teachers for a whole week filled me with terror. I struggled in private with these activities and my family's loving help shielded me from the cold reality of my inabilities. They knew what I needed to the extent that I rarely had to ask them for help. Sensing I might have some concerns about the trip, Ms Kitkat took me aside and assured me that I'd be given any extra help that I needed. She explained that Prudence had selflessly offered to come along and provide assistance. Oh, joy! I could handle the Bible quotes in small doses, but the thought of her breathing down my neck for seven consecutive days was as attractive as the crucifixion she kept banging on about. But, to get out of going, I'd have to tell my parents how unhappy I was and that wasn't going to happen. So, despite the klaxons blaring in my head, I kept schtum.

A sign welcoming us to Sayers Croft Activities Centre struck fear into my heart. Activities…? Requiring coordination? Strength? Balance? We were shown our dormitories, which were long wooden chalets set among trees. I was in one with ten other girls, including Lorna, Stacey and Emma. A tough girl called Denise was assigned the bunk above me. I sat on my bed and unpacked my bag.

Mum had hidden a good luck card in my clothes. I took it and placed it under my pillow. We were called for lunch and made our way to a large canteen. Kushi, a shy Indian girl from science class, stood in front of me in the queue and offered to carry a tray over to a table for me. I gratefully accepted. Maybe this wasn't going to be so bad after all. I looked around. Lorna, Emma and Stacey beckoned me over to them. They kept me on my toes by throwing me the occasional crumb of goodwill. Which was invariably followed by three months of silence. But beggars can't be choosers and I sat down, thankful to be included.

The food was unidentifiable but I'd been assured that it was vegetarian. I picked it, not because of an urge to eat a mass of creamy white goo oozing on to brown stuff, but because it wouldn't require any cutting up. I jabbed tentatively at the slop with my fork, and took a few mouthfuls. It was tasteless – phew! I had several mouthfuls while the girls talked about Stacey's recent encounter with Ben behind his shed. It had involved 'fingering'. I hadn't pegged Stacey or Ben as the kind who were interested in gardening, and I was glad to hear she was taking more interest in the environment.

The girls finished off their sausages and mash, and I decided I'd consumed enough gruel for one day. Stacey, Emma and Lorna picked up their trays. My tray, of food, drink and untouched yoghurt (just too messy to contend with in public) remained on the table. I tried to figure out if there was any way on Earth that I could carry it over to the stack at the side of the hall. It was at least ten metres away. Hmmm. Very slowly, I lifted the tray. The yoghurt pot wobbled precariously before falling headfirst on to the table. Not a great start. I lowered the tray back down. Tray carrying would not be featuring in my future. I turned around to leave and a loud voice rang through the canteen.

'Francesca! What do you think you're doing?' Prudence, who had been sitting with the teachers at the other end of the hall, had stood up and was looking directly at me. Her stomach trembled as she spoke. I stopped in my tracks.

'You need to pick up your tray when you leave.'

'I can't do it.' I cringed at the word 'can't'. The other girls who were dotted around, still eating, looked up.

'Yes you can! Try!' she ordered.

'I did try. But I nearly dropped it. Can I just leave it on the table?'

The clattering of cutlery stopped. So did the general chatter. Silence. Like spectators at a tennis match, everyone turned to Prudence to watch her next shot.

'No. Try again.'

'There's not much point because I've never been able to carry a tray!' I explained, hoping it would diffuse the mounting tension.

Prudence crossed her arms. 'You give up too easily. Now pick up your tray like everyone else, Francesca. Chop, chop!'

Her voice flew through the air, bullets which hit my ears. I recoiled involuntarily. My family felt a million miles away. For a second, I felt Yayo's strong arms wrapped around me. Then I was alone again.

'I can't do it,' I said slowly. Anger rose inside me, reaching my eyes. Don't blink. Don't blink. I repeated the phrase to myself. Prudence would not have the satisfaction of seeing me cry. Out of the corner of my eye, I saw Stacey and Lorna and Emma stone still, watching me like predators.

Prudence turned to the teachers at her table. 'Oh, she's crying.' She delivered this with false concern.

The other teachers looked uncomfortable but said nothing, sitting there like children.

'I'm not crying,' I said, steadily, somehow managing to drag the tears back in. The palms of my hands felt hot as I walked in silence to the door. My legs wanted to shake and buckle but I willed them on, one step at a time. Prudence spoke again but her words flew past me. Soon, fresh air was hitting my face. The door swung shut behind me as green grass filled my blurry vision. I kept walking.

It was pretty impressive work, even by the standards Ethel had set. I decided I wouldn't ask anyone for help for the rest of the trip. It wasn't that long. My main strategy would be to stand next to Kushi in the canteen so that she would, I hoped, offer to carry my tray to the table. Failing that, I could just go hungry. And I could always pick up biscuits and juice cartons myself. I might become a bit thinner but I'd survive. The blades of grass tickled my legs and I pulled a few of them up and wrapped them around my fingers. Time to go back. I stood up and made sure my eyes were dry before heading for the dormitory.

Embarrassed eyes watched me as I walked in. Nobody knew what to say, so nobody said anything. I sat on my bunk, reached under the pillow and rested my fingers on the card my family had given me.

I learnt lots of things on that trip:

1. Biscuits aren't entirely devoid of nutrition; indeed, they can sustain a hungry teenage girl pretty well.
2. Lorna was definitely *not* my best friend.
3. Sayers Croft need to employ a better cook.
4. Giving Denise a stamp for her postcard is no guarantee that she won't stamp on your bare feet a few hours later.
5. Prudence would not be on my Christmas card list.
6. Most of my jeans stay up without the button being done.
7. Teenage girls don't get nicer after 4 p.m.
8. Kushi thought I was stalking her.
9. It's possible not to ask anyone for help for a week and not starve to death.
10. Fingering is not a gardening activity.

Getting on the coach at the end of the week, I couldn't help but feel pleased with myself that I hadn't asked Prudence for a single thing. Better still, I hadn't uttered a single word to her. The day after the tray business, she found me lugging a bag of books up a hill and very sweetly offered to carry them for me. I silently carried on with the speed of an elderly snail. The next day, she came up to me in the art workshop and suggested she tie my apron and mix my paints. I didn't move a muscle (quite an achievement for a wobbly girl). By the third day, she steered clear of me. It was a small victory but one I was proud of. I was surprised by the determination that surged through my veins. Something in me felt that Prudence wanted me to be a victim, someone she could push around, knowing that I'd have to ask her for help later. And I resolved not to let her turn me into a meek doormat who she could happily wipe her muddy shoes on.

Despite the fact that I was becoming less and less sure of myself at an alarming rate, I was acutely allergic to authority figures seeing me as an easy target because of my disability. This power dynamic made me kick back. And hard. The girls could treat me like shit – I could handle that. But not Prudence.

My biggest fear was of being seen as vulnerable and pathetic and, therefore, easy to control. I needed to prove to myself that, even though I needed help in some areas, I wasn't a weakling. If I failed in this, it would have meant that my damaged body had succeeded in defining me. And there was no fucking way that was going to happen.

When my mum opened the door on my return, I let her hug me as I breathed in the familiar smell of home. My rigid limbs began to relax as I watched Raoul play in the front room. I sank deep into the soft pink sofa and shut my eyes. It was good to feel safe again but I was off biscuits for a while.

The confidence I'd once possessed felt as if it had been run over by a ten-ton lorry. Repeatedly. I wondered where that carefree girl had gone. The one who'd seduced boys with afternoon kisses and gleefully gobbled poisonous berries. Was she hiding somewhere? What would she think of me now? Not a lot, I guessed. Some days I got out of school by feigning illness and I'd lie on the sofa reading all day, enjoying the peace and quiet.

There were a few exceptions to all this shit. The first was Mr Gurman, who continued to be very nice to look at. The second was drama. I still thrived on performing and had been top of the year for two years. My teacher, Ms Sanderson, had encouraged me in my passion and spurred me on in class. Everything in life was fine when I was in the drama studio. I spent the whole week waiting for this one hour when I could be someone else. When we had our first one-on-one session with Ms Murray, the Career Advisor, I knew, without a shade of doubt, what I wanted to be.

'I'm going to be an actress!'

Ms Murray looked over the top of her glasses and put down her pen. 'An actress?' she said, softly.

'Yes! I love acting. It's my favourite thing to do in the world.' I replied.

'The thing is, acting is a very difficult profession...' She trailed off.

'I know. But I want to give it a shot,' I said, dripping with enthusiasm.

'Right, but... er... maybe you should consider something a bit more secure. Something like IT.' Ethel had suggested that too. What was it with me and bloody computers? We were being pushed together like two unenthusiastic singles at a party. (By the way, if you are ever saddled with the beautiful label 'disabled', be prepared for people's expectations of you to plummet to frightfully low levels. So low, in fact, that the world's best limbo dancer couldn't scrape under them.)

'I just want to do something I love,' I said, ignoring her. She stared at me for a moment before dropping her eyes to the floor, perhaps remembering some distant passion she'd once held before deciding to spend her days politely crushing other people's dreams.

Besides history and drama, I also enjoyed English. I devoured the books we were asked to study, and I always enjoyed reading plays and poems aloud in class, even if my impassioned recitals elicited a wave of eye rolling from my peers. In my spare time, I was writing more and more poetry but I didn't show the poems to anyone outside the family. My dad was a brilliant writer and my mum had written books too, and they were very encouraging about these rhyming odes on life and love.

One day, our English teacher asked us to write a short story about anything we wanted. I chose to write about an orphan boy who grew up in a cruel foster home and, years later, finds his real parents. I'm not sure what induced me to write this but I threw myself in and savoured the task. My style of writing tended to yank firmly, rather than tug gently, on the reader's heartstrings. Luckily, my teacher wasn't averse to that and gave me an A. I proudly took my story home and handed it to Yayo, who had come to visit. I waited while he read it, watching him as he sat on the sofa, his silver hair swept off his fine face and his dark-framed glasses perched on his nose. When he reached the end, he put the typed pages on the seat next to him, took off his glasses, and placed them on the paper. Pausing for a second, he wiped his face, stood up and walked over to me. Always ready for a Yayo hug, I got up and stretched out my arms.

'That, Chessie, was beautiful,' he said, with tears in his blue eyes. I pressed my face into his soft woollen jumper and breathed in deeply.

As thoroughly delightful as the academic year had been, I found myself, once again, willing the holidays on with desperation. I found it increasingly difficult to walk on my own but there were scant arm-holding options at school, so my walking had settled into a style I can only describe as 'awkward shuffle'. I begrudgingly accepted that it probably wasn't going to improve any time soon. This new way of moving seemed to reflect the self-consciousness that had descended upon me like a foggy mist. I figured it wouldn't be leaving any time soon. Annoyingly, it got worse the more people looked at me. Sometimes, I could barely move at all. I started to develop strategies to deal with it. I'd stop and fiddle with my bag, or bend down to attend to my shoelaces, inventing plausible reasons to stand still until the starers had had their fill.

Much to my dad's relief, I finally agreed to attend physiotherapy once a week. It was not that I'd developed a sudden maturity or a new willingness to endure boredom but more a resigned sense that this darn body was not going away. It was as if I'd been stuck in a loveless marriage for years, before realising that I'd have to sit down with my partner and work something out. Only difference was, divorce wasn't an option. So, with a heavy heart, I decided to try and make this difficult relationship work. It wouldn't be easy. Especially as my body had a mind of its own and a tendency to do whatever the hell it wanted, without having the courtesy to consult me first.

My taxi dropped me off after school at an imposing red-brick building in Hampstead. I was embarrassed about being seen at this place and ducked through the large doorway like a lonely middle-aged man slipping into a sex shop. Once inside, I would go into a large treatment room and the physiotherapist would get me to walk and write and offer constructive suggestions along the way. It was actually rather painless and sometimes helpful. But it did feel odd having these weekly sessions that were dedicated to the part of me that I'd tried to ignore for so long. One week, my therapist told me, with a broad smile, that I carried out tasks more effectively when I was relaxed and happy. I smiled back. If he only knew...

There were a few nice girls in my year that I hung out with when I got the chance but, unfortunately, there didn't seem to be many of them in my class. I have to point out that, by now, my classmates were hardly ever cruel or overtly mean to me. They just didn't talk to me or have lunch with me. As unpleasant as arguments or fights could be, at least they involved interaction and contact and a level of aggression that suggested some degree of caring, some willingness to expend the energy required to get annoyed. That, I could handle. It was the frosty apathy, largely concealed, that was corrosive, that peeled away the thin layer of confidence I held on to. I felt invisible.

It was disconcerting to go somewhere everyday with the feeling that nobody would even notice if you just stopped coming in. I realised how little daily interaction I had with my class and what a far cry it was from my chatterbox days at Salusbury when nobody could shut me up.

Perhaps noticing a shift in my personality, Ms Kitkat took it upon herself to intervene with her signature tactlessness. I'm sure she was trying to help, bless her, but a demented gibbon would have done a subtler job. She'd passed on her observations to Ms Wilson, and I was called into an empty classroom one afternoon. Six chairs had been set out in a semi-circle and Ms Wilson beckoned me to sit. I had an uneasy feeling in my throat. I was about to ask her why we were there when Lorna, Emma, Stacy and Denise walked in and filled the empty chairs. They looked at me resentfully, slouching down and stretching their legs out defiantly.

'I've called you here today to try and work through an issue which is causing concern...' Ms Wilson paused and turned her gaze towards me. My panic quadrupled. 'Why are you being mean to Francesca?'

I nearly toppled off my chair. 'What?' I said spontaneously.

'Ms Kitkat has noticed that some girls aren't treating you well.' My life, I couldn't help thinking, would be a lot easier if Ms Kitkat stopped trying to 'help' me.

'It's okay. We don't need to do this.' I said, hurriedly, eager to wrap up this car crash.

'I think it will help to talk openly about what's going on,' said Ms Wilson, firmly. The girls' sullen faces said otherwise.

'Why aren't you friends with Francesca any more?' She directed this at Lorna, who didn't move a muscle. 'Come on, Lorna, say something,' persisted Ms Wilson.

'We don't like her no more,' said Lorna, slowly.

'Why?' asked Ms Wilson.

Lorna smiled before she spoke. 'Because she's so different from us. She has a typewriter. She gets a taxi to school. She gets help from Prudence. She does gym when we do netball sometimes. And she's clever. She don't need all that help.'

'You do realise that Francesca gets some extra help because she's got cerebral palsy,' said Ms Wilson, calmly. I flinched at this.

Lorna looked back at me and crossed her arms. 'I forgot that.'

'You forgot it?' Ms Wilson looked surprised.

I wondered if I was dreaming. Maybe it would all end in a minute and I'd wake up to the morning sun shining through the dark blue curtains.

'Yeah, we don't think of Fran like that. She's different but not really 'cause of that, you know. She's just… she likes the wrong things and wears the wrong clothes and she uses words we don't.' The others murmured their agreement. 'She's just… different. She's not normal, Miss,' she concluded. I couldn't argue with her analysis. Ms Wilson sighed, visibly baffled.

'Well, girls, I don't want you to hold the extra support against Francesca. Parliament Hill is committed to treating everybody equally regardless of ability,' she said, with a condescending tone. 'Do you understand?' said Ms Wilson to the girls. They nodded vaguely.

Unsurprisingly, this ham-fisted effort failed to deliver renewed offers of friendship. The following week, the girls demonstrated their displeasure by sticking chewing gum in my hair. I hoped no more humanitarian interventions would take place.

At 3.20 p.m. on the seventeenth of July, I rushed out of school, into my taxi and headed for Yaya and Yayo's flat. Raoul was on the doorstep and we hugged each other with excitement. Holidays! Raoul was enjoying life at Malorees but he knew that time off school was always more preferable to time in it. Yaya opened the door and swept us into her arms, pulling our heads to her round, cuddly frame and covering us with loud kisses. She was full of smiles at the prospect of stuffing us with tortilla and salad and beans and garlic bread and Coke and chocolate and apple pie, and we were equally happy at the thought of consuming it all in front of the TV. It was heaven, the perfect way to forget school and ease into the hols. We bounded upstairs and took off our shoes.

'How was last day at school?' asked Yaya in her thick Spanish accent. In thirty-two years, she had not acquired an atom of Englishness. Her love of the country helped her not a jot in mastering its language and she struggled with it perpetually, which never failed to amuse us.

'Okay, but it's good to be off now!' I said.

'Where's Yayo?' asked Raoul.

'She sleeping upstairs,' answered Yaya. Raoul laughed.

'Yaya, it's "he", remember?' he giggled.

'Okay, *he* sleeping!' she said, laughing. Yayo often had a nap in the afternoon. He was undergoing dialysis and often needed to rest in the day. Friday night was family night and he liked to be fresh to talk to my parents when they arrived after work. We walked into the TV room, flopped down on the sofa and settled down for a serious dose of *Neighbours*. Halfway through our mountain of grub, Harold Bishop had a heart attack. The shock was such that we dropped our forks and stared at the unfolding attempts to save the poor fella's life. We sat frozen for twenty minutes to see if he would make it. Yaya reminded us that our food was getting cold and we ate a few bites as the doctors continued to resuscitate him. Madge, Harold's wife, looked on with desperate panic. Eventually, he was brought back to life and Madge cried with relief as she sat by his hospital bed. The emotion was too much for us and we shed our own tears over the tortillas Españolas. As the jolly end jingle kicked in, we turned to each other and gasped. These Aussies certainly knew how to deliver heart-stopping entertainment.

I was already stuffed when Yaya set down a bowl of apple pie and cream. My protestations were brushed away and I resigned myself to more eating. I could always find a way. Sitting back for a moment's breather, I felt the warm glow of the approaching holiday settle over me like a light golden blanket. Upstairs, my grandma screamed. I sat upright. She screamed again and again. Raoul and I turned to each other, eyes wide, frozen with fear. The screaming stopped and we heard Yaya pick up the phone and dial a number. When the call was connected she didn't speak. She just cried into the receiver before dropping the phone on the wooden dresser. Horror filled my stomach and oozed out like black paint. I felt sick. Without knowing, I knew what had happened. We both did. Raoul and I pushed back our tables and walked to the doorway. We stood there, waiting, afraid. The fear spread down to my legs and up to my chest and neck. I felt like I was being strangled and opened my mouth and gulped in air. Yayo had died.

Raoul started to cry. I pulled him to me and heard myself tell him not to cry. But my own eyes were wet and I felt my face break with grief. We stood there, holding on to each other, our bodies shaking, the tears rushing furiously down our faces. Yaya appeared on the landing in her apron, grief drawn in heavy lines across her lovely face. Walking over to us, she moaned softly and drew us close to her. We didn't move until my dad arrived. His face was white but he wasn't crying. In that moment, I thought he was the bravest person I'd ever known.

My grandfather had had a massive heart attack while sleeping on the sofa. He had died immediately. Raoul stopped crying shortly after seeing my dad, declaring that he wanted to be strong for Yayo. I greatly admired his maturity but I didn't share his courage. I sobbed all evening. And the following day. I think I racked up a fortnight of continual sobbing.

Later that evening, my parents asked us if we wanted to see Yayo. I wasn't sure what to do. A part of me was terrified about seeing a dead person but another part just wanted to see my grandfather once more. I crept up the short flight of stairs holding my dad's warm hand. The door to the dining room was on the right. I hesitated.

'Do you want to go back downstairs?' asked my dad.

I looked at his face. He looked tired and sad, his eyes throbbing with pain. Yayo had been his best friend all his life and now he was gone. And yet he was still holding it together and comforting me. I wanted to be strong, just for a minute, for my dad. I shook my head. We stepped forward together and I turned slowly to the open door, pulling my eyes up from the floor. There he was. Sitting on the sofa in his pyjamas and stripy dressing gown, his legs outstretched on the floor, his feet encased in slippers. His head was tilted and resting on the back of the sofa, his mouth was open as if he was about to speak. But it was his eyes that held mine. They were wide open and staring up at the ceiling. Except they weren't staring. They were just... there. Two glass globes with nothing behind them. He had gone somewhere else. Whatever made him Yayo had disappeared and only a shell was left behind. It was a shell I loved but it was still a shell. He was so still. I had never seen him so still. The stillness wormed its way into my brain and stayed there for a long time. I realised I was gripping my dad's hand tightly and not breathing. I gulped.

It was then I noticed that Yaya was sitting beside Yayo and holding one of his hands in her lap as she cried. She was touching him and I wanted to touch him too. To have one last hug. One last feel of his skin. But I just stood there, too scared to move. I hoped that wherever he was now, he knew how much I loved him.

I thought back to the last time I'd seen him. It was Sunday. Yayo and Yaya had come to lunch and we'd eaten together and laughed and talked. He had loved my dad's home-made garlic bread so much that, unusually for me, I'd given him my last piece. He had accepted it gratefully.

A few hours later, two men carried my beautiful Yayo down the stairs in a black plastic bag and I never saw him again.

Only the day before, he'd called my house and I'd answered the phone. He left a message for my dad and I promised to relay it.

'It's the holidays tomorrow!' I told him, barely able to contain my happiness.

'Yes. We will have a great time together. See you tomorrow, Chessie. Bye,' he said, his smile audible.

'Bye. Oh, Yayo…' I said, hoping he was still there.

'Yes?' he said in his soft Spanish voice.

'I love you,' I said, somehow feeling that I might never get the chance to tell him again.

CHAPTER SEVEN

★★★★

I cried in the shower, through breakfast, lunch, dinner – stopping just long enough to shove some unwanted food into my mouth – and at night in bed. I didn't have time for much else. Little things would set me off, like seeing one of Yayo's stray slippers on the floor or catching a glimpse of his handsome – and very alive – face in a photograph. But, after two weeks of this dedicated lamenting, I woke up one morning expecting to embark on a fresh sob-fest to find my eyes eerily dry. Perhaps my tear ducts had gone on strike, in desperate need of a break. This happened just before my fourteenth birthday: my first ever without Yayo. (When the day came, my tears sprang back into action for one more time.) Not normally inclined towards superstition, I couldn't help feeling relieved to move on to the more numerically neutral fourteen.

Heaven was not a concept I was brought up to believe in, but it was comforting to think of Yayo somewhere in the ether smiling down on me. And, judging by the strange-but-welcome incidents of good luck that began to enter my life, it would appear that he was using his mighty after-life powers to make some good shit happen. As a tasty starter, on my first day back at school, I found out that Prudence would no longer be 'helping' me. I tried very hard to mask the ecstasy that pulsated through my body and which threatened to seduce me into attempting an actual jump. I managed to keep my feet on the ground and not scream for joy, deploying, instead, my acting skills to look suitably disappointed-yet-accepting of the vagaries of life.

However, I was not to be completely assistant-free: I was to be assigned a new helper called Carol Carlton. I prayed to Yayo that it would be third time lucky. And being the fantastic dead grandpa that he was, he granted my wish. Carol was just lovely. Soft-spoken, with long greying hair and pale eyes, she was caring and sensitive and as far away from domineering, bullying and tactless as you could be. And she actually seemed to, wait for it, *like* me! I still missed Yayo terribly but the wonder of his God-like meddlings eased the pain somewhat. Very quickly, Carol and I became good friends and we'd spend hours talking about life and hopes and dreams, as well as her complicated love-life as a forty-something single mum of two. Clearly unaware that the last time I'd kissed a boy he was holding an action figure, she seemed genuinely interested in my opinion of her romantic endeavours, and I felt privileged that she confided in me. Finally, there was someone nice to hang out with at school.

Yayo had one more ace up his ethereal sleeve, however, and a few weeks later, my life was to change for ever.

'You've got an audition for *Grange Hill*!' said my mum, unable to keep herself from smiling.

'What?' My eyes widened spontaneously.

'You've got an audition for *Grange Hill*! The show's producer is coming to meet you next week!' She was beaming now. I looked back at her in disbelief, struggling to process her words because they were simply too awesome to be true.

'Really? But what… how…?' The words dried up on my tongue.

'Carol saw an advert in the paper asking for disabled children in mainstream schools to come and audition for a new part and she recommended you! We've been waiting to tell you for two weeks. We were just waiting for the meeting to be confirmed! Isn't that exciting?' She looked at me expectantly. A huge smile pushed itself on to my lips. A laugh exploded from somewhere deep inside me.

'Are you sure?' I asked.

'Yes. I'm sure.' We hugged for a long time.

Aside from the Raoul-being-born business, this was the Best News Ever. In the history of the universe. For years I'd dreamt of being an actress and daydreamed about being cast in a TV show. And now it was *actually* happening. *Grange Hill* was only *the* most popular children's show on the BBC. Okay, Costner wouldn't be in it but you can't have everything, right? And maybe, just maybe, the producers would lure him over to play the hot new American teacher in this North London comprehensive who has an illicit affair with a student. Who happens to be a tad wobbly. A girl can only hope.

I lay in bed that night, a million thoughts flying around in my head. It all seemed just too amazing to be true. Everyone in school watched it and it came second only to *Neighbours* in my favourite TV shows. I would have to buy Carol a BIG box of chocolates for giving me such an incredible opportunity. And I'd have to find a subtle way of slipping it into a conversation with my eternally sceptical careers advisor. I fell asleep with an over-sized smile stretched across my face.

The following day, I gave Carol a huge hug which may have been a bit too crushing in its strength. She was visibly chuffed at how happy I was. Such happiness *in school* felt weird and unnatural. The girls, unsettled by my upbeat demeanour, eyed me suspiciously. Stacey sidled over and perched on the edge of our table.

'What you so happy about?' she asked, suspicion colouring her voice like a faint dye. I was unsure how to answer.

'Francesca just got some very good news!' said Carol, proudly. Stacey did not look pleased. She cocked her head to one side and fiddled with her massive hoop earring.

'Oh, yeah. What's that, then?' her intense interest overwhelming her efforts to appear disengaged.

'Well, I… er, I got an audition for *Grange Hill*,' I said. Stacey stopped playing with her ear hoop and stared at me.

'You w-what?' she sputtered like a failing engine.

'I got an audition for *Grange Hill*.' Curious as to what had rendered speechless the usually highly vocal Stacey, the rest of the gang – Lorna, Emma and Denise – glided over.

'What's going on, Stace?' enquired Emma, eyeing me up as she spoke. Nobody said a word for a while until Stacey blinked back into existence.

'Fran's got an audition for *Grange 'ill*.' The girls looked dumbfounded.

'What?' said Lorna, menacingly.

'Fran's got an audition for *Grange 'ill*,' repeated Stacey as if she'd just learnt to speak. A noise came out of Lorna's throat.

'But she hasn't even got a fucking telly! How the hell did that happen?'

'I recommended her to the producers. I said she'd be perfect for the show,' said Carol, smiling. I wasn't used to appearing in the same sentence as the word 'perfect'. It felt wrong.

'But...' A keen actress herself, Stacey had always made it very clear that she intended to be a star. Although she invested more time on her luscious black hair than on the art of acting, she often spoke of her unfailing magnetism and her future casting couch conquests. When I would join in and voice my acting dreams, she would laugh with pity at such ridiculousness. I looked from her to Lorna, Emma, and Denise and saw the same thing staring back at me from each one. A thing that I'd never seen before. The unmistakable sight of envy. I suddenly felt bad. It was an awful lot to take in and I watched them sit back down in their seats, still reeling from the news. They simply could not believe it. And why would they? I was the wobbly goof who wore the wrong clothes, ate the wrong sandwiches, and sported the winning combo of frizzy hair, big nose and acne-covered skin. A born repeller-of-males. Not, therefore, someone meant to be on TV. Ever. It was against the ancient laws of the universe.

A week later, I met the producer, Christine, at my house. Barely able to stand still, I tried to convince her that there was no teenager on the planet who wanted this part more than me. Amused by the absurd level of enthusiasm, she explained that she wanted to cast a student with a disability so that the show would more accurately represent modern-day schooling. Despite having run for nearly twenty years, *Grange Hill* hadn't yet featured a disabled main character and Christine thought it was about time to do so, it being such a flagship show and all. I heartily agreed. And for the first moment in my life, I felt lucky to be wobbly. But for that, I wouldn't be on the cusp of auditioning for a real TV show. In that second, I thanked my lucky stars for my disability. Christine interrupted this private outpouring of gratitude towards my palsied cerebrum by asking me if I watched the programme. I assured her that I did, even though we didn't actually have a TV. She wasn't put off by this freaky revelation and even laughed at the irony of my trying out for TV despite not having one. Things seemed to be going well. I even refrained from busting out my Tina Turner bit (although I was tempted).

At the end of our chat, she handed me a script to learn and told me that I would be auditioning in three weeks' time at the BBC rehearsal rooms in Acton. I waved her off and then subjected my family to a blow-by-blow account of the meeting. By 9 p.m., I'd learnt the script by heart. The paper was yellow and I was fascinated by it, handling each page with all the care I could muster. This was a real TV script with scenes and dialogue and descriptions. It was a thing of true beauty. I practised my scene over and over again until the words felt easy and natural in my mouth. Then, of course, time slowed right down to a frustrating crawl and I had to endure the three longest weeks ever.

Eventually, the day I'd been waiting for (all my life) rolled around, and I found myself in a big room with about forty other disabled teenagers. Some were in wheelchairs, some were short, some wore leg braces – it was a long time since I'd been around other disabled teenagers. I couldn't help feeling they were a mirror reflecting back an image that I wasn't used to seeing, but I pushed that aside and focused on what I was there to do.

We were divided into groups of three and each group had to perform the scene in front of Christine and three other important-looking BBC people. It was, without a doubt, the biggest day of my life but, for reasons I can't explain, I wasn't at all nervous. In fact, I was itching to get up and perform. This complete absence of nerves is a mystery and I can only surmise that they were obliterated by the delicious thought of winning the role and missing the best part of eight months of school a year – legally! I waited impatiently until it was my group's turn. We stood up and Christine said 'action'. The hours of practice paid off and I launched into the scene with gusto, pleased to see I was the only person not holding a script. I paused before delivering the final comic line. The BBC people all laughed. I knew I'd done well. Jemima's perfect face flashed across my mind as I stood there. Finally I was able to forgive her her theft of Cowgirl #1. I was happy for her. This was so much better.

My ability to assess audition outcomes had improved since the days of dear old Mr Rainbow and, a few days later, I heard that I'd made it to a final group of four. I greeted this fantastic news with commendable maturity: I jumped up and down on the sofa while screaming and then fell off. Stacey was slightly less enthusiastic.

'Did you do that audition?'

'Yes.' She scanned my face as I tried to remain impassive.

'And… what 'appened?'

'I got through to the final four.' I hoped the joy would stay hidden from my face. She looked really annoyed now.

'But… you don't even have a TV…' she said, with irritation.

'I know!' I smiled at her as she looped a lock of hair round her finger and slumped into her chair. Being the class freak wasn't so bad after all.

The second audition took place in the iconic BBC Centre in West London. As the security gates opened for our car, I bristled with excitement. I'd always wanted to visit this famous building and here I was, about to audition for the biggest children's TV show in the country. We waited in the reception and Yayo walked into my head. A devoted movie-lover all his life, I knew he'd be thrilled that his granddaughter was getting a shot at acting. His proud smile filled my mind and I vowed to try and win this part for him, wherever he was now.

Christine appeared and led me down never-ending corridors until we reached a small room with a table and chairs. The same important BBC people sat behind the table and welcomed me as I sat down opposite them. This time, there had been no script to learn and I just read through some scenes with them. Luckily, I'd developed into a confident reader during my toddle-free toddler phase. Once again, I thanked my balance for being so elusive in those first three years.

With the audition over, all I could do was wait. It was early December and I hoped that I would hear the news before Christmas. But the term finished and I still had heard nothing. It drove me crazy and, by extension, I drove my poor family crazy. Each day I would leap out of bed, bump downstairs, open our flat door, bump down the communal stairs to the hallway, plop myself down on the doormat and rifle through the pile of post. Any letter addressed to me would be ripped open (the contents being torn in the process). I'd frantically search for the famed letterhead but... nothing. By the time Christmas Day arrived, I'd convinced myself that I hadn't got the part, and even the prospect of an over-flowing stocking at the end of my bed couldn't lift my mood. I'm not sure what I was more upset by: the thought of not getting the part or the dreaded prospect of continuing at school. My family tried to keep me positive and reminded me that I hadn't heard yet so I shouldn't be so pessimistic. We toasted Yayo on New Year's Eve and, predictably, I let more tears out. Yaya held me in her arms as always – her unwavering bravery in the face of losing a loved one was something I had not inherited. She left me feeling a lot more philosophical and I went to sleep comforted by the vision of Yayo sitting on the side of my bed watching over me.

The next morning I awoke to the sight of my mum in her dressing gown standing next to me. She was holding a letter. Which was addressed to me. I sat up and looked at her, scared to take it. She held it out to me.

'Go on, open it!' she said, encouragingly. I took the envelope and stared at it.

'This is actually a bit scary. What if it's bad news…?' I said quietly.

'Just open it!' My mum sat down next to me. I turned the envelope over and slowly peeled off the seal. I pulled out the white letter, took a deep breath, and unfolded it to reveal the BBC logo in the top left hand corner. I forced my eyes down.

Dear Francesca,

We are delighted to offer you…

And that's all I read before I threw the letter in the air, screaming with joy. Dad and Raoul came running into the room.

'I got the part! I got the part!' I shouted.

'That's amazing, Chess! Well done!' said my dad, smiling broadly. Raoul jumped on the bed and we all attempted a rather clumsy group hug. The joy exploded in my stomach, little bombs of happiness, which kept going off all day. It was the best New Year's Day I'd ever had.

The dread that normally lay across my shoulders as I entered school after a holiday was strangely absent. Instead, I felt a calm distance from my surroundings as I climbed the stairs to my classroom for registration. An unfamiliar feeling settled in my stomach. It was the feeling of hope. Undoubtedly school would continue to be shit but it was the kind of shit that I could endure now because I had something else in my life. Something so amazing that the mere thought of it made me smile. I was going to be a professional actress. And, at that moment the producers were busy creating a new character especially for me. I was sure this would make my classmates hate me even more but, as Clark Gable said in Yayo's favourite film, I didn't give a damn. The girls waited impatiently until first break before approaching me.

'So, did you 'ear from *Grange 'ill*?' asked Stacey, jutting her chin out.

'Yes,' I said, opening a yoghurt and nut bar. The sight of it made Lorna groan.

'Well, what did they say?' Stacey's eyes flitted nervously from me to the floor.

'I got the part. I start in April.' I couldn't help smiling as I said it. I still enjoyed saying it out loud.

'Don't mess around! You never did...' said Emma, squeezing out a tight laugh.

'I don't believe you. They'd never pick someone like you!' said Lorna. Only Stacey remained silent as she dragged her fingers through her hair.

Slowly, word spread around the school that I'd landed a part on TV. Girls ran up to me in the corridors and asked if it was true, a welcome change from the usual hearty 'You're a spastic!'

News of my new role was greeted by girls and (female) teachers alike with the same reaction. Eyebrows raised, eyes widening, mouths hanging open, all combining perfectly to transmit silently – but unmistakably – 'How the hell...?' It was a novel experience for me. I almost apologised. (I'm not sure why, but the only teachers there who seemed intent on making school an unpleasant experience were female. The blokes, on the other hand, were uniformly lovely. Weird...)

Nobody, myself included, expected such a cool thing to happen to me. It took a while for the girls to come to terms with my impending TV debut and they approached the subject with a mix of fascinated suspicion, but I was beginning to care less what these strange people in this strange school thought of me.

Grange Hill turned out to be five years of sheer bliss. I can never thank Christine Secombe enough for casting me.

It was a complete joy from the moment I started. On my first day, I walked into the large rehearsal room at BBC Borehamwood studios to be greeted by faces I recognised from the telly. Determined to remain cool, I resisted the urge to ask them for their autographs and just sat down on one of the chairs that had been set out in a big square. Soon, the room was filled with the large cast and Christine stood up and welcomed us to the read-through of the next four scripts of the series.

'I'd also like to introduce our new cast member, Francesca Martinez, who will be playing Rachel Burns.' She gestured towards me and I felt my face go hot.

'Would you like to say hello, Francesca?' she asked.

'Er, hello, it's so great to be here. And not at school!' The room laughed. They probably thought I was cracking a joke. I was a little intimidated by the fact that many of the young actors had already starred in West-End productions such as *Les Miserables*, and had an Equity card, a cut-throat agent, and an RP accent by the time they'd hit their teens. I, in stark contrast, had never been paid to perform unless you counted the time Yaya's friend Rosina gave me £1.50 when I did my Margaret Thatcher impression for her.

Everything was so new and exciting. I woke up each morning itching to get to the studios. The sight of Borehamwood High Street filled me with a degree of joy that, I'm sure, is rarely associated with an otherwise uninspiring suburban thoroughfare in Herts. By the time my taxi reached the studio gates, I'd be buzzing so much,

I'd have to consciously regulate my breathing. It was that intoxicating. Who needs drugs?

On Mondays we'd read through the scripts for that block (we'd film twenty episodes a year and these would be done in five blocks of four), then we'd rehearse for two weeks, and film for a month. I'd receive each set of scripts and eagerly scan them for my name, often counting the number of lines I had. The more lines you had directly correlated to how much school you missed and that fact alone, coupled with my hunger to act, meant I regularly prayed that the writers would write me into every storyline.

The first scene I ever filmed took place outside Rachel's house one morning as she waits for her taxi to take her to school. (Sound familiar?) The sight of all the cameras and crew gave me goose bumps. I'd always been so fascinated whenever I'd spotted film crews as a child and I couldn't believe that I was part of one now. When the director shouted 'action', I nearly squealed with glee but just managed to stop myself. (I was sure that such an explosion of happiness would not have been appropriate for someone about to go to school.)

Unlike other cast members who seemed to be relieved when a scene was in the can, I always felt disappointed when it was over. Secretly, I wished we could spend all day doing scenes over and over again so I could bask in the thrill of the process. It always made me smile when someone forgot a line because I knew we'd have to do it again. And that, to me, was heaven.

To my surprise, I began to make friends with the other cast members. Most of them behaved as if they actually liked me. Which was a bit of a shock. It took some getting used to as I'd half expected the same cool apathy as at school. And there were boys. REAL boys. Oh, how I'd missed them. Dodgy walking had become a permanent fixture in my life but some pretty good associated benefits were becoming apparent. Boys would see me lurching along a corridor and offer me their lovely boy arms. I began to link arms with them whenever we walked around the expansive studios, and they would escort me like proud fathers on their daughter's wedding day. I'm not sure if part of the appeal was that my lanky arms and bony fingers made their biceps feel impressively strong, but I was more than happy to play along and let them assume the role of heroic and masculine gentlemen towards me.

Of course, I couldn't completely avoid education and, for reasons I struggled to understand, the BBC was legally required to provide actors under the age of sixteen with three hours of tuition a day. Whoop-de-fucking-doo! It was, I begrudgingly concluded, a small price to pay for spending my days acting and hanging out with (and on to) lots of gorgeous boys. Still, I tried my hardest to avoid doing any actual work and, thankfully, our tutors were often happy to file activities such as 'random fun quizzes' under the 'viable educational tasks' banner. I soon discovered a myriad of ways to reduce my three hours of attendance. Granted, they were supremely more enjoyable than school but not as enjoyable as pretending you needed to go to the toilet and then whiling away an hour wandering around trying to bump into someone famous. This was easy, because the BBC also filmed the famous cockney melodrama, *EastEnders*, and the hit music show, *Top Of The Pops*, at the same studios. And the possibility of bumping into Phil Mitchell or Wet Wet Wet beat tuition hands down every time.

My fellow cast member and loyal arm-in-waiting, Kevin Bishop, clearly shared my dislike of classrooms (what eleven-year-old boy doesn't?) and would often accompany me on my mission to stalk soap stars and music icons. ('Stalk' is too strong a word: my 'stalking' would be punctuated with plaintive requests to 'slow down, please' or 'can I take your arm?') Our disappearances usually occurred on Wednesdays as this was when *Top Of The Pops* was recorded (even though viewers often thought it was live – my first inkling that TV lies). And, while the thrill of seeing the latest *EastEnders* heart-throb scoffing scrambled eggs in the canteen was substantial, it didn't quite match up to spotting Madonna pecking at a cheese sandwich. Our jaunts were routinely successful; we ran into Take That in the corridor, witnessed a tantrum from Elton John, and watched Aerosmith rehearse while sticking our fingers in our ears. One Wednesday, I walked past two unshaven and scowling men who were sitting on the floor in a corridor. I took them to be cleaners on a break. They turned out to be Oasis.

As we were professional actors, we weren't allowed to behave like 'normal' teenagers around these megastars. One afternoon, I left my dressing room, turned the corner and walked straight into David Bowie, who was standing against the wall looking cool (of course). I stopped instinctively and stared at him. He brought his eyes to mine, his poised expression unruffled by the sight of the wobbly, gawky girl in a school uniform that confronted him.

'All right, Dave?' I said. There was a slight flicker in his penetrating eyes.

'All right,' he replied, not moving a muscle. I wobbled through the double doors, heard them close behind me, stopped, and attempted an air punch, which almost threw me out a nearby window. I regained my composure and continued my slow walk to the studio as 'Ashes To Ashes' played in my head.

A few months later, I met Gary Kemp of Spandau Ballet at an evening do. This was rather exciting in itself, but even more thrilling was the fact that I successfully steered our conversation around to the topic of Gary starring alongside a certain Mr Costner in *The Bodyguard*. Gary indulged my curiosity and regaled me with stories of Kevin as I listened intently. He was a lovely guy, although I was slightly disappointed that he didn't facilitate an introduction to the delightful star himself.

It felt like I was leading a double life. At the studios, I had friends, was part of a hit show, and enjoyed engaging in small talk with musical legends. At school, I was still the odd-bod. I'd finally made friends with a sweet girl called Gemma who had the distinction of being My Only Friend In The Class. And I'd also learnt an interesting lesson. Contrary to my long-held assumption that niceness begat niceness, I was beginning to see that this wasn't true at all. In fact, I could not have been more wrong. As I became less bothered about gaining the affections of my classmates, I started responding to their jibes instead of ignoring them with lowered eyes and pursed lips.

'Fuck off you spaz!' said Justine. The smell of Wotsits assaulted my nostrils. I paused as I dealt with the cheesy tidal wave.

'Why don't you fuck off yourself?' It wasn't the most imaginative comeback but I'd concentrated most of my energies on forcing my eyes to stare at her as I stood my ground. Justine gazed back at me in disbelief before skulking off like an injured animal.

I deployed this new tactic more and more, and couldn't believe the results. Some of the insultees would actually approach me a few days later wanting to be friends. I was mystified. Far from pushing the girls away with my increasing array of colourful ripostes, this sticking-up-for-myself shtick was actually making me less unpopular. It seemed that the sniff of self-respect was a potent weapon, and the girls soon started to go elsewhere for their kicks. I was bewildered by this discovery but it was one I never forgot.

My teachers soon got used to me missing weeks on end and the girls would simply raise their eyebrows when I showed up. Occasionally, they'd casually enquire if I'd met any famous people. When they found out I'd met the apparent boy-gods that were Take That (I failed to see it myself) I was deemed interesting enough for the girls to engage with me. However, I'd stopped caring, since *Grange Hill* was so much fun.

As my first series drew to a close, I began to worry that I'd be let go and have to return to my old life. It was with huge trepidation that I walked into Christine's office and perched myself on her soft, green chair.

'How have you found this year, Francesca?'

'It's been incredible. Like a dream come true. I've loved every minute!' I gushed, failing epically in my attempts not to appear desperate.

'I'm so glad to hear that. We'd love you to come back next series, if you'd like to?' She smiled widely. I paused for what I judged to be an appropriately professional time – a full ninth of a second – before blurting out a loud 'Yes.' I wanted to jump up and hug her for everything she'd done. But I just smiled. Very emotionally.

'Great! See you next year, then. And enjoy watching the series in February when it airs.' She got up. I got up too.

'I will. We've already bought a video recorder for my grandmother so we can tape it every week!' Christine laughed at this and I kissed her on the cheek.

'Thanks again. I owe you big time,' I said as I walked out the door and heaved a huge sigh of relief that the fantastic dream would continue.

Some of my teachers had not been best pleased that I'd missed nearly eight months' worth of classes, and were looking forward to a period when I would be attending school full-time again. Unfortunately, my parents had planned a month-long trip to Australia in December, which turned out to be bang in the middle of my GCSE mock exams. I was elated at the brilliant timing, having had as much interest in mocks as in taxidermy. Ms Kitkat, appalled by the disgraceful planning, called my mum to try to convince her that I shouldn't be taken away at such a crucial time. My mum explained that she was sure I'd be fine and that Australia was bound to be an educational experience too. She also explained that, with the passing of my grandfather, they felt it was important for us to connect with Yayo's other son, Francisco, and his family. Kitkat couldn't trump the dead-grandpa card. We went to Australia and I missed half my mocks. Blooming perfect!

I spent a novel Christmas on the beach in Perth. As I watched parrots flying over the ocean, I indulged in smug imagination of my classmates sitting in the exam hall. I returned to school in January 1994. My concerned teachers needn't have worried. I was more resolved than ever to work hard. This was not an inexplicable personality shift or some proof of a new-found maturity. (If that existed, it remained well and truly hidden.) No, I'd adopted this new determination because some kids had been forced to leave *Grange Hill* as a result of falling behind in their schoolwork. And there was No Bloody Way that a few poxy essays were going to ruin my dreams. No. Way. So, I knuckled down and worked harder than I'd ever worked before. I even brought myself textbooks to do extra studying at home. It was a strange sensation being this academically focused but I had no choice if I wanted to carry on this wonderful life.

And so, it was with huge anticipation that I sat down with my family to watch my first episode of *Grange Hill*. We had come down to Yaya's to watch it live on a Friday afternoon in late February. I'd experienced no nerves while acting but now, oddly, my stomach felt like a sick knot at the prospect of seeing myself and I positioned myself by the door so I could easily escape if it got overwhelming. The theme music kicked in. Yaya put her hand on my arm and squeezed it supportively. And there I was on the screen standing outside my house, leaning against the wall and reading a book. I pulled my knees up to my chin and held them tightly. I was not used to seeing myself and it was a rather uncomfortable experience. Is this how everyone sees me, I wondered? My curly hair was huge. It looked like it should have had a series all to itself. A spot on my chin also seemed impossibly large. As the taxi driver pulled up on screen, I heard myself talk for the first time. The voice emanating from the telly was a far cry from the smooth sounds I heard when I spoke. It sounded... slightly slurred. It wavered gently. Frankly, it shocked my ears. Is that how I sound to others, I thought? The voice in my head always sounded strong and clear. I liked that voice. This other voice was the voice of someone I didn't know and didn't want to be. Then I saw myself walk towards the taxi. I felt my toes curl up on the floor beneath me. Fuck the voice, I thought, is that how I walk? My eyes were transfixed by the slow, jerky, laboured movements.

The knot in my stomach tightened. I couldn't believe how vulnerable I looked, as if a gust of wind would send me flying. My thin legs looked spindly and delicate and, when I walked, the concentration on my face was clearly visible. I had no idea that my internal efforts were so clearly displayed on my face and how transparent a vessel my body was.

Above all, I looked, well, disabled. You'd think that by fifteen this would have been undisputed and accepted, something that was not up for negotiation. But no. In my mind, I'd been strong and feisty, but this creature didn't fit that image at all. Instead, she looked weak and a bit broken. I was massively disappointed in Rachel Burns. Millions of people would be watching her at that very moment. Suddenly, I felt utterly naked. The camera had stripped away all my self-delusion and forced me to see myself as I was. And it hurt.

'Well done, Chess! You were very natural!' said my dad. He looked very proud. As did the rest of my family. I smiled at them, ignoring the pool of embarrassment that was collecting around my tense feet.

After the initial shock, I learnt to enjoy watching the rest of the episodes by routinely ducking out of the room when I was on. I was confident that my acting was not atrocious and that I appeared quite natural on screen but it was still incredibly hard to see myself as others saw me, so I avoided it whenever possible. When the sight of my erratic walking popped into my head, I'd experience a stab of humiliation before quickly thinking about something more pleasant. These first TV appearances were greeted with a mixture of silence and lukewarm comment by my peers. My old adversary Ms Bunt chose to congratulate me with 'You think you're a star now, don't you?'

Another thing that had been well and truly confirmed

for me as I occasionally caught sight of myself on the box was that I was Definitively Not Attractive. At all. Whichever way I looked at my face, I just saw big hair, big nose, and big teeth. Despite the shock of seeing my wobbly self on national television, I couldn't wait for the new series to start. I loved the process of rehearsal and recording so I decided that I'd focus on enjoying them rather than the final product.

We started work on *Grange Hill* again in April 1994 and, once more, I threw myself into this brilliant life. No longer the new girl, I had a group of good friends and I settled into another eight months of fun. The only marginally negative aspect was the appalling quality of the food in the canteen. The chef's generosity was legendary and he/she/ it would make sure there were added extras like hair or pieces of paper in our 'food'. Very quickly, I switched to pre-packed sandwiches and crisps. In the rare instance that I missed hot food, I'd buy a bowl of chips (perhaps they should have been called 'potaturds') and I would rapidly be reminded why sandwiches were preferable. One lunchtime, after finding the latest random inedible in their foods, my friends, Aidan, Rochelle and Jenny, decided it was time to fill in some canteen feedback cards. I suggested that the comments would be taken more seriously if they came from proper stars. So, the constructive criticisms were 'signed' by such influential figures as Gary Barlow, Kylie Minogue, and Prince. We popped them into the feedback box, convinced there was no way that such VIPs would be ignored. No such luck.

I had taken on the role of a joker and loved making people laugh. I was still convinced it was the best way to kick pity in the nuts. Often, I would try and make the crew chuckle on set and my favourite scenes, by far, were the comedic ones. We were filming in the school playground one day and, as usual, were freezing. For reasons unknown to me, we filmed the summer scenes in winter and the winter scenes in summer. This meant that we were often in thin shirts with bare legs in temperatures of five degrees. The playground seemed always to have a wind chill factor of minus fifty and my friends and I were huddled together like Arctic explorers. The executive producer, Babs, stood by us. Eager to take my mind off my ice-block legs, I started up a conversation.

'So, how was your break?' I asked, trying to stop my teeth from chattering.

'Lovely. I heard you went to Australia?' said Babs. My eyes suddenly caught sight of a hair hanging off her chin. It looked like it shouldn't be there.

'I did. It was amazing!' I paused. 'Erm, Babs, there's a hair on your chin...' And I grabbed it and pulled. Babs yelped. The hair was attached to a mole.

'Oh, no! I'm so sorry. I didn't know...' I went bright red. Babs rubbed her chin. A lot.

'Please don't sack me! I would hate to be fired over a mole!' My friends dissolved in fits of laughter. By the end of the day, everyone knew about my unfortunate antics. Thankfully, Babs forgave me and I learned that most invaluable of lessons: never offer to rid a woman of seemingly unattached facial hair. Especially if said woman is your boss.

The second series sped by. It felt strange to be paid each week and I wondered if the BBC knew that I would quite happily have done the job for nothing. In fact, I'd have paid them to let me do it. It didn't feel like a job at all. I couldn't help thinking that it would have made more sense to pay me to go to school instead. That was the real grind. Intermittently, I began to get recognised, often by the local schoolkids who would spot me and yell 'Grange Hill!' Sometimes they would approach me and enquire if I was a millionaire yet or if I owned a limousine. They would always look disappointed when I told them that the family car was a slightly battered mint green Peugeot. On the odd occasion, they'd ask for my autograph. Anticipating the time and effort this would entail (and the quality of the end product), I usually asked them if they were sure they wanted one. Shoving a scrap of paper and pen into my hands, they would stare at me expectantly.

'Is it possible for me to lean the paper on your back?' I'd ask, apologetically.

'Yeah, sure!' they'd answer with a fleck of surprise as they turned around dutifully. Bringing the pen to the paper on their back, I would steady my hand for a second before attempting an autograph. What came out of the pen was a complete mystery to me, the only constant being that it looked nothing like a signature. I'd hand them back the now crumpled piece of paper and they'd study the curious markings with perplexity.

'I have no idea what it says either but I promise you it's unique!' I'd offer as an explanation, hoping that they'd eventually derive some pleasure from the messy scrawl.

Throughout the year, I continued to study, ferociously keeping up with all my classes. My GCSE exams were steadily approaching and I knew my teachers would be looking for any excuse to keep me from missing school. I foiled them by working solidly at home during the evenings and weekends, thereby continuing to use the BBC tuition session times to indulge in the ever-fascinating sport that was celebrity spotting. I saw Marti Pellow storm out of rehearsal, shot the breeze with East 17, saw Gabrielle eat a Mars Bar, and was invited, along with my friend Fiona, to a party by Peter Andre and his impossibly muscly dancers. We were too shy to go but it was nice of them to ask. When the second series came to an end, I was asked if I'd like to return the following year. I managed to wait a whole second this time before saying yes. Cool or what?

Finally, after what had seemed like an eternity, the end of high school was approaching fast. Many of the girls had decided to stay on in the sixth form. I was not one of them. I decided that, as soon as my exams were over, I'd never set foot in Parliament Hill again. Ever. I'd been offered a place to do my A-levels at Greenhill College in Harrow and had gratefully accepted. In preparation for my exams I had (regretfully) asked the BBC to write me out of the show in May and June that year. It was only temporary but I was still annoyed at having to sacrifice six juicy weeks of Borehamwood delights. David Bowie would surely notice my absence on his next visit.

For obvious reasons, it had been decided that I should

dictate my GCSE answers to a teacher instead of writing them down myself. So I took all my exams in an empty classroom while one of my teachers or Carol Carlton wrote down my answers. A few girls were incredibly nervous about these exams; one girl had even fainted from the intense pressure. I didn't think exams merited any form of collapse and, although I wanted to get good grades, I knew what I wanted to do in my life and it did not involve academia. My approach was to do my best, avoid stress, and get back to acting as quickly as possible. As the last exam came to an end, Carol put down her pen and smiled at me.

'Well, Francesca, that's you finished!'

'I suppose it is. I can't believe it,' I said, looking at her.

'How do you feel?' she asked, as she packed away her pen.

'Weird. I can't believe it's over. It's been a long five years.' My half smile said a few last words, which Carol understood.

'I can't thank you enough for what you've done for me. I'll never forget you.' I felt my throat tighten as I spoke. We remained friends for many years.

I went to my form room to pick up the last of my stuff. Lorna, Stacey, and Emma were lounging around like big cats.

'You off then, Fran?' said Lorna, throwing a look over her shoulder.

'Yep. My exams are all done.' I gathered my belongings and headed for the door. The girls looked at me briefly, their eyes passive and their mouths silent. I walked out, passing more of my classmates and teachers in the corridor. I'll never walk through here again, I thought. I pushed open the door and walked outside. Balancing my bags on both shoulders, I slowly went down the steps. I got into the taxi and we drove off down the empty path. As we passed through the gates, I turned to look at the school buildings. I felt nothing. I'd spent five years of my life there. Five years! And, apart from Carol, not one person had said goodbye on my last day. For a moment, I felt a profound sadness pour over my body and I closed my eyes. When I opened them again, we were nearly home. Somewhere, deep inside, I felt the flicker of a flame and a long-dormant part of me sparked back into life.

I was free.

CHAPTER EIGHT

****

I learnt a lot of things on my sixteenth birthday:

1. I could carry off a dress that veered dangerously close to sexy.
2. Make-up was my friend.
3. 1 and 2 could get me into nightclubs.
4. There were boys in the world who didn't find me hideously unattractive.
5. If I stayed very still in the nightclub, I could look normal.

These five lessons were revelatory in their own way. I'd lived in jeans and baggy tops for years, covering up as much of my body as possible. It was my new best friend Fiona who forced me to try on a tight, short dress in Brent Cross Shopping Centre. Yes! I had a real, living, breathing *best friend*! Fiona had joined *Grange Hill* after me and was playing one of my classmates. She was popular and funny and always up for a bit of mischief, and we quickly became inseparable. It turbo-boosted my somewhat scant confidence to know there were teenage girls on this planet who actually wanted to hang out with me on a regular basis. Finally I had an actual social life! Full of parties and sleepovers and all the stuff that had passed me by at school. Some pinching of myself was required.

I stood in that fitting room for an awkward moment before daring to raise my eyes to the mirror. I had never seen an outfit on me that displayed so much skin. And there was a *lot* of skin. My long legs were barely covered and my cleavage line was clearly visible. For a girl who didn't even know she had a cleavage, this discovery was quite a shock. I was a late developer in that department but, at some point, I'd sprouted a pair of actual boobs. Boobs that had gone unnoticed, since being naked was not a state I enjoyed. I was rather prudish about my body, preferring to dress and undress as quickly as possible. I simply couldn't understand those women in public changing rooms who willingly partook in a very public – and prolonged – towel-drying of their lady bits (flossing would be more accurate) before ostentatiously patting their cha-chas with talcum powder. This dress clinging to my body like a frightened animal revealed more of my flesh than I'd ever seen, certainly more than I'd ever shown in public. I wasn't sure how I felt. Fiona, on the other hand, was very sure.

'You look fab, Chess! Who knew you had such great boobs? And look at your legs! They're amazing,' she squealed in delight. I stared at my legs. They didn't look bad, just very skinny and very long. I felt like I hadn't seen them all before.

'But…' I started.

'But what?' said Fiona, placing her hands on her hips.

'It's too sexy. And I'm not,' I said, curving my shoulders with embarrassment. Fiona, the sexiest girl I'd ever met, laughed at the palpable fear on my face.

'Rubbish. You're hot, Chess. You just don't know it!' That was the first time anyone had attributed the word 'hot' to me and not been referring to my body temperature. I looked at her, unconvinced.

'Look, you'll never be sixteen again. You might as well enjoy looking it,' she said. I couldn't disagree with her, despite trying hard to.

Neither of us had been to a club before. We were excited and a bit terrified, mostly because we were worried that we'd be turned away for being too young. To combat this dangerous eventuality, we leant heavily on the wonders of make-up. I'd never been near it, naïvely allowing my teenage acne to be seen by all. Occasionally the make-up artists at the BBC would spare the nation the sight of a particularly angry zit but, on the whole, it had never occurred to me to treat my face with anything other than soap and water. So, with much anticipation, I let Fiona apply the mysterious stuff to my face. It took ages. I could have read half a book in the time it took. Obviously it was a big job. Finally, I was allowed to look in the mirror. I gulped. The spots were miraculously gone and my skin looked flawless. The lashes around my eyes were long and dark and there was a shimmering pink colour around them, which made my green eyes pop. And I had cheekbones!

'Where were they before?' I asked.

'I just brought them out with blusher,' she answered, as if it was patently obvious. I stared at myself in awe. The gawky teenager had disappeared and, although I was not beautiful like Fiona, perhaps, just perhaps, Jesus might find me attractive after all. I turned to Fiona and smiled. Now I knew why women spent so much time and money on this shit.

'Let's party!' said Fiona, as she admired her handiwork.

We chose a club near Oxford Circus called Bar Madrid. I liked the name and imagined it would be full of dishy Latino boys that I could impress with my Spanish. It wasn't. The bouncer at the door was huge and, for a moment, I wanted to turn around and go for pizza instead. But Fiona smiled at him and he let us through with a big soppy grin on his face. I was learning that Fiona's smile had mystical powers and, as long as I was on her arm, people (well, men) bent over backwards to please us. Once downstairs, we took off our coats and a pang of self-consciousness echoed around my body as I stood there in my tiny dress. I tugged at the hem but it didn't budge. I pulled at the top to find an extra inch of coverage but this proved unsuccessful too.

Weirdly, nobody else seemed bothered by the fact that my dress covered very little. In fact, the male clientele seemed pretty appreciative of the scant material on display. They let me know this through a mixture of smiles, winks and compliments – most of them lost on the way to my ear in the deafening music that pulsated through the air. It was a strange sensation, being noticed by grown-up boys. True, most of them swarmed around Fiona but a few actually tried to talk to me. I soon discovered something rather amazing: the combination of loud music, low lighting and heavy consumption of alcohol meant that, if I remained quite still, they thought I was *normal*! Brain damage in this environment was apparently invisible. I was keen to keep it that way, so I stood at the bar and kept very, very still.

A cute guy approached me. He had jet-black hair and a lovely smile.

'Can I buy you a drink?' he asked, flashing a set of pearly whites.

'Sure. Can I have a Coke?' I said, making sure I didn't move much more than my lips.

'Just a Coke?' said Mr Charming, raising an eyebrow.

'I don't drink,' I replied. My taste buds had never learnt to embrace the metallic tinge of alcohol. The merest drop of it on my tongue made me screw up my face like an angry toddler. And I guessed that face would not be an appropriate one to pull in front of this young hottie. Mr Charming looked confused. He leaned in close and I felt his hot breath on my ear. It made my neck tingle.

'What do you mean, you don't drink?' He pulled away slightly and smiled cheekily at me.

I leaned towards him, careful to keep my movements smooth and fluid.

'I just don't like alcohol!' I said into his ear. He laughed, revealing deep dimples on his freshly shaved cheeks.

'So what you on, then?' His eyes looked directly into

mine. 'And can I have some?' I paused, not quite knowing how to answer.

'I'm just high on life. It's my sixteenth birthday!' He took my hand in his. It felt warm and strong. The first I'd held since Clint's.

'Then we should celebrate! Let's dance.' He tugged gently at my hand. And that's when I realised that this normal game wasn't going to work. Checkmate.

'Er, no thanks...' I slid my hand out of his.

'You don't want to?' His brown eyes looked surprised. He brought his head close to mine and smiled. I could smell his aftershave. My stomach jumped a little.

'Sorry. No... not tonight!' I smiled apologetically. He stared into my eyes.

'Well, at least let me give you a birthday kiss?' I looked at his mouth. It was very kissable. I was sure it would be quite pleasant and I knew it would be an appropriate indulgence on my sixteenth birthday. But I was a hopeless romantic, remember? And hopeless romantics don't settle for first kisses in dingy basement clubs with inebriated strangers. No matter how nice their dimples.

'Sure, you can,' I said, and turned my cheek towards him. The first in a long line of kiss-scuppering. Mainly because I found the thought of kissing someone utterly terrifying.

Fiona and I began to go clubbing regularly, sometimes on our own, sometimes with other cast members. The 'normal' act was addictive and I loved it when men thought I was just pissed or high. The irony is, I didn't drink or do drugs, not out of any puritanical leanings but out of a fear that the little control I had would bugger off. So I clung on to my sobriety with the fervour of a drunk gripping his whisky bottle. Everyone thought I was off my head on these nights, anyway, so I fitted right in. Nowhere more so than in Leicester Square at 3 a.m., when my walking blended in perfectly with the unsteady lurching of the other revellers. For a brief moment, I walked 'normally'.

Despite not snogging or getting pissed or high, I found these nights out incredibly exhilarating. I loved to dance. (Yes, I use the term loosely.) There were not many group activities I could join in with so I let myself enjoy the collective dancing. And it was usually dark enough for me to assuage any self-doubt. I also became an expert at throwing compliments back in men's faces. I didn't mean it but I was just so profoundly uncomfortable at receiving them that chucking them back seemed the only possible response. In one club, a good-looking guy came up to me on the dance floor. We chatted and laughed and I thought he was very sweet. After a few songs, he brought me close to him, clearly unperturbed by my unique 'dancing'.

'You're perfect,' he whispered into my ear. I looked at him like a panicked deer.

'You're a bit short,' I blurted out. Not surprisingly, he looked hurt at this reply and sloped off into the darkness. I stared after him, feeling helpless and idiotic. Being ignored by boys for so many years had been painful but I knew how to deal with it. It was a lot easier to deal with than this.

After a summer of thwarted kisses and pretended normality, it was time to start the new sixth-form college.

Contrary to the predictions from several of my teachers that I'd fail my exams because of my TV gallivanting, I passed my GCSEs with As and Bs. And a C for drama! I chose English literature, history and sociology. However, I was also given my biggest storyline on *Grange Hill* so far, which meant that I attended the new college for only three days in the first month. Those days were perfectly pleasant and refreshingly different from Parliament Hill. The students and teachers seemed to be nice human beings, too, which was a relief. But my infrequent appearances were worrying to the staff and, at the end of September, I was called into the head's office.

'Francesca, I hear you've only attended college three times in a month,' he said, raising his eyebrows with concern.

'Yes, I have. It's because I've got a big storyline on *Grange Hill* so I've been at the studios a lot,' I replied.

'I know. The thing is that your teachers and classmates barely know you.' He crossed his arms and waited for my answer.

'I know. It's bad timing. I'm sorry!' I smiled at him to acknowledge the tricky nature of our predicament.

'We're very happy to have you here but I think this isn't working. You're going to have to choose between us or *Grange Hill*. You can take some time to think abou—'

'*Grange Hill*. Sorry,' I said, as I closed the door.

It was the easiest decision I'd ever made. I'd spent eleven years waiting for the moment when school would be over and, now, suddenly, it was. I'd happily have gone to no college at all if I'd thought it was an option. The thought of giving up my life-long dream so I could spend time sitting in a classroom being talked at made me physically sick. Luckily, my parents supported me in my decision.

'Go and follow your dreams and, if they don't work out, then you can reassess,' said Dad when I explained what had happened. It remains one of the best pieces of advice I've ever been given. (He mightn't have been quite so encouraging if he'd known that this career choice would keep me living at home until I was thirty-two.) I was beginning to realise what absurdly cool parents I had. They are the sole reason I do what I do. They were happy for me to leave formal education at sixteen and spend my nights surrounded by leery men and cocktails with sexually explicit names.

The no-TV thing meant there was still plenty of time in the day to fill and my family spent most of it talking to each other like friends (how abnormal!). I could always talk to them about anything. We have a very open relationship and they were ridiculously trusting of me. So much so, in fact, that I was the only girl in my group of friends that didn't have a curfew. The only thing they ever wanted to know was where I was going and how I was going to get home safely. Not once was there the exhortation not to smoke, drink, kiss random men or do drugs. I don't know if they were using some kind of super reverse-psychology but it proved spookily successful. I was about as debauched as a nun in a coma. There was nothing to rebel against, so I didn't rebel.

My mum even suggested that I lighten up a bit and not wait until I found my true love before kissing a guy. I responded by sighing deeply and rattling off a love poem, the like of which only a hormone-ravaged teenager could inflict on the world. And my hormones were in overdrive. I'd fallen completely in love with a new cast member, a Frenchman called Dominique. For such a devout romantic, my passion for him was born less out of an intense spiritual connection – a meeting of two souls and a profound sharing of values – than by something rather simpler. He was DREAMY. So dreamy that, when he'd walked into the rehearsal room a few months earlier, I'd almost fainted. He had curly brown hair, bronzed skin and a face so darn beautiful that I felt guilty just looking at him – it gave me such joy. Within five seconds, I'd imagined in detail our wedding and the birth of our first child. Blame the hormones. I knew we'd never be together. He was too perfect for a mere mortal like me but, somehow, that made my unrequited love more satisfying. I could pine over him and write him reams of poetry (which I did) but never have to deal with anything approaching reciprocation. So I felt totally safe, which was just how I wanted to feel. Okay, a small part of me did want him to rip my clothes off and devour me with kisses but, mostly, I just wanted to stare at his face and listen to his spell-binding French accent, which poured into my ears like golden honey. That was enough for me.

My new life was wonderfully free of the education system and full of the joys of performing and intense unrequited love. I was delighted that I could, at last, dedicate all of myself to acting. Always keen to support my dreams, my dad proposed an idea one evening over dinner.

'Chess, I've been thinking. You're an actor, I'm a

writer, so why don't I write a TV script for you?' He was an accomplished writer and I was honoured that he'd even thought of writing a part for me.

'Yeah, go on! Make it the main part!' I laughed. I adored *Grange Hill* but having to share the screen with a cast of sixty was a tad frustrating for someone who wanted to be in every scene. And I was aware that I only had a couple of series left.

'Okay, I will!' he said, and he picked up his fork and started to eat again. I was already bursting with excitement to see what he'd write.

Dad clearly didn't suffer from writer's block. A week later, he presented me with a typed script. The title read 'LADY SOD'. I laughed. Mum had recently misheard me when I'd called myself a lazy sod. I read the script immediately. It was amazing. I couldn't believe that my dad had written it so quickly. And I had so many lines! There was just one problem. For some inexplicable reason, Dad had made my character a stand-up comedian.

'Dad, this is a brilliant part, but why did you make her a stand-up? That's like the scariest job in the world ever!'

'I don't know why I picked it. It just came to me. And I think you could be a good comedian, actually,' he said, with a quiet and unnerving conviction.

Granted, when I was younger, I'd declared that I wanted to be a comedian, after watching the genius of Little and Large. But that once invincible performing confidence had been so successfully hacked away that I no longer believed I could rise to the challenge. Now, the thought of standing onstage in front of people simply petrified me. And, surely, to win the part, I'd have to go all Robert De Niro and practise stand-up for real. I still loved TV acting but that was done in a closed studio in front of a small crew that knew me. It was an entirely different premise to do a live gig in front of strangers. If you fuck up in a live performance, there's nowhere to hide: you can't just laugh it off and start again.

But there were more inscrutable reasons for my discomfort at playing such a character. On the surface, I appeared happier and more confident since leaving high school and, in many ways, I was. I finally felt judged on what I could do, not on what I couldn't. However, the scars of those five years were embedded deep in my subconscious and my self-worth was still rock bottom. Despite my recent induction into the world of fashion and make-up, despite having friends who seemed to like me, and despite attracting the attention of a few members of the opposite sex, I couldn't shake the feeling that I was fundamentally abnormal and unattractive.

I kept this negativity largely hidden from others – even my loving family – but its presence undermined my self-esteem, as if a streak of thick black paint had been splattered across my inner self. I felt that the shape of my body was fine but I still felt disconnected from it and had an intense dislike for how it did things and how it moved. I would often privately berate it for working differently, and the disparaging voice in my head became normal, constantly pointing out my glaring and freakish defects.

This paranoid commentary became more and more intrusive and I didn't know how to turn it off. I rarely liked to be alone with my own thoughts and religiously sought out the company of others. It was because of this innate anxiety about myself that I was so scared by what my dad had written. Somehow I was aware that I wouldn't be able to convince as a comedian, even pretend to be one, while I harboured such epic self-doubt. My dad was oblivious to the turmoil I felt inside and he thought I'd be wonderful in the role. I was just relieved that I'd kept my unease hidden from him. I didn't want it upsetting my family.

The script was fantastic. My dad had created a compelling drama about a timid, disabled teenage girl who creates a sexy, confident alter-ego, a comedian called Lady Sod, and I read the comic routines with excitement. But I knew, deep down, that I hadn't the balls to bring his sassy creation to life.

Dad said we should start thinking about who to send the script to, and I said I'd keep an eye out for people who might be interested. I couldn't confess my monumental cowardice to him, of course, so I just hugged him once again and thanked him for writing me such an incredible part.

The Jekyll and Hyde element that was so alive in the script had also become a distinct quality of my life. The people around me thought I was happy and confident, and my growing circle of friends saw me as a natural confidant. If there was a problem to be shared, I was the girl to come to. I grabbed this role with both hands because it made me feel strong and capable, and I carried it out with aplomb. I loved being perceived as so 'able'. Fiona was my primary 'patient', often calling me two or three times a day to discuss the complexities of love, life and fashion choices. There was no better feeling in the world than having somebody lean on me. I adored solving other people's problems. And it was the perfect distraction from having to deal with my own.

The following year, I was invited to attend the Children of Courage Awards at Westminster Abbey. The idea of going as a 'celebrity' was daunting – I felt as far away from celebrity as you can be – but I couldn't come up with a viable excuse not to celebrate the achievements of brave children. If they were able to take on terminal cancer and armed gunmen, I could handle being looked at by a few strangers.

The ceremony was very moving and I was honoured to receive an award on behalf of one of the children. Unwisely, I chose to walk up to the Duchess of Kent by myself. This took a minor eternity. The poor dear had to stand there with a smile plastered across her face for an unreasonably long time. When I eventually got to her, I was hot with embarrassment. She was just grateful to relax her cheek muscles. The applause ran out when I'd only made it a third of the way back and an awkward silence descended on the abbey as I wobbled to my seat in shame. Much as I admired those plucky kids, I decided I wouldn't be doing that again. Afterwards, at the reception, I got chatting to a blonde man in his late forties. He asked me about myself and I told him all about *Grange Hill* and how much I loved acting. It was some time before he managed to get a word in.

'Yes, I love acting too,' he said, smiling at my unbridled enthusiasm.

'Oh, are you an actor?' I asked.

'Yes, I am,' he answered. He seemed amused by the question.

'Cool! What have you been in?' Well, it turned out he'd been in quite a lot of stuff with quite a lot of people and that he was quite a bit famous. He was Anthony Andrews! He'd acted with Laurence bloody Olivier! I turned to my mum who was laughing her head off at my ludicrous gaffe.

'This is what happens when you don't have a TV!' I turned back to Anthony. 'If it helps, I once mistook Oasis for cleaners.'

'So I'm in good company, then?' he said, charmingly.

'Yes, well, I'm just going to go and die of embarrassment after regaling you with my Zammo anecdote.' Anthony didn't mind being mistaken for someone's uncle and we carried on talking. He asked me what I planned to do after leaving *Grange Hill*. I told him about Dad's script, at which point, he asked me to send it to his production company. He gave me his card. I promised I'd send it and we said goodbye.

A few weeks later, Anthony rang my dad and told him he loved the script. He wanted to buy it and produce it. His only request was that Dad write it as a film. This wasn't particularly difficult for Dad to agree to – he's a big movie buff. Anthony also said he was keen for me to star in it. This struck both joy and primal fear into my heart. My long-time dream of starring in a movie was beginning to look strangely possible. But, I'd have to embody this strong and sexy woman. And I didn't know how the hell that was going to happen.

Another unexpected piece of news came my way: I might be able to learn to drive. Me! The girl who reduced cupcakes to heaps of crumbs with a single twitch. This startling revelation came to me through Lisa, my other best friend (ooh, get me now), who was of restricted height and who'd started *Grange Hill* at the same time as me. Apparently there was a centre that assessed disabled people to see if they were able to drive. Lisa was very excited about this – she was fearless in a way I was not. I secretly looked up to her, even though she wasn't much more than three feet tall. She was awesome, and I envied the way she took everything in her stride. Lisa was often in pain but you'd never know it. She was staggeringly ballsy when it came to physical discomfort. I was rather less so. Recently, I'd gone to have my earwax removed (nice). Once on the hospital bed, I had to regulate my breathing. When the nurse placed the little hoover next to my ear and began to suck out the wax, my mum was obliged to point out that I was digging my nails into her hand. I apologised as sweat ran down my cheek.

Yep, Lisa trounced me in the bravery stakes, a fact illustrated by her infectious excitement at the idea of learning to drive. Unsurprisingly, I was highly dubious about the possibility. I couldn't imagine myself driving around London without leaving a trail of death behind me. I didn't want to end up in prison. My parents, however, were very keen that I should take the assessment, possibly because they'd played the role of taxi-driver longer than one could reasonably expect of them. After various assurances that nobody would be killed, I reluctantly agreed to go.

Dad came with me to Banstead Mobility Centre. As we pulled into the car park, my heart sank. Here I was again, attending a 'special' place because I was 'handicapped'. We were led into a large room. After a minute, a middle-aged man with glasses walked in and sat behind a desk.

'Hello. Are you Francesca?' he asked, with a grin on his face. (The kind of grin one adopts for interaction with a human being who has been alive for days rather than years.)

'Yes, I am,' I replied.

'Ahhhh! And this must be Daddy?' he said, turning to my dad, who remained motionless.

'Yes, that's my dad, Alex.'

'Lovely. Well, I'm Dr Green, like the colour...' He paused and waited for our guffaw. Not getting it, he continued.

'... and, eh, I'm going to assess your perception and ability to follow instruction.' He looked at me intently to check whether I'd understood this complicated sentence. I nodded.

'Right, the first thing I'd like you to do is look at these blocks.' He opened a box and emptied an array of red, green, and yellow wooden shapes on to his desk. He clasped his hands together as if he was about to make a momentous announcement.

'Can you place the circles with the circles, the squares with the squares, and the triangles with the triangles?' His eyes looked at me eagerly. I held his gaze for a moment and let out a laugh.

'Seriously?' His expression didn't change.

'Yes, go on. See how quickly you can do it!' he said, as if challenging an infant. Turns out those nine GSCEs had prepared me well for trials of such complexity. Dr Green appeared to be genuinely delighted at my performance.

'My, you're a clever lass, aren't you?' I felt Dad bristle silently next to me.

'Now, can you place the shapes in three colour groups? So all the red shapes together, all the—'

'I get it. Yes.' I moved the shapes around. I hadn't anticipated that playing with coloured toddler blocks would be so essential for driving. Once again, I managed to solve the puzzle and was rewarded with another smile of sincere admiration.

'You're really flying through these, aren't you?' Dr Green beamed at me.

'Well, I'm doing my best,' I said, sweetly. Dad cleared his throat.

'Next task, then. More of a question this time. What colour is the wall in this room?' He said this slowly.

'Pardon?'

'What colour is the wall?' He pointed at it to clarify the brainteaser.

'Why are you asking me that?' I asked, making sure I finished with a gentle smile. For a moment he was thrown.

'Erm, because I want to check you can accurately identify colour...' he offered. I wanted to tell him that, though I was wobbly, I wasn't fucking blind. Instead, I just said, 'White.'

The other sessions tested my reflexes and road awareness. The day ended as I made my way around the test track in a specially adapted car, at the speed of a cataract-ridden pensioner, with an instructor beside me trying not to look nervous. Dad and I chewed over the events of the day on the drive back home, imagining ripostes to Dr Green.

'I should have said "most colours are fine. Occasionally I mix up green and red but that doesn't matter, does it?"' I joked.

'Yeah, or maybe you could have asked what you should say to the police if they ever stop you and ask you to walk in a straight line!' We laughed all the way home.

I was convinced that Dr Green would deem me unfit to drive and that was fine by me. So, a few months later, I was amazed to receive a letter informing me that I was permitted to take driving lessons. Hadn't they seen me demolish my sandwich in their canteen?

I remained sceptical about the whole thing. And who on Earth would teach me? The instructor would be more frigging terrified than me. And who could blame him? I wouldn't get into the car with me. I felt sorry for them already.

Driving wasn't the only thing I was terrified of. Take water. Well, large amounts of it. I could be on a lilo, wearing armbands, and a rubber ring, in four feet of water, my parents on either side, and I'd still be hanging on to them as if I were clinging to a tree in a tropical tsunami. Me and water were not cool. At all. Unsurprisingly, my strategy was to avoid it. However, the doctor had been telling me for years that swimming would be beneficial for my body in many ways. So Mum kept pushing me to learn to swim. I had managed to squirm out of it for seventeen years but, with the perseverance that only a mum can possess, she finally persuaded me go to a swimming club on Friday evenings. I kicked up a fuss but she was adamant that I try it once. So I agreed to go once. Just once. I sat in a moody silence as Mum drove me to the pool. I made sure that she knew just how annoyed I was.

'After tonight, I'm never going again,' I reminded her. 'You can't make me.' She sighed but said nothing. I followed her into the pool complex, determined to take as long as possible. Andrew, the instructor, came over to say hello. He was alarmingly cute. I learned to swim in six months. I stayed for two years. And I loved every single lesson.

I discovered I was willing to risk drowning in exchange for ninety minutes of splashing around with this semi-naked hottie. I'm only normal, for God's sake. In water, I finally experienced what it was like to have balance. Actual balance! I didn't have to worry about falling over. For the first time in my life, I felt physically free. It was as if I'd been given superpowers, and I realised what able-bodied people felt like all the time. The lucky buggers have it so easy, I thought. I imagined how great life would be if I had this ease of movement and I couldn't understand what other people possibly had to moan about, when moving around required such little effort. I wondered if it was possible to live more of my life in water – if someone would design me my own portable water tank. That would be inconspicuous, all right.

It wasn't disloyal to pine after Andrew, because my French crush, Dominique, had left *Grange Hill* at the end of the previous series. I was momentarily devastated by his departure and wondered if I could ever love another again. I managed to nab a slow dance with him at the wrap party and we swayed to 'You Are Not Alone' by Michael Jackson, as the hormones galloped around my body. I cried all night over the tragedy of it all when we parted. A few months later, Fiona gently told me that he'd expressed an interest in her that night. This didn't surprise me. Every man with a pulse seemed to fall for Fiona. At any given time, she usually had at least forty men chasing after her. I kept her away from Andrew for a very long time.

Still intent on saving myself for 'the one', I continued to avoid any kissing-type activities. I was happy to indulge in one unrequited crush after another and convince myself that I couldn't kiss anyone because I had to remain loyal to my current crush, whoever he was. So, I'd meet guys at clubs and parties who seemed interested in me and I'd rebuff their advances. Sometimes this was objectively the correct course of action but other times I was annoyed at myself for being so stupid. Most of my close friends were dating and I was lonely. I longed to be held and kissed but the thought of that terrified me. I still believed I was unattractive and that nobody could love me, and I sought out men who would reject me so I could confirm this belief to myself again and again.

Perhaps spurred on by the 'normal' act that I'd assume in clubs, I became increasingly obsessed with trying to hide my disability. It's not easy to hide brain damage but I gave it a damn good bash. My strategy was simple: never ask for help and minimise the amount of physical tasks I carry out in public. My mantra was 'the stiller, the better'. I even managed to convince myself that if I ignored my disability, it would be invisible. As if I was gay!

One evening, during the filming of my final series of *Grange Hill*, I was invited out to dinner by Mickey Hutton and Danny Peacock, two TV presenters I'd recently worked with on a show. We'd had a real laugh together and, this evening, they took me to a fancy restaurant in town. I ordered a tomato and mozzarella salad which appeared to be the only vegetarian dish on the menu. The salad arrived and looked delicious. I was ravenous. However, a quick survey of the dish told me that the huge pieces of tomato and mozzarella would require cutting up before I could fit them in my gob. Still engaging in upbeat conversation with these two funny men, I assessed my options. I could try to cut the salad up myself but, given my history with knives, this wasn't viable (or legal, probably). I figured all three of us would end up covered in a pesto-tomato-cheese goo and that that wouldn't be very polite of me. Especially as the boys were paying for dinner. Of course, I could have asked Danny or Mickey to cut it up for me. But this would have meant revealing my brain damage. And that was not something I wanted to burden them with (certainly not over dinner). I decided the only possible option was not to eat it. I was starving but I could eat when I got home. I managed to lob a couple of smaller pieces into my mouth, but left most of it.

'Is your salad not nice?' asked Danny as he finished his meal (which had looked delicious).

'No, it's lovely! I just, er… felt a bit sick today so I'm not eating much,' I replied, as my stomach growled loudly, and that inner voice lambasted my hands.

It became increasingly harder to be myself. I devised more and more elaborate ruses to conceal my disability. This was futile but it didn't stop me trying. I'd go to parties and not drink because I didn't want to ask for a straw, and stand for hours on end because I didn't want to ask for a chair. When I was out, I'd stop in my tracks if someone was walking towards me, hoping they'd think I was normal (although there's nothing normal about a girl suddenly standing still in the middle of the pavement and staring intently at her feet). The incessant monologue that dominated my thoughts got louder and louder any time I found myself surrounded by strangers. It kicked in whenever I left the house. If I spotted teenage boys, I'd hear 'Look at those boys. Yeah, them. I bet they're thinking what a freak you are. I bet they're going to talk about how crap your walking is and laugh at how ridiculously shaky you are. And they'd never go out with someone like you, even if you were the last woman on Earth. They'd rather let the human race die out than engage in any physical contact with you.'

On spotting a mother and toddler, I'd hear 'She's thanking God that her baby is beautiful and perfect. Unlike you. You're making her feel good about her lot in life right now. She's feeling so grateful that she doesn't have to deal with damaged goods. And she's also pitying you and your parents for having to cope with such a sad situation.'

Seeing a pretty young woman, I'd hear 'I bet she's

thinking "Oh my God, look at that poor girl! Look at the way she walks. I am so glad I'm not her. I think I'd actually kill myself. I mean, I'm a strong person but I'm not that strong. I just couldn't cope with being stared at and pitied. It must be so awful… poor, poor girl.'"

On having to ask a stranger for help, 'Yeah, go on, ask for help. Let them think you're a baby. A pathetic little baby who can't even cut up her own food. They'll just feel sorry for you and think you're useless and weak and stupid. And you are!'

That voice persuaded me that I had to be seen as strong and independent at all costs. So I made sure I tried to help everyone else and never asked for anything in return. With my close friends, I allowed myself to take their arm when I walked, and managed to ask them to cut up my food. But they were the only demands I made. I was convinced that these more than filled my asking-for-stuff quota.

Several factors conspired to induce such high levels of paranoia and stress in me. *Grange Hill* was coming to an end and, although I was satisfied with my five-year stint, I was worried about what to do next. I found it hard to imagine my agent's phone ringing off the hook with parts for wobbly girls. I also dreaded the idea of returning to the education system: I'd only just crawled free of its insidious clutches and I was determined not to go back. Dad's film project was progressing nicely and he was working closely with Anthony Andrews on another draft of the script but it was some way off being finished. And anyway, I still had major doubts about my ability to do it. There was no way I was *that* good an actress.

Unable to put them off forever, I also attempted a few driving lessons. My mum had arranged for our car to be adapted for me, and there was now a steering ball fitted on the steering wheel and levers fitted on the indicators, gears and brakes to make them easier to operate. My instructor was a scarily upbeat chap called Tony. Even the sight of me fighting with the steering lock for three minutes hadn't wiped the grin off his face. I was impressed by his courage. He actually cheered when I switched the engine on. I managed to drive round the block a few times without injuring anyone but I was rigid with fear behind the wheel. My body was unaccustomed to such intense levels of control and, once again, I felt I had to suppress my disability in order to succeed. I had to find a way of being normal in that car. Sleep was easy after those lessons.

Finally, although my close friendship with Fiona had been very positive in many ways, I was beginning to feel as if our sisterly bond was adding to my deep insecurity. It was largely my own fault because I'd been so successful as an agony aunt that I'd created a dynamic where I was always strong, never had any problems, and was the 'together' one, while Fiona openly leaned on me emotionally. Into the bargain, I was, without a doubt, the plain one. The opposite sex flocked around Fiona like dizzy birds, all eager to win her affection. She was flawless in her beauty and whenever we were out she would receive multiple marriage proposals, notes with phone numbers scrawled on them, and offers of free clothes, meals, flowers. In many ways it was a lot of fun and I'm sure I'd never have played late-night strip poker with a Calvin Klein model (we remained fully clothed as we gawped at his six-pack) had it not been for Fiona's magical charms. But I couldn't shift the feeling that this friendship was feeding an unhealthy part of myself. Being around such physically beautiful people all the time just highlighted the gnawing feeling that I was ugly and inferior and faulty and abnormal. The act of keeping up the pretence that I'd no insecurities or problems or unhappiness or brain damage – along with the pressure I placed on my body by constantly demanding it to be 'normal' – was reaching breaking point. Something had to give.

The cracks started to show when my body began to develop mysterious aches and pains. I began to feel increasingly disconnected from my surroundings, as well as my body, and that rotten voice in my head nagged at me ceaselessly, becoming more and more biting in its analysis of what it thought others thought of me. The vitriol that it directed at my body's efforts intensified and every physical movement of mine was judged and scorned and ridiculed.

I stopped going out. My brother, who was the only person I knew who had known me his whole life, became my closest friend. We loved hanging out together which, I'd been told, was pretty unusual. To Raoul, I was still completely normal. I adored being with him. At thirteen, he'd already grown into a remarkable human being. We had shared a room together since he was born, until he was twelve and, far from it being a problem, we loved being able to chat late into the night whenever we liked. My parents eventually spent a lot of money splitting their bedroom into two so that Raoul would have his own room, and they were not best pleased when, during the first night in his new bedroom, he crept into mine because he missed it and me.

I had fewer scenes in *Grange Hill* during the last episodes of the series so I spent most of my time hiding away at home. I felt fully accepted by my family. They were like a life raft on a stormy ocean. But I couldn't share the turmoil that was raging inside me. I had become a ball of rabid self-loathing, but had concealed it from the world. Those who knew me saw me as robustly confident and those who didn't often looked up to me because they thought I was slightly famous. The gulf between how I was seen and how I saw myself became unbearable.

On the fifth of September, shortly after my nineteenth birthday, I went to bed. I lay there, unable to turn my neck without shooting pains while my tight chest struggled to breathe. Pins and needles filled my body. This is it, I thought, I'm dying... I've contracted some awful disease and it's going to end my life. I obsessed all night over what I'd say to my family and how I'd spend my last few hours. As the room grew light, I thought about Yayo and how I hoped he would be waiting for me if there was an after-life. I wanted there to be one. I got up and made my way down to the kitchen, pausing for a moment as I took in my family. My lovely mum was at the sink in her fluffy dressing gown, her blonde hair catching the sunlight. My brother was at the table, munching through a bowl of Shreddies, while flicking through a Superman comic, his beautiful face absorbed by some fantastic adventure. My gentle dad was standing by the stove making his beloved morning cup of coffee. My stomach lurched. I didn't want to say goodbye to them. The overwhelming love I felt for my family at that moment brought tears to my eyes.

'I'm dying,' I said, calmly. Everyone looked over to me, standing in my garish pyjamas in the doorway.

'What do you mean?' said my mum, concern written in her face.

'I've got some disease and I'm dying. I can't breathe properly. My neck's on fire. I've got pins and needles that won't go away. And I feel faint and sick. I think I'm dying.' My mum led me into the living room. She sat me down on the sofa and put her hand on my back.

'I love you,' I blubbed, the tears escaping from my eyes like grateful prisoners.

'Chessie, you're not dying. You're having a panic attack,' said Mum, softly.

'Are you sure?' I asked.

'Yes. Just concentrate on breathing. Breathe in and out, in and out…' We sat there for a while as I tried to breathe normally. Dad and Raoul came in and sat quietly with us. When I had calmed down, Raoul gently asked me why I was having a panic attack. I told them everything. Torrents of words and tears tumbled out of me like a wild river breaching a dam.

CHAPTER NINE

****

It took over a year for my shredded nerves to stop jangling. With a lot of love and extreme patience, my family finally convinced me that brain damage was not something to be brushed under the carpet. No matter how vigorous the sweeping.

I stepped back from the outside world and buried myself in the bosom of my home. I'd always prided myself on being mentally robust so it shook me to realise just how fragile I felt. Especially as I'd dismissively judged people who had panic attacks as somewhat hysterical with a melodramatic tendency to exaggerate. I was ashamed of myself for not having taken them seriously. I felt like a weary boxer after a long, hard fight who has finally accepted defeat. In many ways, it was a relief.I didn't have to pretend to be normal, or obsessively project strength or confidence any more. But it was also a shock. A shock to have to admit to myself that I was disabled. And that there was nothing

– nothing – I could do to change it. I stopped fighting it and begrudgingly accepted the damn label with the same grace with which I'd accept a parking ticket. I didn't bloody want it but I could see there was no other option. It took nineteen years of kicking and screaming to admit that I was brain damaged. I was a slow learner.

I finished *Grange Hill* in November 1997, shortly after the panic attack. A few tears were shed at the end-of-series party. It had been a wonderful experience and one I knew I would treasure forever. The nostalgia I felt was intense but, surprisingly, I knew it was the right time to move on. This calm acceptance was unexpected because I'd always feared the time when this amazing dream would be over. On many nights, I had lain in bed worrying what I would do without it. Yet here I was, happy to leave all that fun behind and scuttle back home to my family like a frightened rabbit. As much as I loved acting, I knew that some fundamental change had taken place inside me and I was still reeling from it.

The following spring, I fell out with Fiona and Lisa and lost their close friendship, which upset me deeply. I still miss Lisa. Much of it was my own fault. My personal insecurities had crept into both relationships and I handled the resulting mess terribly. I spent most of my time with Raoul voicing my woes to him, stuff I'd never talked about before. Remarkably for a fourteen-year-old, he sat and patiently listened to my shit. He had grown into a wise and compassionate teenager (very abnormal) and he comforted me with gentle words and lots of brother-hugs. I knew he was one of the best people I'd ever have the pleasure of knowing. My parents, too, let me come to them day after day, to air my worries and insecurities. They listened like friends and were always there to make me feel loved when I felt lost and scared. It was strange and unnerving to share my private anxieties with them, and it left me feeling acutely vulnerable. I didn't like it but I swallowed my pride and boldly embraced my new persona of negative, moany whinger with admirable success.

Yaya provided me with grandma cuddles on a regular basis as well as mountains of delicious food. It was hard to share the complexities of my feelings with her pidgin English and my elementary Spanish, but she could see that I wasn't ecstatically happy with life. As ever, she was devoted to her granddaughter. Her favourite term for me was '*mi vida*'. She would often tell Raoul and my cousins, with a glint in her eye, 'I love you but no as much as Francesca! She number one!' I would tell her off for saying those things but secretly felt a glow at her operatic expressions of love. She was never satisfied with the amount of time I spent with her. It could get annoying sometimes but I learnt to appreciate it. After all, how many people on the planet never get sick of you? Grandmas rule.

I often took her to her fortnightly medical visits and enjoyed her valiant attempts to flirt with the doctor only half her age:

'How are you feeling?'

'You very handsome today!'

I realised that my family were my rocks, and used their

unwavering strength to root myself in a more positive place. Which took some time.

As predicted, my agent wasn't bombarded with offers of parts for me, and I stopped waiting for the phone to ring. Despite this early-life crisis, I hoped I could be an actress again one day. My dad's film project was still going strong and had been an unexpectedly emotional journey. Through the different drafts, the story had evolved and one of the key elements now was the complicated relationship between my character and her father. Anthony Andrews was keen for my Dad to write about the battles he and I had fought over those bloody exercises. At first, he'd been reluctant to delve into such a personal and painful area but he sat down and wrote a draft that openly explored the conflict we'd been through. It was an incredibly cathartic experience for him and he cried on to the keys of his computer while recalling our fights. When I read the script, I was moved to tears too at the vivid reconstruction of our clashes. It opened a door for us to address something that we'd never talked about before. Still holding the script, I went to him, after drying my moist eyes.

'I thought you didn't love me the way I was, that you wanted me to be normal,' I said, not quite able to look at him. I'd never said those words aloud. Dad took this in for a moment.

'That's not true. I just wanted you to have the best chance you could have to be independent, to live a full life,' he replied.

'I understand that now. But, back then, it made me feel

not good enough. I thought you didn't love me because I wasn't perfect.'

His face looked heavy with guilt.

'I've always loved you, Chessie, more than I can say...' His voice cracked a little.

'I know you do. But I was more confused when it was all happening.' My voice threatened to break too under the weight of honesty in those words. They hit my dad with a force that was almost visible. He wiped the corner of his eye.

'Well, you tell that little girl that I love her. And that I'm proud of her. And she's perfect in my eyes, okay?' There was a shyness in his face at how open we were being. I could feel it in mine too.

'Okay. I love you, Dad.' Our hug was inevitable and we both held each other tightly, struggling not to cry. We've never really fought about anything since.

Finally, I felt accepted by my dad in a way I'd always longed to be. I'd known he loved me but hearing his words finally gave me permission to stop trying to be someone else. He was proud of me as I was.

Throughout this period of self-examination, emotional breakthroughs, and jangled nerves, I was still taking driving lessons. And would be until the next Ice Age, by the look of it. It was challenging but I slowly trained my body to behave in a roadworthy manner. Cheery Tony turned into Passive-Aggressive Tony, so I traded him in for Cuddly Michael, who was just what I needed. Soft, gentle and, yes, cuddly, his lilting Irish accent went some way to calming my often frenzied state when sat bolt upright behind the wheel. Impressively, he showed not a flicker of nerves when we got on to the North Circular for the first time. As cars sped past me and I struggled to keep in the unbelievably narrow lane, he just hummed a ditty and chatted about the weather. I wondered if he'd fortified himself with a tipple before getting in the car with me. Frankly, I hoped he had.

I took my first test that winter and failed on a minor technicality (nobody died). I nearly passed but this rejection sent me into a major funk. I bid goodbye to Cuddly Michael (who I suspected had been a bit *too* nice), and refused to take another lesson for six months.

My mum tried to lift me out of my negative state by suggesting I start a college course. Her suggestion did not go down particularly well. When she pushed the issue, I admitted that I harboured a primal fear at the thought of having to enter another education establishment. The floodgates opened and I blubbed about how unhappy I'd been at high school. Mum was shocked to hear about Ethel and Prudence and Bunt and the girls, and she couldn't understand why I hadn't said anything earlier.

'Because I thought it was normal to be unhappy at school,' I told her.

'Well, we would have moved you to another school,' she said, annoyed that I'd kept silent.

'And I would have beaten them up for you,' chipped in Raoul. I smiled. Sharing my high-school horrors felt good, as if some of their power over me was dissipating as we spoke. The college suggestion was dropped and I was free to continue my moping, which had reached professional level.

Eventually I pulled myself together enough to get back behind the wheel with Nice Michael who was a better teacher than his Cuddly namesake. I was heading towards my one hundredth lesson – it was lucky that I'd saved a lot of my BBC money. I wonder how many wobbly people have bankrupted themselves learning to drive. Yep, it was taking a long time to get my body to respond the way I needed it to. A very long time. But Nice Michael was very patient and kept telling me that I could do it. I'm not sure I believed him but I stuck at it, mainly because I'd spent so much money on lessons already. I took my second test in early summer and, once more, failed. Nice Michael was determined that his 100 per cent success rate was not going to be ruined by something as trivial as a bit of brain damage, so he booked me in for a third test a few weeks later. At the end of the test, I pulled into the car park and looked nervously at the examiner.

'I'm pleased to tell you that you've passed, Ms Martinez,' he said, smiling.

'What? Are you sure? I mean… are you sure?'

'Yes, I'm sure. Well done!' He held out his hand to shake mine, and I took it.

'Thank you. I thought I'd never be allowed to drive!' He looked slightly unnerved by this and quickly got out of the car, perhaps regretting his decision.

Well, it may have wiped out my life's savings but learning to drive was worth it. I could now go places. *On my own.*

(Providing someone could meet me at the destination.) Of course, I didn't have anywhere to go but it's the principle that counts. My family were very proud of me and no doubt relieved that I no longer had to rely on them to take me everywhere. They were happy that I had a degree of real independence, even if it was only in theory. Passing the test made me feel a bit more positive about my life. And, when Mum delicately mentioned that I could start a part-time course in October, I agreed. Without a fuss. I decided to do an A-level in English literature, and drove myself to Kensington and Chelsea College every Friday. The teacher was lovely and so were the students, who were of various ages. On the first day, I made friends with a pretty girl called Natasha Bedingfield. Yes, that one. After the lessons, I offered her a lift to the station. I could see her hesitate slightly. Her survival instinct was right to kick in but I assured her that my erratic walking did not accurately reflect my driving skills. Clearly I was persuasive because she faced her mortality with aplomb and happily jumped in the car. I delivered her safely to the Tube, thereby ensuring that the world would not be denied her future pop songs.

Slowly I began to replace those painful high-school memories with more pleasant ones, and I found myself actually enjoying the course. Often, after the class, I'd go and visit my new friend Freddie, who lived in Chelsea. I met Freddie when she had had a guest role on *Grange Hill* during my last series. Coincidentally, she also happened to be related to a certain Mr Anthony Andrews. Freddie is short and walks around with two sticks. I remember thinking how visibly different her body looked when I first met her. I even felt a bit nervous. But, within a week, I concluded that she was the least disabled person I'd ever met. She raced around London in her car, smoked like a chimney, and had a love life that would have fuelled *EastEnders* for a year. Constantly talking and with a laugh that strayed into dirty territory, Freddie took great pleasure in shocking me with detailed accounts of her filthy antics. She cracked up when I spoke about my idealistic desires to meet a man who would write me poetry, and who I could have passionate and scintillating... conversations with. We were very different – her romantic entanglements made me blush and I could not believe the things she got up to. Freddie may have looked 'disabled' at first sight but she led a wild and fun-filled life, and didn't care what anyone thought about her. She was much more confident than many of my able-bodied friends on *Grange Hill* and her vivacious lust-for-life had a deep impact on me. She lived her life exactly how she wanted and I couldn't help being in awe of her. I wanted to do the same. I just didn't know where the hell to start.

In the autumn of 1998, my family were invited to a gala dinner with Anthony Andrews. Wanting to show him that I could convince as the sex-bomb that was Lady Sod, I wore a stunning red cocktail dress. The outfit seemed to have the desired effect. Anthony told me that he was still holding out for me and had turned down several offers from high-profile actresses who were desperate to play the role. He then asked if I would consider doing some comedy training for the part. There was no way I could refuse, so I smiled and nodded enthusiastically. As the cold fingers of fear slowly tightened around my neck.

I was trapped. With a reluctance bordering on pathological, I signed up to do a comedy workshop in January at the City Lit in central London. The minute I'd enrolled, the worrying began. What was I doing? How was I ever going to succeed? And, above all, how could I get out of it? The only thing that stopped me backing down was the fear of losing the part. The part that my dad had written especially for me. I'd never live with myself if Cameron Diaz won an Oscar for wobbling it up because I'd been too chicken to play. And I was hoping that George Clooney would be my leading man (sorry Costner – you had your chance). It was these two thoughts that I focused on when my nerves started to go crazy. I warned my parents repeatedly that I was doing the workshop purely – *purely* – for research.

'Don't expect me ever to do a gig! I will never do a gig, okay?' I asserted, my arms crossed defiantly.

'Okay. We know. Just go and see how it goes,' replied my dad, calmly.

'I will. But I will never do a gig. Do you understand?' I said, with a slightly maniacal laugh.

'I think you've made that pretty clear several times now,' said my mum, a smile on her lips.

'Good. I just want us all to be on the same page…' The stress had made its way into my voice.

'We hear you, Chess,' said Dad, casually.

'Good. Okay. Great. Right. That's all agreed...' I sat there as the nerves whizzed around my body like sugar-loaded toddlers. With ADHD.

On a dark January evening, I pulled up outside the City Lit and turned off the engine. I sat there, wondering what the hell I was doing. With a deep breath, I got out of the car and headed into the building. Thankfully, I was early (I still hated walking into rooms full of people) and I introduced myself to the teacher, Jill, before sitting down in one of the plastic chairs that were laid out in a circle. People began to arrive and, before long, there were twenty-five of us, all different ages, sitting facing each other. Jill spoke for a while about how she wanted to create a safe environment for people to give stand-up a try. Then we all had to say a few words about why we were there. I said I was researching a part. And that was the extent of my verbal contribution for the week. And the next. And the next. In fact, I managed not to say anything else for six whole weeks. I was that terrified.

For a natural chatterbox like me, this was a novel experience. Every week, the class would play some warm-up games, which I'd watch; then people would have the chance to perform short routines and receive feedback. It was obvious from the start who was funny and who wasn't. Sometimes it was horrendously awkward, watching people who were devoid of any comedic talent whatsoever trying to make us laugh. It was a real mix – there was Lizzie who was naturally funny, Tom who was quick and confident, Eric the pensioner who was slightly bonkers, and Dylan who clearly came from another planet. I loved watching all of them perform but I couldn't help feeling angry at myself for being so pathetic. I'd happily acted in a TV show for years and here I was, paralysed with fear at the thought of delivering a few lines in front of two dozen people. Three of whom clearly had mental health issues. It didn't make any sense. Except it did. It was gut-wrenchingly simple. I knew why I was filled with horror at the prospect. I couldn't stand in front of these people and *be myself*.

Jill didn't push anyone to perform who didn't want to but, by the time the seventh week loomed, I felt the pressure building on me. I would have to say something. I woke up on the day feeling stressed. I had no idea what to write about. Luckily for me, that was the day the English football manager Glenn Hoddle chose to make some choice comments about how disabled people came to be disabled. Because of karma from a past life! I privately thanked him for being such a twat and quickly wrote a short routine.

That evening, I sat in the workshop and waited. And waited. The session was nearly over.

'OK, guys, we've got time for one more person… anyone?' Jill glanced over at me. I felt my body stiffen. It was now or never. I shoved my hand up before I had time to change my mind.

'Francesca? Great. Come on up…' Jill smiled and gestured to the stage area in front of the audience. I stood up shakily, gripping my piece of paper that was now a crumpled rag after an hour of being pulverised by my nervous fingers. The stage area was only a couple of metres away but it took me about ten seconds to get there. As usual, my body was doing a sterling job of reflecting my inner state – at this point, a frenzy of panic and adrenaline – and my limbs decided to move with the jerky shakes of a 1960s' sci-fi robot.

By the time I positioned myself centre-stage, I craved a cup of tea and a nap. I could feel my pulse throbbing in my neck as I looked at the faces in front of me. Faces that – despite the admirable effort at English politeness – bore the unmistakable shadow of unease. Only Dylan looked unperturbed by the bead of sweat that ran down my left cheek. And then my legs started to shake.

'When you're ready…' said Jill, in some distant realm. My eyes focused on the paper which shook as well. I opened my mouth. It was parched. My saliva had fucked off too with my balance and coordination. Bloody deserters.

'Glenn Hoddle thinks that if you're disabled, it's because of karma from a past life…' I paused and tried to stop my legs shaking. 'So what the fuck must I have done, then?' The room laughed, loud and long. I looked up in surprise. The veiled panic had gone from their faces. They were smiling now.

'I mean, I must have been a bloody axe-murderer…' More laughter. I performed the rest of my short piece to laughter and applause. I knew I had delivered the routine badly with a voice that was thick with nerves. And I knew I'd only managed to 'breathe' three times in two minutes – and at exceedingly badly chosen points. But I also knew that, for me, in that moment, something revelatory had happened. Somewhere, buried beneath the panic and fear and terror and shaking and embarrassment, I felt something totally unexpected. I felt a pull I'd never felt before and I knew, there and then, that this was what I was meant to do.

'Well, I think we've witnessed the birth of a new comedy star tonight!' said Jill, warmly. 'Well done, Francesca.' I was just grateful to sit down and feel the solidity of the chair instead of the jelly of my legs.

I went straight home and told my family how well it had gone. The following day, I wrote my second routine and waited impatiently for the week to pass.

In the next session, I flung my hand up and volunteered to perform early on. I'd like to say that my legs shook less on the walk to the stage, but they didn't. It was less of a shock, though, and I tried to embrace their wobbles instead of fighting them. A part of me ached with embarrassment at having my disability so starkly on display but I tried not to dwell on it. I took a breath.

'As a disabled person, I feel I am denied access to a lot of things… like drugs! I mean, I can't even thread a needle, let alone stick one in a tiny vein!' I paused, gratefully soaking up the laughter that rolled around the room.

'It's not fair… I can *always* remember what happened last night! I mean, I want to know what it's like to stare at my carpet for hours and find it fascinating!… And even if I could do drugs, how could I fund my habit? Bank robbery? Getaway car? No disabled parking space!… Pick-pocketing?' I moved my very shaky arm towards someone's pocket. 'And credit card fraud? Well, I can't even repeat my *own* signature twice!' I was beginning to enjoy myself.

'And can you imagine me rolling a bloody joint? The amount I'd drop would mean I'd have to set my carpet alight to get high!… And if I ever moved flat, the removal men carrying out my carpet would never know they had just rolled the biggest joint ever!'

I was still shaking like a leaf in the wind but it didn't seem to matter. People were laughing and clapping in front of me. For a second I wanted to cry and I gulped back the emotion that was climbing up my throat. Standing there and looking at the faces staring back at me, a blinding realisation pulsated through me. I had been so damn certain that the only way to acceptance was to hide my differences. How utterly wrong I'd been. I was finally seeing that if I was honest about who I was, people would be *more* likely to accept me. My jokes had obliterated any nerves in the room. More than that, I could feel that people wanted to hear my perspective. They were actually interested in my difference. This was the first time in twenty years that I'd willingly referred to my disability in public. Despite my quivering legs, a rock-solid determination throbbed through me. I wanted to be a comedian.

After the workshop, I went to the pub with the other students. It was amazing to hear their feedback on my routine. They were all incredibly positive. People were offering me lines and making suggestions, and they felt free to make jokes about me in a way that nobody had ever done before. It was unfamiliar but welcome, and the nerves that usually accompanied me in public places were strangely absent. Towards the end of the evening, I found myself alone for a moment. As I got up to join a small group at the bar, Dylan walked over. We hadn't really spoken before. He was a bit odd.

'I love the way your body shakes onstage. It's electric.' He stood still as he spoke. I didn't know how to respond to this so I laughed.

'Well, I hate the way it does that! It happens when I'm nervous.' My eyes flitted down to my feet.

'You shouldn't hate it. It's you and it's beautiful and different and musical.' His voice was soft and delicate.

'And abnormal!' I added, trying to deflect one of those dreaded compliments.

'Why do you say that, Francesca?' That was the first time he spoke my name.

'Because I am… Don't you think I am?' He regarded me for a moment.

'Yes. You are abnormal. Most people in the world live in dire poverty. You are lucky. So take your head out of your arse and open your eyes.' That was the first time he smiled at me. I looked directly at him.

'Okay, Mr Brilliant-Answer Man. But I am abnormal in other ways too!'

'I've got a hole in the heart. Am I abnormal?' he asked.

I wasn't sure what to say. So I just reached into my brain and grabbed for something. Anything.

'But I'm not normal!' I looked at him defiantly. Standing there in the middle of a pub in Soho.

'What do you mean?' His hair was the colour of dragonfly wings and his eyes, pale blue, stared at me and saw more than I wanted them to. I smiled to break the tension that was creeping slowly up the back of my neck. Tension that he seemed to embrace while waiting for me to speak, his eyes watching me with faint traces of amusement. I decided to go for it.

'I'm brain damaged.' The words shot out of my mouth, clumsy sounds that halted awkwardly in the air between us. After twenty years, they still made me jolt inside, and that annoyed me. Dylan's eyes didn't flicker.

'What do you mean?' His words sounded soft, calm, sensible, in stark contrast to the ugly ones I'd uttered that were still hanging, like dirty clothes, in front of me.

'I mean...' I meant what I said. I didn't want to say it again. Once should be enough. It wasn't.

'I mean... my brain was damaged. At birth... so...' The words couldn't even fall out awkwardly now. They just clogged up my throat like pieces of wet tissue. A few strands of the dragonfly hair fell in front of his eyes and a hand swept them away. I noticed then, suddenly, that he was beautiful. Astoundingly so. His beauty hit me in the stomach and I gulped.

'Who said your brain was damaged?'

'Er, the doctors?' Uncertainty had crept into my mind and was crouching there. An unwanted predator.

'The doctors.'

'Yes. They said I was… brain damaged.' I nodded as if to clarify the statement but I was unsure where this was going. 'And that caused my cerebral palsy.' I added this to try and sound as if it was no big deal, as if the rug was still firmly under my feet. Dylan took a sip of his beer. I looked at his lips. They were glistening.

'They're only words made up by other people. Sounds. Words that don't mean anything. You're not "brain damaged". You don't have "cerebral palsy". Those words are vague attempts to try and define you. Your brain is your brain and you are perfectly you.'

I let those ideas into my head one by one, each gingerly walking in with hesitant steps. All the people and the chatter and the grey smoke around me faded away and all I could see was Dylan. I fumbled for an answer in the new space I found myself in.

'But I'm… different.'

'Everyone's different.'

'I'm not normal.'

'Nobody's normal.'

'But people think I'm different.'

'How do you know what they think?'

'I don't. But I think they're thinking it.'

'But what you think they think is coloured by your own perception. Therefore, it's a pointless exercise. It will never lead anywhere.'

'But I want people to accept me.'

'Do you accept yourself?' Silence.

'No.'

'Then you can't expect anyone else to.'

'So I shouldn't care what anyone else thinks?'

'The only opinion of you that matters, is yours.'

This hit me hard. In the gut, in my legs, in my arms, my feet. For the first time, I hated myself for hating myself.

'You mean, I can just… choose how to see myself? I don't have to be "disabled" or "brain damaged"? I can choose to be… me?'

Dylan drank more beer.

'If you want. The only power we have in life is the power to choose what to think.' I laughed without wanting to, a bubble of joy escaping from me.

'So, I'm just… me.' I felt invigorated, as if I could see everything all at once.

'If anyone else wants to call you another label, that's up to them. But you choose how you see yourself. And that should be all that matters to you.'

I looked at his face, delicately marked by time, and glanced quickly at his eyes, which stared back at me calmly. He spoke once more.

'You are Francesca. Full stop.'

And that was the moment everything changed. And the moment when, for the first time in my life, I fell hopelessly, recklessly, wondrously, magically, painfully in love.

As I lay in bed later that night, a million thoughts exploded in my head like shooting stars. My mind had been well and truly blown. Dylan's words echoed in my body and the vibrations shook my veins. I wasn't wrong or abnormal or faulty or disabled. I was me. I was just *me*.

I had spent years accepting other people's definitions of me and doing so had filled me with shame and negativity. All my life I'd hated saying 'I've got cerebral palsy.' And now I realised that I never had to say it again. I was just Francesca and Francesca was wobbly. My neighbour's kids had called me 'wobbly' years ago and I loved it. It was accurate and non-judgemental and *cool*. I hadn't realised that I could *choose* how to view myself. I hadn't even realised that, somewhere along the way, I had given that vital power away – the only power I possessed – and I had given it away without even knowing it. It had stripped away my happiness and confidence and self-worth. But Dylan had handed them all back to me. With a few words. He changed my whole life with some words. And I loved him for that. With every atom of my beating heart.

Yes, he was from another planet. And I wanted to be on it too.

He convinced me that I didn't have to worry about what anyone else thought of me. It didn't matter. All that mattered was what I thought of myself. I decided in that instant that whenever I had a choice how to view myself, I would choose to be positive. Life was hard enough without me being my own worst enemy.

I felt I would burst at the seams with the happiness that soared through my cells. And suddenly, lying in bed, I became aware of every inch of my body and I apologised to it, quietly. I apologised for being so ungrateful for so long. Then I thanked my arms, hands and fingers for always trying so hard. I thanked my legs and feet for holding me up all the time. I thanked my brain for working so amazingly well and conjuring up thoughts and dreams and sentences and images and crazy poems. And I thanked all my organs for working together and giving me life. It had taken four and a half billion years for me to be here. Right now. In this universe. And, in that moment, I felt totally overwhelmed at being alive. There could have been nothing but there was everything. I didn't want to waste a single second more of my life worrying about trivialities. Worrying that I'd never match up to an ideal that didn't even exist. Nobody is normal. We are all different. I had to make sure that every moment I had left on this planet counted.

I knew that nothing would be the same again after that. A jolt of appreciation for everything I had experienced surged through me, pure as raw diamond.

'I like myself,' I said out loud into Night's listening ear. 'I like myself,' I repeated, with more conviction. I said those words every night for a long time.

And I never looked back.

CHAPTER TEN

****

got out of bed the following morning, stood in the middle of my room and looked at the white patch of sunlight that fell by my feet. I felt different. I breathed in deeply and wondered what had changed. Then it dawned on me. My shoulders felt incredibly... light. There was no heavy weight pushing me down, crushing my hope. It was gone. Completely. I looked around me slowly, to see if the dark presence was hiding, ready to drape itself over me again, but all I could see was the bedroom bathed in warm dappled hues. The brooding negativity that had clung to me like a leaden cloak for so long had disappeared, melting away silently into the black night while I was sleeping.

The first thing I wanted to do in this new state was go for a walk. I wanted to go outside and feel good about walking down my street without shame or guilt or worry. I threw on some clothes, went downstairs and opened the door. The sun was shining and the sky was a soft March blue. I shut the door behind me and wobbled slowly down the path. The paranoid voice in my head started up but I just let it spout its useless crap before politely telling it to fuck right off. Which it kindly did. Then, I told my legs that they were doing a brilliant job of transporting me along the pavement (albeit in a rather unique manner).

'Well done, legs. Keep up the good work. Don't listen to that pathetic little demon. It's full of shit and is of no benefit whatsoever.' I continued along the road slowly, marvelling at the fact that I was here, alive and walking on the outer crust of a rocky ball in space. A young couple crossed the road and walked towards me. For a moment, I slowed down to a crawl before remembering that I didn't have to stop, that I could carry on walking, that I had a right to be there. Don't be embarrassed, I thought to myself. Just keep walking. Let them get on with their journey and you get on with yours. I felt my legs stiffen a bit but I kept on moving, determined not to stop. They passed me with no more than a sidewards glance, which I was happy with. I was beginning to accept that, frankly, my walking did merit the odd peek. I even felt a tinge of pride that my movements were so interesting that people took time to clock them for a fleeting moment.

I sat down on a low wall and smiled. It had been so many years since I'd actually enjoyed being out in the world. As I listened to the birds chirp away, I was overcome with a longing to see Dylan again. It had only taken a day but I'd tumbled headlong in love with him. And I had never felt anything like it before. My stomach jumped at the thought of those blue eyes and that smile and the way his hair fell on to his forehead. Everywhere I looked, I saw him. In the crystal sky, in the wispy clouds, in the swaying branches and budding seeds, in the daffodil heads that nodded, and in the fallen petals that danced along the pavement. And his voice! His soft beautiful voice sang in my ears and spilled out into the air around me. I felt that the rays touching my cheek were his lips, that the dew glistening around me was the glint in his shiny eyes, and the breeze playing with my hair was his slender fingers. I felt that the cosmos was purely a reflection of Dylan's ethereal beauty, and I was in sheer awe of it.

Yes, it took me a mere twelve hours to develop these somewhat extreme feelings of love, epitomised by the conviction that all universal matter had been brought into existence for the sole purpose of worshipping this man. Evidently, the concept of 'taking it slow' hadn't entered my stratosphere.

By the time I got home, I had mentally undressed Dylan fifty-odd times (my walking was still snail-slow despite the new-found pride in it). I was desperate to see what his hair looked like after we kissed, to undo his shirt buttons – or rip them off if this turned out to be too time-consuming – and to feel his hands in mine. He was going to be my first kiss. I was sure of it. I went into the bathroom and had a shower. A long and very cold one.

'Sod the research. I want to be a comedian!' I declared to my family over dinner. My dad stared at me in surprise.

'But you assured us several times that you would "never, ever" do a gig. What's changed?'

I smiled with embarrassment.

'Well, I know I can be quite… er…'

'Headstrong? Stubborn?' Offered my mum, helpfully.

'Yeah, okay, those. But I was wrong. I think I'm meant to be a comedian,' I said.

'Why?' asked Dad.

'Well, I think I can do it and it feels amazing to make people laugh, and I can be honest about who I am.' The sentence bubbled out of me like fizzy champagne.

'That's great, Chess. I'm so happy to hear that! So, you're no longer struggling to be honest about who you are…?' said Mum, a trifle amazed.

'Not any more. I'm happy with who I am. This is going to sound weird but, last night, I had the best conversation of my life… and I decided to like myself…' Then I relayed the entire exchange – in far too much detail (I'm sure my dad didn't need to know how gorgeous Dylan's lips were) – and told them how Dylan's words had changed my whole outlook on everything.

'It's incredible! I'm still wobbly, obviously, but I don't see it as a problem any more. I'm going to be proud of being wobbly because it's me! And I feel so bloody happy to have you all in my life. Thanks for putting up with my negativity for so long. You deserve flipping medals.' My family were visibly bowled over by this profound transformation, although they gently suggested that perhaps we should wait and see if I managed to sustain it for more than twenty-four hours before celebrating it too enthusiastically.

'Fine. But I know I've changed forever!' I stated,

emphatically. I could see the amused relief in their eyes as they smiled at my words. And I was grateful that neither my parents nor Raoul chose to point out that they had been telling me for years exactly what Dylan had told me. I was clearly a lot more receptive to the message when it was delivered via The Most Beautiful Lips On Earth.

I continued to walk around with an intensity of happiness that was, frankly, sickening. I'd fallen deeply in love and had opened my eyes to a whole new way of thinking – it was a powerful combination. Every day I woke up buzzing with super-charged joy. I didn't feel disabled any more and the realisation that I could tear up that shitty label and throw it away for good filled me with strength.

I no longer felt like a freak. I just felt part of that wonderfully diverse species we call human. And, the truth is, every single one of those humans is different. Every person has things they can and can't do. I finally felt beautifully, and utterly, normal.

Dylan had given me the confidence to choose how to view myself and the world around me, and I felt a powerful liberation that I hadn't encountered before. I felt mind-bogglingly free. And I didn't quite know how to cope with such an incredible sense of empowerment. It was as if I was drunk on the heady myriad of new possibilities. I felt almost indestructible, like I had all those years ago when I was tearing around school and upsetting nuns. It was true that the inner devil still sometimes spoke up when I left the house. But it was beginning to fade into the background. And, just before venturing out into the world each day, I took to standing on the doorstep for a second and closing my eyes briefly. I'd tell myself that anyone could think whatever they wanted about me and it didn't matter – it couldn't affect me any more. And it always seemed to work. Even if standing with your eyes shut on your doorstep does make you look slightly insane.

I even managed to walk the four streets to Yaya's house all on my own, navigating across several roads without getting run over. There was one hairy moment when I was crossing over by the local park and a rusty three-wheeled banger suddenly appeared on the horizon. It chugged towards me slightly more quickly than a toddler on a scooter, but I reached the kerb and avoided a head-on collision just in time. This was an epic journey for me, despite the walk being less than a kilometre long and, when the going got tough, I just focused my mind on Dylan. I pictured him walking along without a care in the world, and was filled with renewed strength and a belief that I could make it in one piece. His image was my secret weapon and, whenever I needed a surge of confidence in the following months, I simply filled my head with Dylan and was recharged immediately.

When I made it to Yaya's, she was incredibly impressed that I'd walked down to her all on my own. It had taken a degree of exertion that I later judged to be a preposterous waste of effort so I never did it again. I reasoned that there were far better ways to expend my time, energy and sweat. But I was really happy that I managed to do it once.

My excitement about the next workshop session

reached fever pitch. Not only would I get to perform my new routine – which might feature jokes about a certain Bunt – but, more importantly, I would also get to see Dylan again. I'd have the chance to convey to him (in a non-scary way, of course) that he'd changed my whole life and that, as a result, I now wanted to have his babies.

I was the first person to stick my hand up in class and I wobbled the now-familiar route on to the stage. My legs kicked off as usual as I stood there but I told them they could do what they bloody well wanted.

'My PE teacher was scary. Bulging biceps, perfect six-pack, well-trimmed moustache… she was a bitch!' The room laughed. My eyes landed on Dylan and his dragonfly-wing hair and I momentarily forgot what planet I was on.

The routine went down well, which I was very pleased about, although I was somewhat distracted during the feedback session because I couldn't stop wondering if Dylan was going to come to the pub afterwards. I was worried that he'd just dash off, and the thought of not being able to talk to him made my stomach hurt. But I was in luck. After a tense couple of minutes in the pub during which I didn't hear a single word anyone said to me, I saw him walk through the door in his long navy coat with his scarf hung loosely around his neck. He looked around and I waved at him, trying (and failing) to appear casual. He walked over and sat down next to me. His thigh pressed against mine. I thought I might have a seizure. I gulped too loudly and looked at him. We hadn't been this close before. My thirsty eyes drank in his face. He was older than me, perhaps even in his forties, but I didn't care. His face was finely drawn and his eyes were deep enough to lose yourself in. His hair was a work of art, ruffled strands of silver-blonde that fell across his eyes when he laughed. I had to stop myself reaching out to touch them and then running my fingers down to the nape of his long, delicate neck. He was tall and strong and, through his cotton shirt, I could see the defined lines of his collarbone and chest. His sleeves were rolled up, revealing his forearms, which were slender and sensual, and made for wrapping around me. My heart ached at the wild beauty of him.

'How are you?' he asked me, a smile hovering on his lips. Those lips. I was aware I would have to speak before long. And I warned my brain that it needed to focus on constructing coherent sentences. I dragged my eyes from his lips, which were commanding far too much of my attention.

'I am fine. I am better than fine… because you've changed my life.' I brought my eyes to his, confident that I could handle their power now that I wouldn't have to speak for a second.

'Really?' Dylan smiled and his perfect teeth caught the light. It was a smile that reached into my lungs and sucked out all the air. 'How did I do that?' he asked. I yanked my eyes away to gather my thoughts into some kind of sensible order.

'Well, you gave me back the power I'd given away. The power to think for myself. And you reminded me of the overwhelming beauty of life and how I don't want to waste a single second more worrying about crap. I chose to like myself and I didn't know I had that choice. Thank you for helping me to extract my head from my arse, in which it was very firmly placed.' I felt his eyes on me but didn't know how to look back at him.

'Last night I was thinking about kissing you.' His words burnt themselves into my ear and down my neck. I coughed out the nerves that sprang into my throat. That was the only answer I could manage. A slightly phlegmy cough. My seduction technique was nothing if not sophisticated.

'So, tell me a bit more about yourself. What do you do?' I managed to shove out the words while my skin tingled with the heat of what he'd said.

'Lots of things. I paint. I make art. I sing. I do music. I play instruments. I teach. I read. I write poetry...' The hairs on my arm bristled.

'You... you write poetry?'

'Yes, I love poetry.' He smiled again. This was all getting a bit too much.

'I write poetry too.' I managed to look at him.

'Let's write poetry to each other.' His eyes looked into mine. I remembered to blink.

'Okay. What shall we write about?' The voice that asked him was clearly in need of more oxygen.

'How about we write poems about each other?'

I nodded. I could do that. I could DEFINITELY do that.

'We'll swap addresses.' He got up. 'Do you want a drink?' I shook my head in a daze, watched him as he walked to the bar, and, finally, gulped in some mouthfuls of air.

As well as being determined to nab Dylan, I was serious about becoming a professional comedian. So serious that, once again, I chucked in the A-level course to concentrate on my new passion. My teacher and classmates were very supportive of the decision and wished me luck. The main reason for stopping – aside from the looming deadline for a *King Lear* essay, which had been the object of some serious procrastination – was a growing sense that comedy was about to take over my entire life. I felt that it wasn't something you simply *did* but something that you *lived*, something that consumed you fully. And I was ready and willing to give myself completely to it. I felt that I had finally discovered my calling.

I became addicted to the buzz of making people laugh every week. Acting was fantastic. It had brought real joy into my life – and at a time when I desperately needed it – but comedy fed a part of me that hadn't been fed before. A part of me that seemed to be waking up from a long hibernation. A part that was longing to express itself. I knew that, in order to become a real comedian, I would have to fully accept who I was. And, at some level, despite feeling sick with nerves every time I imagined doing a real gig, I knew I *could* do it and I knew I *had* to do it. The magnetic pull that comedy was exerting on me seemed to coincide perfectly with my new personal awakening, and both of these filled me with a piercing clarity and a dogged determination to challenge myself.

My dad's film, meanwhile, had entered into that delightful phase known as 'development hell'. The process of having your highly personal project slowly murdered – repeatedly, and in a plethora of violent ways – turned out to be a painful one. There was growing disagreement over what the film should be, and a rapidly decreasing amount of common ground. I felt very sorry for my father who had written this beautiful script but I was still utterly grateful to him for bringing comedy into my life. And Dylan. Who was, of course, the other reason why I had to leave the English course. Turns out that the dual pursuit of stand-up comedy and a passionate first love affair doesn't leave much time for anything else. Especially not detailed analysis of Shakespeare.

I may have given the Bard the finger but his influence was clear in the poem that I gushed out to Dylan in a matter of minutes, when I got home from that heady evening in the pub. The words had flooded out of me in torrents, soaking the pages with inky desire, but I held off from sending it to him. I thought it probably wise to receive his poem first so I could gauge whether mine oozed a level of intensity that was out of proportion to his. Okay, I had no doubt that my poem *would* trump his in terms of passion and longing and inventive lip compliments, but I didn't want the poor man never turning up again to the workshop for fear of being jumped on. I had to attempt some pretence of sanity. Even in my love-drunken state, I had enough self-awareness to know that.

Three days later, I received an envelope. I knew it was from Dylan right away because the stamp was not in the top right-hand corner. Oh no. It was in the bottom left-hand corner. I stared at it for a very long time and decided that he was, indeed, a genius. Having calmed my breathing, I took out a typed letter. It had been written on an old-fashioned typewriter and the lines wobbled at points:

```
                    Dear FM
         I will not labour with this task
    Having already considered you a flower and
                  compared you
      To the petals of a rose opening to fall
              Delicate as fine thread
       A glass of champagne freshly poured
               A dandelion's sneeze
             Shiny nosed fragmentation
              Wild body like a vine
```

It went on but I stopped reading. The beauty of his words made my eyes water and my heart pound like a tribal drum. He thought these things – these incredible things – about me. It wasn't exactly a marriage proposal but it was surely a positive step towards that first kiss. I would just have to train myself not to have a coughing fit next time he mentioned kissing. I read the poem again and again until I knew the words by heart. Eventually, I placed it under my pillow, and read over the first verse of my poem to him:

> Your smile overwhelms me
> Smouldering radiance and power
> Cascading forth from deep within
> Transforming those dreaming eyes
> To a pair of suns in scorching skies

I could see that it wasn't exactly neutral. But it didn't occupy an entirely different hemisphere to Dylan's poem. A different continent perhaps but, on the whole, I thought I could just about get away with sending it. So, I popped it into the post box and hoped I wouldn't be issued with a restraining order.

'Have you got a stamp impediment?' I said to Dylan at the next post-workshop drink.

'Why do you say that?' he asked, raising a glass of beer to his lips. I envied the beverage, which was enjoying an intimacy that had, so far, been denied to me.

'Because you don't stick stamps in the top right-hand corner. Why do you stick them in other places?' I said, trying not to stare at his mouth.

'Why not?' he answered. Try as I might, I couldn't offer a counter argument. Why not, indeed? How was it that a choice of stamp placement could be such a turn-on?

'You like challenging norms, don't you?' I said.

'I like difference. I like creativity. Life is art. That's why I like it when you shake while performing. You're like a tree swaying in the wind.'

'You mean, you like my unreliable balance?' I laughed at this idea.

'Your balance isn't unreliable. It's just yours. You don't walk badly or talk badly. You do them like you do them. Don't put judgements on them. I love your walk. It's full of energy and effort and anarchic rhythm. It's like a dance with gravity.' His eyes flashed.

'More like a fight with gravity! It's funny, I hated my

walk for years. I wished I walked normally,' I said, the shame swelling in my belly like an ugly pufferfish.

'Nobody walks normally. And you might as well like your walk because it's your walk, and it ain't going to change.' Yet again, I couldn't find a reason to disagree. 'Did you get my poem?' he asked.

'Yes. I loved it. Did you get mine?' I felt a shyness flutter over my voice.

'Yes. It was one of the most beautiful things I've ever read,' he said, with a smile that threatened to stop my heart.

Dylan and I continued to exchange poems every week. I couldn't believe I was at last living out my cherished fantasies with a man who could not only write poetry himself but wasn't scared shitless by my own rhyming odes. It was the kind of idealistic courtship I'd craved, full of heady dialogue, mind-blowing ideas, and challenging stamp sticking.

Not surprisingly, Dylan didn't own a phone – that would have been far too conventional a possession for him – and, one day, he called me from a public pay phone (remember those?) and invited me to dinner at his house. I tried to keep my voice steady as I said yes, and we agreed that I should come over the following evening. I put the phone down and composed myself. What would I wear? What would I bring? How would I hide the undying devotion that radiated from my pores like the Ready Brek glow? I had tried to picture his apartment, what it would look like, how it would smell, what he'd look like in it. Now, all my questions would be answered. The excitement welled up in me. Time for another cold shower.

Twenty-four hours later, I pulled up outside a tall and imposing red-brick block of flats in South London. Dylan lived on the top floor, which meant I had to climb ten flights of stairs. But nothing could dampen my spirits as I ascended, not even the sight of several large puddles of urine, which I managed to circumnavigate with surprising agility. Finally I reached the top level and stopped outside the third flat. The door was wide open.

'Hello… Dylan?' I said, tentatively. Dylan appeared from a doorway and walked towards me. He was wearing a purple shirt and looked delicious. I hoped *he* would be dinner.

'Welcome!' he said, kissing my cheek and sending a ripple of electricity down my spine.

'Thanks! Why is your door open?' I asked, trying to appear as if the kiss hadn't shaken every atom in my frame.

'I always leave my door open,' he replied.

'Haven't you heard of burglars?' I said with a puzzled look.

'Nothing they can steal belongs to me anyway.'

'Have you ever been robbed?'

'No. But everyone knows they can come and get a cuppa if they need…' As if on cue, a man with long matted hair and beard appeared. His clothes were full of holes and his face had grimy marks all over it.

'Ta, Dylan! And thanks for the chat.' He walked past me and stopped. The smell of alcohol darted up my nose like two fingers. 'This man here is a diamond fella,' he said, before tottering off. I looked at Dylan and, with supreme effort, managed to stop myself mounting him. Just.

The apartment smelt of incense and herbs and flowers. I followed Dylan into the small living room. The walls were covered in paintings, drawings and material. Everywhere I looked, my eyes fell on some kind of art – sculptures, models, brightly coloured mosaics, woven fabrics of deep dyes and intricate patterns. In the corner, by the window, sitting on a shelf, was a large clay model of a TV. And covering the main wall was a series of large black and white photographs of different people staring at the camera.

'Is this a project?' I asked him.

'Yes. I tell everyone to think of nothing and then I photograph them.' I laughed. 'Can I take your photo?' He picked up a bulky camera from a low wooden table.

'Okay.' I tried to think of nothing and Dylan took my photo. 'It's kind of hard!' I said.

'I know. That's why I'm fascinated by what people look like when they try.' He took my coat and I sat down on the sofa which was covered by different pieces of Indian quilt. I spotted a guitar sitting in a corner.

'Do you play?' I asked him.

'Yes, I've been in many bands over the years.'

'Will you play something for me?'

'Okay.' He walked over and picked up the guitar. He sat down opposite me in a small chair.

'Any requests?' he asked me, as he cradled the guitar in his arms.

'Erm, I love Van Morrison…' I said.

'So do I.' And he closed his eyes lightly and began to play 'Brown Eyed Girl'. His voice was gentle and soulful and beyond perfect. The world stopped moving as he played and I felt as if I was flying through space and all I could see were silver stars out of the corners of my eyes.

'Are you hungry?' a distant voice asked me. I think I nodded.

He brought out several bowls of vegetables and rice and laid them out on the table.

'Shall I serve them for you?' he offered.

'Yes, unless you want your carpet covered in food!' I joked.

'I wouldn't mind. It might look beautiful. We could create carpet art together.' He smiled as he served me out a full plate of food. 'You can eat with your fingers if it's easier. I love eating with my fingers.' He sat cross-legged in front of me and began to eat. 'Don't worry about making a mess. I love mess.' He laughed a hearty laugh that pulsated around the room. I looked at the food. A few weeks ago I'd have been riddled with anxieties about eating in front of my future husband but now I didn't care what chaotic movements my body might try out. I ate a forkful of rice. A few grains fell on my indigo satin dress. Dylan looked at me with a glint in his eye.

'Francesca, you're beautiful. And your body has a wild mind of its own. I like that.'

'Well, now I'm a rice-covered beauty!'

'I love rice. So it's a winning combination!' His eyes darted over me with a restless energy.

'You love things most people are scared of, don't you?' I asked him.

'I love all of life. That includes what some people may call the messy, ugly, awkward bits. They are interesting and profound and alive and beautiful and affirming. I don't discriminate.'

'I've never met anyone who sees the world like you. It's like you live in your own world.'

'We all live in our own world.'

'Yes, but, I mean… you choose how to view everything around you.'

'That's the only power I have.'

'But most people don't do that. Most people adopt society's values and live by them… I did it, for God's sake! How do you not care at all about what people think of you?'

'Because it doesn't matter at all. My life will be over in the blink of an eye and I want to value each second of it. That's what matters to me. Nothing else.' My heart groaned with a desire so strong that I was sure he heard it.

'I think you're the happiest person I've ever met.'

'Sometimes I'm happy. Sometimes I'm sad. But I have everything I could ever wish for. Society can call me poor, which I am, but I am free from their chains. Time to think and be and create is what I treasure most. And I don't need much money for that… Do you want more rice?'

Did I want more rice? I wanted more than frigging rice. I wanted to tear off his purple shirt and bite him, drown in his kisses and stare into his devastatingly seductive eyes until the end of time itself.

Alas, Dylan's shirt remained annoyingly intact and there was no drowning of any kind. But the evening was utterly beautiful and I drove home in an intoxicated – though legal – state. Unfortunately, the comedy group were far less enthusiastic about him, sharing my initial judgement that he was 'from another planet'. They thought he was strange and odd and a bit bonkers. I thought he was all these things too but in a totally endearing way rather than a what-the-fuck-are-you-on way.

Despite our differing views on Dylan, I had made good friends in the class and we often went out together to see comedy gigs in London. These were a fascinating experience and I felt like I was discovering a whole new exciting and edgy world. We would turn up at tiny rooms above pubs and watch as endless new acts performed to audiences of, often, single-digit numbers. Some people were funny, some had potential, and some belonged in a high-security prison. I was hooked. I loved the electric vibe, the different takes on life, the rawness of it all. It was very different to the well-groomed and glossy world of TV. Here was an underbelly where outsiders came to muse, where difference was considered a positive, and where physical appearances just didn't matter. There was nothing to hide behind, no crew, no props, no character. It was just you and the microphone. My friends had taken to ribbing me about how lucky I was to be wobbly and how they envied my immediate uniqueness. And I often ended up comforting my friend Tom as he shared his woes at having to try and stand out as a white middle-class male comedian.

In May, the group was getting ready to do the end-of-course show at the Actors Centre in central London. I had been given the headline spot, which I was honoured and terrified by in equal measure. This would be the first time I'd be performing to the general public and I was certain that it would be a very different experience. In between writing reams of poetry, I'd been working religiously on a five-minute routine for the show. Jill had come up with a great idea to help combat my shaking legs onstage. She suggested that I hold on to the back of a chair with one hand while I performed. It was a masterstroke and steadied my body without looking too ridiculous or distracting. The day of the show came and I couldn't eat a morsel. I veered between the desire to develop a life-threatening (and rapid-onset) illness and the temptation to get in my car and drive far, far away. Alas, I had no choice but to turn up at the theatre. It was a small, black, studio space with raked seating, and was jammed with about sixty people including my very excited (and nervous) family. They, also, had not managed to ingest much that day.

I had to wait until the end of the show for my spot, which was not very pleasant, especially for my bowels. Just as I was contemplating pleasing my careers advisor after all and running off to work with computers, I was announced on to the stage. My friend, Lizzie, walked me to the centre. I have never been so grateful for the presence of a chair, and I reached out and clasped my left hand tightly around the wooden back. It was wonderfully steady. I tried to steal a bit of its solidity and drag it down to my legs, which were engaged in some form of tribal dance. I looked up and blinked at the bright lights. The faces that were out there were invisible to me but I could feel their eyes burning through the darkness. It was deathly silent. Glassy nerves hung like stalactites over the crowd. My heart was beating fast and my tongue felt too big for my mouth. I wanted to run but I could barely stand up.

'In case you're wondering what the correct word for my condition is… it's sober.' Through the black dusty air came laughter, flying towards me like butterflies.

'When I am drunk, I walk in a really straight line!' The laughs were followed by applause this time, applause that shattered the icy tension into tiny fragments.

'When I learnt to drive, I felt so sorry for my instructor… he was so fucking nervous!' I didn't notice my legs any more or the pain in my fingers from gripping the chair so tightly. I simply soaked up each laugh and clap from the audience. And then it was over. Drenched in sweat, I walked off the stage with Lizzie, and slumped into a chair in the cramped dressing room. I'd done it! I'd made a roomful of strangers laugh for five whole minutes. Without fainting. Or crapping myself. And the palpable tension that had initially gripped the room when I'd wobbled on had melted quickly into a warm and friendly vibe. It felt amazing. I couldn't wait to do it all over again. I felt so grateful for Jill, for her support and encouragement and help. She had opened up a whole new world for me and I could never thank her enough.

My dad was overjoyed at finally seeing me perform stand-up.

'Whatever happens with the film, I think you've found your vocation. And that's all that really matters. Well done,

Chess. I'm very proud of you!' He put his arms around me and I squeezed him tightly back.

'Thanks for saving me from a life in IT,' I said, with genuine relief.

I threw myself into gigging with a passion. It was so thrilling to dive into this whole new scene, so rich with ideas and secrets waiting to be discovered. The thought of learning a new craft was exciting and I felt I'd found something that was endlessly fascinating, which could never bore me. Part of the appeal was the ability to create my own world onstage. For the first time in my life, I didn't feel I was being compared with anyone else or measured against someone else's standards. When I performed, it was my take on life that mattered. I chose what labels were used and what perspective was shared with the audience. It was an empowering feeling to turn parts of my life into comedy and I felt a sense of freedom unlike ever before.

No gig was too far away and no crowd was too small. I've performed to two old men and a dog, one old man and two dogs, one barman and two bouncers, four grumpy women, and a man who shouted 'alligator' at random moments. Some shows were great, others less so (it's hard to compete with a live England match blasting out from the telly at the side of the stage), but they were all valuable learning experiences and I tried to get as much stage time as possible. I was beginning to enjoy the tension created by my wobbly appearance onstage. If comedy is about the build up and release of tension, then I was lucky to be able to create mountains of the stuff just by walking out. The experience of facing those collective nerves head on and then smashing them to pieces in a few seconds was highly satisfying. This process was cathartic and I felt myself settling into my own skin in a way I'd never done before. I felt that audiences opened up to my honesty and quickly felt relaxed and free to laugh. With them on my side, I could begin to challenge their preconceptions about various, often taboo, topics in an entertaining and light-hearted way.

It was slowly dawning on me that it was possible to use comedy to present new ways of looking at the world, and this seemed hugely exciting. After all, my life had fundamentally changed because of Dylan's words and I wondered if, one day, my ideas could have the same positive impact on someone else. Being able to share these mind-blowing concepts with strangers was a thrilling possibility and it ignited a passion in me that has driven my comedy ever since.

After my third gig at the King's Head in Crouch End, I was offered a paid twenty-minute slot by the booker. Someone wanted to *pay* me to do comedy! Sadly, I had to admit to him that I had only five minutes' worth of jokes, maybe seven, if I spoke very slowly. He asked me how long it would take to build up a twenty-minute set. It was July and I asked him to give me a slot in January. I was incredibly grateful for his support. I now had a deadline to work towards and the thought of getting paid twenty-five quid to perform was almost too much to handle.

My other passion was not proving such a success. It got to the stage where I was so in love with Dylan that I barely heard a word he said. When I was with him, all I could think about was how I was going to express my overwhelming love to him. The more time I spent in his presence, the deeper in love I fell, even though I had a nagging feeling that he was not really the marrying-type. I concluded this for a number of reasons:

1. He'd already been married twice.
2. He'd had more dalliances than I'd had dinners.
3. He used the word 'dalliances'.
4. He was a free spirit and this probably encompassed 'free love'.
5. He was far too beautiful a hippy to be tied down.
6. He played the guitar in a way that did not indicate a propensity for romantic loyalty and commitment.

Much to my regret, I knew I had to shift my goals a little. Maybe we wouldn't be having babies but we could still partake in baby-making activities. Regularly and with much enthusiasm. The burning question was: how could I let him know my feelings? How could I communicate my romantic desire in a cool and charming manner? After much deliberation and heartfelt analysis, I settled upon the form of poetry. To this day, I still don't know why I decided this because my poems were neither cool nor charming. Heavy, intense and soul-searching, perhaps, but definitely not anything approaching light or funny or non-stalkerish.

Armed with zero relationship experience, I proceeded full-steam ahead with my diabolical plan.

Not only did I decide to relay my passion in poetic form, I also resolved that I would give Dylan said confession in person. In short, I saw no problem with being in close vicinity to him while his eyes took in my words of longing. Why I couldn't just send it to him is anyone's guess but my love not only made me blind but seriously deaf and dumb too. So, it was with naïve optimism that I set about constructing the perfect poem that would accurately capture how profound my love was, and win Dylan's heart. These were two lofty aims but I felt my poetic skills could rise to the challenge and, after putting in some long hours at the computer, I added the finishing touches to my romantic declaration. It was ready. Now I just needed the guts to give it to him. Guts that turned out to be strangely elusive.

Slowly, I began to get more and more gigs, and was kindly encouraged by other comedians to keep at it. It was a strange feeling to have a sense of belonging, and a certainty that I would evolve into a proper comedian. But I was in no rush and felt confident that I could take my time and enjoy the ride. If I wasn't gigging, I was watching comedy or writing new jokes or talking about comedy with my new group of friends who I felt so comfortable with. Never before had I felt so accepted by people outside my family, so relaxed about myself, so able to ask for help when I needed it. It was incredible how I no longer worried about what people thought of me, how content I was in my own skin. I even developed strategies to calm my nerves before going onstage. First, I'd tell myself that there would be at least one person in the audience who wouldn't like me and that was fine. I couldn't please everyone. Then I'd tell myself that I was a tiny speck in a huge universe and that what I did in my tiny life didn't really have any significance whatsoever. Finally, I reminded myself that it was an amazing privilege to be given someone's time so I should try and communicate something of value. These thoughts didn't wipe out my nerves completely but they reduced their power to that of an annoying mosquito rather than a soul-crushing rhinoceros.

My family were delighted that the overnight trans-formation that had taken place on that March morning seemed to be here to stay. Our house was decidedly mope-free and I flounced around with a smile almost permanently plastered across my face. Dylan had infused me with a sense of urgency about life, and I was hell-bent on appreciating every new day that greeted me. This new-found perspective made me so grateful to be alive. I was still as wobbly as ever, but I now felt not only happy with my life, but overwhelmingly lucky to be me.

I thought about how amazing it was to be able to pursue my dreams when so many others were stuck in jobs they hated. I thought about how lucky I was not to live through war or in terror or hunger or poverty like the majority of human beings. I thought about how my body was healthy and strong and gave me life. I thought about how Dylan made me feel beautiful and proud of who I was. And I thought about how I had the perfect excuse not to do any housework or manual labour. Ever. I was one lucky bastard.

After a few abortive attempts at giving Dylan the poem, my frustration at myself was reaching epic levels. We'd meet up and I'd spend the whole time debating when the right time would be to pull out my love note. Then we'd part and I'd feel annoyed at how cowardly I'd been. One day, determined to defeat my fear, I vowed to myself that I would hand over the poem the next time we met. So, the following week, armed with my carefully folded A4 sheet of paper (which may or may not have been signed with a lipstick kiss), I went to the cinema with Dylan. I didn't hear or see any of the film because my mind was preoccupied with run-throughs of the impending exchange. I was sure there must be a way to hand someone a love poem in a nonchalant manner. I just didn't know what the hell that way was.

We made our way back to my car and got in. August rain began to patter on the windscreen. It's now or never, I thought. I'll be dead soon.

'Dylan?' I said, watching the drops chase each other along the glass.

'Yes?' he answered, calmly, unaware of what was to follow.

'There's something I want to tell you… but I haven't known how.' I kept my eyes on the falling rain.

'Why not?' I could feel him looking at me. I felt sick.

'Because it's difficult… so… I… wrote it in a poem.' I reached into my pocket and took out the piece of paper. 'Here it is,' I said, daring to glance at him quickly.

'Thank you,' said Dylan. He unfolded the page. I stared ahead into space. This is what he read:

You astound me
Confound me
Surround me
In a haze
For days
Your voice plays
In the garden of my mind.
Drench me in bliss
With your kiss
Like summer rain
Falling, pelting
Each pouted drop melting
Into me.
You, I adore
And implore
To explore
My uncharted seas
Please.
You arouse me
You douse me
In sexual petroleum
Then ignite me
Excite me
With a smile
A touch
It's too much.

My hands long to trace
To embrace
The hills and valleys of your being
And my eyes beg to drink
From the pouring
Roaring
Soaring
Fountain of beauty
That is your face.
Your beautiful face
Is such a place
That on inspection
And much reflection
I deem it to be drowned in perfection.

Dylan sat very still. And so did I.

'You write beautiful poetry,' he said, quietly.

'Thank you,' I said.

'I feel as if I should kiss you right now,' he said, turning towards me. I managed not to cough. Instead, I laughed. Awkwardly. Yep, both responses mature and sexy. At least there was no phlegm. I finished off the borderline maniacal laugh by staring far too intently at the steering wheel.

'Sorry for giving that to you. I just…' The words lay beached on my tongue.

'Don't be sorry,' said Dylan, still holding the poem.

'You don't feel the same way, do you?' Somehow the words escaped my mouth.

'I think you're amazing and sexy and kissable and brilliant,' I heard him say.

'But you don't love me?' I said, feeling a cold grip on my heart.

'What is love?' he said, as he rifled his hand through his hair.

'What I feel for you,' I answered quietly.

'I don't feel the same, no.' He looked at me. And I looked at him.

'I'll drop you at the bus stop.' I turned the engine on and bit my lip. Hard.

I sat outside my house and cried. Huge sobs that shook the car. It felt good to let those tears out. A part of me had already known that Dylan didn't feel the same way but I'd still needed to express to him what he meant to me. Yes, I was embarrassed and humiliated and hurt, but I also felt oddly at peace. I'd told him how I felt and, as painful as his rejection was, I was glad I'd shared it with him. I would survive. If I was going to have my heart broken, I wanted it to be Dylan who did the breaking. I got out of the car and the rain chased the tears down my cheeks.

I figured that declarations of love via poetry probably weren't going to feature heavily in my future. But I was strangely glad that I behaved in such an outrageous way just once in my life. My wildly romantic side was pleased that I'd carried out such a reckless act. As the days passed, I felt more able to accept that my love was unrequited. There was nothing I could do to make him love me, a fact that was both frustrating and crystal clear. However, I knew I wanted Dylan in my life and I was prepared to bury my deep feelings and remain friends. So I wrote him a letter, apologising for laying such heavy shit on him, assuring him that I could keep my hormones in check, and that I was more than happy to have his friendship. I ended the letter with a firm promise that I would not declare eternal love for him in my Volkswagen Polo ever again.

My letter must have allayed any suspicions that I was bat-shit crazy because, a week later, he got back into the car with only a couple of droplets of sweat on his brow. We drove to the outskirts of South London where he was housesitting for a friend. I took the opportunity to reiterate that I had recovered my sanity and that I was happy – more than happy – to put the whole cringe-inducing episode behind us and just be friends. Dylan listened to my emphatic assurances with amusement in his eyes.

'I don't need to label what we are,' he said, after I told him for the tenth time how I could cope perfectly with friendship. I realised in that moment that I couldn't even begin to understand this man and that I probably never would.

The day was scorching and we sat in a park and soaked up the summer rays. Dylan looked radiant as his hair shone in the yellow light and small flames of desire caught light in my stomach. Friends, I reminded myself. Just friends, remember? This whole 'friends' thing was turning out to be harder than I'd anticipated. I shifted my eyes from the tantalising triangle of flesh revealed by the neck of his shirt and focused instead on the significantly less arousing sight of tarmac.

We returned to his friend's house that evening, sleepy from the heat but still glowing from the sunshine.

'It's a long drive back. Why don't you stay over? There are three bedrooms,' said Dylan, switching on the kettle. My heart paused for a moment.

'Okay,' I said, trying to sound relaxed.

'Cool.' Dylan began unbuttoning his shirt. 'I'm so hot. I have to change.' He pulled his shirt off to reveal a tanned and toned torso. I grabbed a nearby worktop to steady myself.

'Apparently there might be a storm tonight.' Dylan rifled through a bag and took out his purple shirt. The purple shirt. Great. How was I meant to be friends when he looked like… that?

'Oh, God! I hate thunderstorms… they scare me!' I blurted out, as he buttoned up the shirt. My pulse stabilised a little.

'Really? I love them! If you get scared, I'll hold you, so don't worry.' He smiled.

All my life, I've been terrified of thunderstorms. As a child, I'd lock myself in our windowless bathroom, put the loo seat down and perch on it, limbs tightly held, as I rocked back and forth. I'm still not sure what I was so scared of but seeing the symbol for lightning hovering over London on the TV weather map would spark off a wave of panic in my stomach. I'd hope and pray for the storm to steer clear of us and spare me those clammy moments in the overly bright light of our bathroom. And, now, here I was, for the first time ever, praying with every cell in my body that there *would* be a storm. A big one. Love is fucking weird.

Dylan led me into a child's bedroom a few hours later.

'This okay?' he said, as I looked round the room.

'Yes, fine. Thanks.' I sat down on the single bed.

'Goodnight, then,' said Dylan.

'Goodnight,' I said. He walked out and went into the bedroom next door. I took my top off and lay down on the bed in my bra and skirt in the dark. This wasn't how I'd pictured our first night together. At all. I was beginning to question the wisdom of staying over. In this child's bed. Surely the only thing worse than leaving someone you love at night, is staying over with them in a *different* room. In my fantasies, there definitely had not been a wall between us. I sighed loudly. I willed the thunder and lightning to come but nothing happened. Bloody typical, I thought, the one night I *want* a thunderstorm... I closed my eyes. There was no way I was going to get a wink of sleep knowing that Dylan was lying in the next room. This was going to be a long, hot, night.

Thirty minutes later, I was still lying on my back staring at the ceiling. Something in me snapped. Fuck it, you only live once, I told myself. I got up and walked out on to the landing. Dylan's door was open. I stood in the doorway and yanked my courage out of its hidey hole.

'Goodnight, Dylan,' I said into the darkness. Silence.

'You can sleep in here if you want,' came through the night. My heart did a somersault.

'Okay!' I don't think I have ever moved so fast. I bounded into the room and got into the far side of the bed. Dylan lay still next to me.

'Goodnight, Francesca,' he said.

'Goodnight,' I said, scared that he would hear my heart, which was thumping away in my chest like a jackhammer.

Sleep eluded me for much of the night and, when the morning came, I stole glances at Dylan's peaceful face. It had a calmness that I hadn't seen before, free from the restless energy that usually set his eyes alive. If anything, he was even more beautiful now, and I bathed in the pleasure of watching him sleep. I hoped he wouldn't suddenly wake up and jump out of his skin at the sight of this girl staring insanely at him. Thankfully, he didn't catch me in the act. Eventually, he started to stir and I quickly looked away.

'Hello. Did you sleep well?' He turned to look at me, his hair tousled and alive.

'Yes, thanks,' I lied.

'Good.' He smiled at me. I felt too hot all of a sudden.

'I'm hot!' I said, a tad too loudly.

'Take the cover off, then.' It seemed a logical thing to do so I did. I lay there in my black bra.

'Wow,' said Dylan. He looked into my eyes and leaned over slowly. Oh my God, I thought. He's actually going to kiss me. I stopped breathing. His lips parted gently as they touched mine. I melted into him. And finally, after twenty years, eleven months and two days, I had my first kiss.

Anyway, he turned out to be an arsehole.

CHAPTER ELEVEN

****

Even an arsehole can change your life.

Dylan may have broken my heart but he also taught me how to be happy. Not a bad trade-off. And he did it simply by opening my eyes to a few beautiful and powerful ideas. This awakening was both a personal and a political one...

Before long, the neurons in my brain were firing off questions like Kalashnikovs. Have I ever met a normal person? What do they look like? Where do they live? Or work? Or play? What do they wear? What films do they like? What books do they read? What food do they eat? What do they like to do with their leisure time? Are they married? Single? Divorced? Living in sin? Old? Young? In between? Are they good with people? Or computers? What shampoo do they use?

Now, it could be that over the thirty-five years of my life, I have managed, by a series of extraordinary accidents, not to have bumped into one of these normal folk. However, given that I've visited all five continents, I guess that's not very likely. So, after much contemplation, I've concluded that the more plausible reality is that these fabled creatures do not exist. Anywhere. On Planet Earth. Normality is a myth.

How could I have bought into the fiction of a 'standard' person, who is right and correct and proper in thought and physical form – an imaginary someone we are expected to aspire to be? It's such a ludicrous, childish idea. Yet this doctrine had me tied up in knots for a major chunk of my life. It sucked the confidence out of me like a Dyson on steroids.

I craved to be the one thing I could never be. I'd fully absorbed society's verdict that I was not-quite-right, without ever thinking about it. But the cast-iron judgements that had hemmed me in so expertly, crumbled away like sand the second I saw myself as a normal member of the human race. NEWSFLASH! As far as we know, we're the only human beings in the universe. Doesn't that makes us all a bit freakish?

Dylan reconnected me to my body, the Earth, and everyone on it. For the first time in so long, I felt comfortable, at home in the world, and part of the beautiful diversity of life in this tiny corner of the universe. I felt incredibly lucky to have been given the opportunity to exist on this rocky sphere and share it with so many other wonderful creatures. I knew that this lust for life streaking through my veins at lightning speed would stay with me until my last breath.

Yes, of course, this life-altering realisation hasn't changed the fact that there are still things I can't do (I'm not too hot at Jenga, for example) but that goes for everybody. So I'm nothing special in this respect. It's true that the bodies of many people function as though operated by a highly disciplined team of microscopic pin-striped civil servants, whereas my control-panel seems to have fallen into the hands of a rowdy band of rum-soaked pirates. But, amazingly, there are things I *can* do that many others can't (or won't). Such as walk onstage and tell jokes. Crazy, huh? For some reason, public speaking tops most people's list of fears. It usually trumps death, for God's sake – most people would rather be laid out in the coffin than deliver the flipping eulogy!

In 2005, I was invited to perform to a large group of medical professionals at their annual conference. They asked me to speak about 'Living With Cerebral Palsy'. Cracking title, I thought, that'll bring 'em in in droves. After years of those awkward looks and slow-paced questions, I was more than happy to pimp my peculiar self out in the hope that one or two of them might learn enough to chill out when confronted with someone different from what they're used to. Plus, I could patronise them for a change – yesssss!

The lecture theatre was cavernous and, as I walked on to the stage, I felt every step being scrutinised by hundreds of expert eyes. Helpfully, my body responded by tensing up and throwing a few new dance moves into the mix. I hoped nobody would faint at this clumsy entrance. When the slightly unsettled applause died down, I surveyed the sea of serious-looking faces that were studying me intently. I introduced myself and delivered a joke. It was met with tentative laughter but nobody bolted for the exit. I almost congratulated them on their bravery.

'I'm defined by what I can't do. But we all have things we can't do, except nobody says stuff like: oh, David Beckham is a great footballer but have you seen him play Trivial Pursuit? He's shit!' The room warmed up a little.

'Why should only some people be burdened with big flashing neon labels like *brain damaged*, *paraplegic*, *blind*? Let's define everybody that way: meet Sally, *she can't sing a fucking note*! Say hi to Rob, *he's shit at DIY*! Here's Danny, *watch him play golf – you'll piss yourself*!' They laughed out loud – that was promising. I paused and my eyes fell on a young male doctor sitting in the front row.

'Hello, sir. What's your name?'

'Er, Derek,' he said, a little self-consciously.

'Hello, Derek. Nice to meet you. Can you tell us something you're really crap at?' Derek laughed awkwardly.

'Well, I, er… I can't dance.' He squirmed in his seat. I looked at him in mock shock.

'Shit! Were you born like that?' I asked him with wide-eyed astonishment. Ripples of laughter; Derek relaxed a little.

'Yes, I was, unfortunately,' he replied, with mock sadness.

'Fuck… that's awful!' The swearing evoked more laughter.

'Sorry if I'm a bit nervous, Derek. I just… well, I've never met anyone who can't dance before! Not quite sure what I should say…' I trailed off, 'nervously'. 'I've actually read about people like you! Tell me have you got a partner, Derek?' He pointed to a brown-haired woman next to him who was giggling at his public humiliation.

'Yes, Katie. She's a doctor too.' I turned my attention to her.

'Great to meet you, Katie! First of all, can I just say how lovely it is to know that there are people like you in the world who aren't superficial. You obviously met Derek and thought, "OK, you can't dance but, fuck it, I love you!" It's so heart-warming!' I put my hand on my heart and nodded my approval to her. The audience were clearly enjoying this little scenario: they'd been laughing and clapping throughout.

'Can I ask you an important question, Katie? Do you get any respite time away from Derek? Carers need breaks too.' Katie shook her head, unable to speak. I turned back to Derek.

'One last question. Can you… have sex?' I asked, with studied curiosity. Katie doubled over as he looked around smiling and embarrassed.

'Derek, you're a very brave man. Well done! It's been a real inspiration meeting you!' Derek's cheeks turned red as the crowd cheered.

After the performance, the audience felt comfortable enough to ask me questions. Normally paced ones! The first one came from a young man in his early thirties.

'Hello, I'm a GP and I was just wondering how I should react when someone enters my surgery with a disability I haven't encountered before?' I told him he should stand up, put his hands to his head, adopt a look of sheer horror, scream as loud as he could, piss himself, and run out shouting 'It's alive! The monster is alive!' Had this man really gone through seven years of university education?

If the audience's response was anything to go by, I think I managed to get my point across, but I spelled it out anyway.

'Well, actually, just imagine that that person was you and think about how you'd like to be treated. I don't think it's rocket science!' He looked surprised.

'Oh, okay, yeah, I'll do that then.' His colleagues chuckled.

The next question came from a woman in her fifties with glasses and greying hair.

'It's my job to advise parents carrying disabled babies on whether or not to have an abortion. And, I have to be honest here. I think we should try to reduce the suffering in the world. What do you think?' She sounded almost apologetic but I appreciated her honesty in raising the issue.

'This answer might be slightly longer than my previous one,' I said. The audience relaxed a bit from the tension that had invaded the theatre.

'First of all, I'm pro-choice. I believe in the right of the parents to choose what is best for them in any situation. But I also believe the debate is never really framed correctly. To look at it in terms of suffering is wrong and pointless. Firstly, suffering is part of life. We all suffer. If you don't want your child to suffer, then don't have any in the first place. Period.

'Secondly, it's impossible to predict how much suffering a person will endure throughout their life. There is no magic "sufferometer" that can accurately determine the amount of suffering a baby will experience. Thirdly, having a so-called disability doesn't mean that someone will suffer more than an able-bodied person. Here's an example: A week after I was born, my mum's friend gave birth to a boy. This child was physically and mentally healthy. He exceeded me in ability from a young age and learnt to walk and run far earlier than I did. However his family life was chaotic and difficult, and he was subjected to a lot of stress and unhappiness. In his teenage years he developed mental health issues, which resulted in a decade of moving in and out of psychiatric institutions. As an adult, he is fragile and emotionally vulnerable. Despite having a perfectly able body, he has suffered far more than I ever have. I may have been born "disabled" but I received all the love and care that I needed and, because of that, I am a happy, well-adjusted person. Yes, being wobbly presents its own challenges but, as Derek has illustrated perfectly, we all have our challenges. My challenges may be visible but that doesn't mean I suffer more than people whose challenges can't be seen.

'I've seen that happiness doesn't come from having a "normally" working mind or body. It comes from being loved and growing up in a healthy environment. If you are lucky enough to receive these things, like I was, then you'll be well equipped to deal with life's challenges – whatever body you inhabit.

'Finally, any "suffering" I've endured hasn't come from being wobbly but from people not knowing how to handle difference. So, instead of focusing on eradicating disability, maybe we should focus on creating a world that embraces it as a natural part of life. Let's prioritise extra financial aid and emotional care for families with disabled children so that a strong support network is provided and parents don't have to fear a life of struggling on their own.

'Most disabilities are acquired during life so we are never going to get rid of "disability". "Disability" is normal. It has always existed and always will. Let's stop being so bloody shocked by it. And let's start educating parents that any child, no matter what body they have – apart from very rare cases – can be happy if they're loved.'

The woman looked at me for a few moments.

'I'd never looked at it like that before…' she said, more to herself than to me.

'If you need to be "able-bodied" to be happy, then how is it that I'm wobbly *and* happy?' I asked. In the semi-darkness, I could make out hundreds of faces staring back at me. The room was silent for a while.

Don't get me wrong. I'm not saying that having a disability is easy, or that disabled people don't require extra support and help in certain areas. I'm just saying that every person on the planet faces problems and obstacles and needs help at times. Everyone has something they find difficult or impossible to do. *That* is what is normal. And nobody wants to be defined by what they can't do.

An instinctive dislike of being reduced to a label wormed its way into my body from an early age. The first time I felt it squirm inside me was when I was taken to a clinic at Great Ormond Street Hospital. I was about three years old. I remember being in a large room packed with other disabled toddlers on various mats spread out on the floor. Everyone had a different set of abilities – some could walk, some couldn't, some could speak, some would just make unidentifiable sounds, some were missing limbs – and we were all there to do physical therapy, aided by a therapist.

Shortly after the session began, the crying started. One child began to wail, then the floodgates opened and, within minutes, the walls throbbed with a cacophony of sobbing, moaning and shouting. I lay there on my mat, stunned at the symphony of misery swelling around me. I looked at the boy next to me. He had twisted knees and feet that pointed inwards. A nurse was trying to move his legs up and down while he balled his fists into his eyes and screamed. Then I looked the other way to a little girl, who was sitting up while supported by staff. Her head flopped forward on to her chest and her arms hung limply by her side. Tears streamed down her face, soaking her bib. It was all too much to handle. So, without further delay, I joined in. With gusto.

When my mum came to get me, I threw myself on her and bawled my eyes out. By the time we arrived home, the sobs had subsided and my breathing had become less shallow. I was exhausted from the effort of such copious weeping. Mum sensed I was finally able to string a few words together.

'Why were you so upset, darling?' She held me close.

'Because the other kids were crying.' My lip quivered slightly.

'But why did you cry?' she asked, as she brushed away the remnants of a failed tear that was hovering dangerously on my lower eyelid.

'Because they were so sad. And we all found the exercises hard...' My voice wobbled.

'And that made you sad?' Mum hugged me tighter.

'Yes, I felt bad because they find things even harder than I do. It's not fair!' I let my mum hold me, comforted by her touch but unable to shift the painful realisation that there were other children with different broken bodies. We'd all been in that clinic *because* of our broken bodies. And *that*, I couldn't help feeling, was not a happy reason to be there.

Mum took me back a week later in the hope that my initial upset would disappear. It did not. The tears sprang almost horizontally from my eyes and I never went back.

So, I guess I'm not a huge fan of labels. Especially ones that make the labelee feel inferior or unfortunate or an object of pity. My own experiences have made me shy away from labels altogether – I've never joined a party, group or religion. Any word that creates division between me and another human being makes me run a mile. Metaphorically, of course.

Many people have argued that labels are useful and that we need them, but we have to be careful they don't obscure the human being they are applied to. More often than not, labels dehumanise people by reducing them to lazy stereotypes. Labels invite you not to think. For example, we define and isolate people with the label 'gay' because their choice of sexual partner differs from what we believe is (or 'ought to be') the norm. But, who you sleep with is just one aspect of the complex human being you are. And, in any case, we *all* differ from the norm in some way or other. It's normal to poo only once a day, apparently. So if you're someone who goes twice or three or – God help us – four times a day, should you have to 'come out' as a multiple shitter? Should you be allowed to marry and have kids? Should these particular questions be up for (interminable) public debate?

The gay label has encouraged homophobic societies to reduce living, breathing human beings to nameless, faceless entities who are undeserving of compassion, or support, or the opportunity to live their lives as they want. 'They're wrong and bad because... eh... well... because they've made different choices... So there!' We could so easily eliminate all prejudice and render 'coming out' unnecessary by accepting that it's totally normal for some people to be attracted to others of the same gender. Like disability, it has always existed and will always exist. End of.

If we are to create an inclusive society – one that doesn't fear disability or difference – before the sun peters out, we're going to have to make sure our kids grow up exposed to all kinds of people. I've often wondered why 'able-bodied' kids don't attend 'special' schools. It would benefit everyone in general and them in particular. For starters, we could dump the term 'special school'. (All schools should be special.) The 'disabled' kids would be part of society and not be defined by their disabilities and fenced off in some ghetto, and the 'able-bodied' kids would experience difference as 'normal' and be comfortable with it. Both groups would evolve, as a matter of course, to relate to each other as human beings, and that knowledge would be carried through to adulthood. I'm pretty sure it would radically transform society. Real exposure to difference is the only way to combat the fear and prejudice that arise out of ignorance and lack of experience. If we ensure that difference is present in daily life from a young age, then it will cease to be a big deal. People will be far less likely to bat an eyelid at someone's choice of partner, or clothes, or lifestyle, if society chose to embrace diversity as a precious resource and not something unsavoury to be brushed under the carpet. With a different value system and approach, this could easily exist.

Most parents-to-be still fear that their beloved newborn will turn out to be – oh, the horror of it – disabled. My personal fear is that my future child will turn out to be unhappy. I don't really care what he or she can or can't do, how they talk or walk or how many fingers and toes they have. Because I don't think the number of fingers and toes anyone possesses is a particularly good indicator of happiness. I just want my kid to be happy.

Of course, nobody dreams of having an unhealthy baby, do they? I used to imagine that dreaded scenario where I'm sitting in a hospital room being told, 'I'm really sorry, but your baby boy does carry the defective gene and he will be... a right-wing politician!'

'Oh my God! Are you sure?' I'd say, the blood draining from my face.

'Yes, I'm really sorry, but we've located the low taxation gene, the privatisation gene, and the smarmy bastard gene.'

'God! You just don't think it'll happen to you, you know?' My head would drop at this point as the full ramifications hit me.

'Can you talk to your husband about this?' she'd ask, trying to comfort me.

'Yeah, but he's busy writing poetry... And I can't tell my parents. They're so old-fashioned. They'll just say, "get rid of it or bung it in a home."' I'd look at her imploringly. 'Is there any way I can keep my baby? What about therapy? Would that help? I could read him Michael Moore. Play him DVDs of Bill Hicks. Or only feed him on my left breast.'

'Well, there are some support groups set up you could join like, Parents Of A Neo-Liberal Baby...'

'What about school? Will he need to go to a special school?'

'Yes, I'm afraid it'll have to be Eton or Westminster.'

'But I want him to grow up with normal kids!'

'Look, if you keep this baby I can't say it will be easy.

There's going to be a lot of heartache, prejudice, bullying, suffering. And that will just be his foreign policy...'

I guess it's a complex situation. It comes down to what you value. All I know is I'd rather my son had a dodgy leg than invade Iraq.

Forget about aborting babies because of the suffering they might endure. What about the suffering they'll create? Wouldn't it make more sense to develop a test to check for the arms-dealer gene, the advertising-executive gene, the corporate-overlord gene, or the gossip-magazine-editor gene? Surely that would eliminate quite a lot of suffering. While we're at it, what about isolating the boy-band gene too?

Despite the amazing technological advancements we've made as a society and culture, it seems we still assess someone's right to live on the basis of whether or not their bodies fit in with some arbitrary 'ideal'. Had my wobbliness been detected in the womb, my parents would probably have been advised by a softly spoken but firm doctor to have an abortion. To spare me (and them) a life of suffering! The concern is touching but I think I'd rather take a punt at living than be scrubbed out of existence because of the vague possibility that I might be exposed to a dose of 'suffering' at some point. So, here are a few tips for those deeply 'concerned' white-coats when dealing with parents-to-be:

1. If you care so much about the suffering of disabled people, maybe you could stop scaring the shit out of

parents when you spot a sign of difference. Just an idea!

2. Instead of pushing to rid the world of difference, you could point out that disability is a natural part of life and then suggest that they love and accept the child as normal. (Crazy, I know!)

3. You could acknowledge that everyone has their own disability (or even many disabilities, like Jeremy Clarkson) and that, even though someone isn't born disabled, they could become disabled at any time. Hence, their baby is actually beautifully unique *and* bog-standardly normal.

4. And you could remind them not to worry because inner happiness doesn't depend on having a 'perfect' body. Otherwise we'd all be buying self-help books by Lindsay Lohan.

By the by, I can't help noticing that the few people I've met in my life who haven't 'suffered' much have also been monumentally *boring*. All in all, I'm certain that I'd much rather have the handwriting of a spider on LSD than drive someone into a coma with my incessantly dull conversation. (Note to self – ensure future child suffers, just a tad.)

Other 'reasons' are being introduced to scare parents into getting rid of their disabled child. It's now common to hear the suggestion that disabled babies should be aborted because of the financial 'burden' they'll impose on the state, at a time when money is supposedly in such short supply. Yep, how much it's predicted to cost is now, apparently, a legitimate factor in determining a human being's right to be born. Civilised, huh?

Many people are appalled that filthy lucre has been brought into such a sacred realm. However, to be honest, I don't think it's a terrible idea if applied differently. If we're going to weed out potential financial black holes, then we need to target the real burdens on society. We should be aborting the greedy bankers who caused the global meltdown and the CEOs who avoid tax on an industrial scale. And let's not forget the politicians who fiddle their expenses claims and siphon off shiploads of public cash into the pockets of their corporate chums. Disabled people are small fry in comparison. I don't remember seeing a news report that said, 'The world economy was thrown into chaos as a result of the collapse of Lehman Brothers and Reggie Unsworth of Sidcup needing a new wheelchair.'

Far from being something to eradicate, difference and diversity are what bring spice and vividness and interest to life. Some people have two arms, some have one arm, some have none, some are small, some use wheelchairs, some are wobbly, some think differently, some don't see with their eyes or hear with their ears, or speak with their mouths, and some have legs that don't walk. Some people are white, some are brown, and some are black. Some boys love girls, some boys love boys. Other boys love girls and boys. And the same goes for girls.

Encountering difference is an opportunity to learn, to grow, to reach out, to connect. A chance to expand as a human being and challenge afresh your ideas, beliefs, assumptions, insecurities and prejudices.

Regardless of the body you're born into, regardless of skin colour, or gender, or choice of partner, or country of birth, or working status, or income, or 'ability', or belief, we all share the same universal human experience. We're all born and we all will die. In between, we live, love, laugh and cry.

Everyone's different and that's what makes us all the same. So, don't let anyone make you feel abnormal because it doesn't exist. And who wants to be ****ing normal anyway?

CHAPTER TWELVE

* * * *

Your boobs aren't big enough.
Your car isn't flash enough.
Your legs aren't skinny enough.
Your handbag isn't sexy enough.
Your teeth aren't dazzling enough.
Your eyelashes aren't long enough.
Your suit isn't sharp enough.
Your bum isn't tight enough.
Your lips aren't pouty enough.
Your forehead isn't smooth enough.
Your phone isn't new enough.
Your laptop ain't sleek.
Your shoes ain't sexy.
Your wedding ring ain't bling.
Your perfume ain't alluring.
Your hair isn't luscious.
Your TV isn't flat.

Your nose isn't cute.

Your glasses aren't stylish.

Your house isn't beautiful.

Your nails aren't manicured.

Your stomach isn't toned.

Your neck isn't long.

Your shampoo isn't luxurious.

Your arms aren't muscly.

Your ears aren't small.

Your face doesn't stop traffic.

Not exactly life-affirming, is it? You might even describe it as – oh, I don't know – a touch *soul-destroying*. What a message to have shoved down your throat, day in, day out. And now, thanks to the wonders of Wi-Fi, you don't even have to open a magazine or walk past a billboard to be told you're not good enough – you can be reminded of your numerous shortcomings in the comfort of your own home. Twenty-four/seven. No wonder we're all a bit bloody antsy.

Think of all the possible alternative messages we could be bombarded with:

You're lucky to be alive!

It took us 4.5 billion years to get here!

We're currently whizzing round in space!

Life is awesome!

You'll be dead soon so live life to the full!

Look after the planet – it's our home!

Appreciate what you have!

Try to make a difference!
It's good to help each other!

If we chose to live by and promote any one of these messages, we could create a very different society – one that might actually encourage people to feel, well... NOT SHIT about themselves.

Dylan lifted the veil from my eyes and left me blinking in the brightness of the new world around me. Once I'd seen that nobody is normal, it got me thinking about the next logical question: why are we are led to believe that normal people exist?

I used to think it was just me who felt negatively judged by society. I'd assumed that my past struggles with acute insecurity were caused by having a disability. I was profoundly wrong. I was flabbergasted to discover that I wasn't the only one who felt abnormal or struggled to like themselves. Far from it. I started to see that just about everyone I came into contact with had major self-esteem issues. And, most astounding of all, those who would readily be labelled young, able-bodied, or staggeringly beautiful, seemed to hate themselves the most. Yes, these lucky gits who'd won the genetic lottery were crushed by the sheer weight of their own self-loathing. I couldn't understand why. Their bodies worked perfectly, they were attractive to a degree that was, frankly, offensive, and they were in the bloom of their youth. So what the fuck didn't they like about themselves? I'd meet my brother's teenage female friends – the kind of sexy girls who seemed untouchable when I was in high school – and discover that they all suffered from eating disorders. I'd be introduced to top models teetering on high heels and the edge of a nervous breakdown.

I tried to understand why people who should have been luxuriating in their youth and beauty were crippled by self-doubt instead. And it wasn't just teenage girls. Practically everyone I met – male, female, young, old – was unhappy in some way or other with their body. I discovered the rather depressing fact that not liking yourself seems to be completely and utterly normal. (As well as war, poverty, hunger, dirty water, inequality, environmental destruction, disease and death. Nice.)

It was a huge shock to realise it was the world around me that had made it so darn difficult to accept myself. The superficial values that dominate so much of our culture had stripped me of my confidence and turned me into a miserable wreck. And I was not alone.

So many people, no matter who they were or what body they had, were being undermined in the same way and burdened with the same preoccupations. Am I good enough? Am I attractive enough? Am I normal enough?

My disability, it transpired, was the least of my problems. The real question became: how do I defend myself against the constant onslaught of pressures to conform to unrealistic ideals?

It's odd that society has chosen to promote such destructive ideas. Who decided that? And when? I must have missed that meeting. Surely it's not just an accident that the Western world has adopted 'YOU'RE NOT GOOD ENOUGH' as one of its primary slogans. And, why has it been so furiously promoted when it creates such damaging beliefs in people? The society I was born into proclaims that people shouldn't have to 'suffer' from disability but is more than happy to embrace values that cause widespread suffering. It doesn't make sense. At all.

Then the answer hit me as I walked through the local spanking-new Westfield, which is probably the size of Wales. Raoul had come with me. Our usual non-stop conversation had lulled and we fell into silence. An unease descended on me.

'This is awful,' I suddenly said, quietly.

'What?' asked Raoul.

'This. Westfield.'

'I know. I'm only here for you. I hate shopping,' answered Raoul.

'It's not just the shops. It's the adverts, the lights, the lack of windows… it's all so…'

'… manipulative?' he volunteered.

'Yes. And I'm falling for it. Every time I walk past a shop, I can feel myself being pulled towards it…'

'Like Gollum and the ring?'

'Totally! I don't want to but I can't help it. Everything combines to make me feel like I need these products. Like my life will be better with them.'

'Advertising works. Otherwise companies wouldn't spend billions on it,' he smiled.

'It does work! I hate it. I don't want to be part of this bullshit! I'm fine as I am already.' I stopped walking.

'Shall we go home?' Raoul looked excited by the change of plan.

'Yes.'

We turned around, walked to the car park and drove off. I didn't go back for years.

The unsettling truth is that, in order to survive and thrive, a consumer society needs good consumers. Good consumers buy things they don't need. And, in order to make us buy things we don't need, advertisers have to make us believe that we need them. Desperately. So they prey on our insecurities and make us believe that we need their product in order to be 'normal', to fill that gaping hole – the very hole they've dug out of us so tenaciously in the first place.

Let's face it: consumerism wouldn't work if we were a population of confident, secure and happy people. We'd see an advert proclaiming:

Hey you! Yes, *you*!

That bag you're carrying looks a bit shit.

In fact, it's bringing you down.

But *this* bag will make you fit in and stand out – in a *good* way!

Buy it.

Now!

THIS BAG WILL MAKE YOU HAPPIER!

And we'd reply, 'No, it won't. It'll just make your shareholders richer, so piss off!'

When I decided to like myself, I didn't become more beautiful, or less wobbly, or richer, or the proud owner of a luxury iGadget. I simply chose to accept myself as I was. And it wasn't that I'd attained spiritual enlightenment or some higher wisdom – I didn't out-Dalai Lama the Dalai Lama – I just made a decision born out of a desire to enjoy life as much as possible before I croaked it. That's it. I finally realised that this hating-myself malarkey was rather hard work – and I nearly always plump for the least taxing option. It turns out that liking yourself requires a lot less energy. Problem sorted. Hurrah!

People who feel good about themselves are far less likely to believe that a flatter TV is going to make them happier or a swish coffee machine will make them more popular. And that is why we're made to feel so inadequate. There's nothing more to it.

It's the 'Normal Trap'.

I've got to hand it to them – it's a pretty genius ploy:

1. Erode people's self-esteem to a pathetically low level through carefully targeted advertising.
2. Jump in and offer the perfect solution. (Which just happens to be *your* product.)
3. Wait for the initial satisfaction from the purchase to wear off (quickly).
4. Jump in and repeat steps 1–3 again with something else. And again. And again.
5. Ker-ching!

Happiness is always one more purchase away, one more promotion away, one more investment away, but numerous studies show that once a person's basic needs are met, material wealth tends not to make them any happier. So, next time you feel you're not good enough, just remember there's a very rich bloke sunbathing on a yacht somewhere because enough people believed this crap and spent their hard-earned cash on shit they don't need.

It's an effective way to ensure mass inadequacy – create the illusion that people aren't 'normal' unless they conform to certain narrow expectations. There's a longing in most of us to belong, to be accepted, to fit in, and consumerism plays on this human trait like an expert Pied Piper. Our culture has the power to convince skinny people they are fat, young people they are old, old people they can be young, beautiful people they are plain, plain people they can be beautiful, poor people they can be rich, and rich people they're not rich enough. It's a mind-boggling achievement that requires a lot of hard-work and dedication…

'What did you do today, honey?'

'Well, today I devised new ways to make people feel bad about themselves so they'd buy my product!'

'Well, thank fuck you were born!'

When I was at Parliament Hill, the undisputed king of footwear was Nike Airs. Everyone wore them. After a year of sustained begging, I became the proud owner of a pair of Nike trainers. (Not Airs but still…) I walked into class with the firm belief that I Had Arrived.

Alas, the wonder shoes did not transform my life. They were quickly viewed as a tiny anomaly in the ocean of my overwhelming gawkiness. Apparently it wasn't enough to wear Nike trainers, you also had to lace them in the correct manner. There are strict rules. Laces can never, ever, be done up – the ends MUST be neatly tucked inside. My walking didn't benefit much from having shoes that regularly fell off. I held out for nearly a week, during which the right trainer fell off nine times, and the left one twice. I almost fell down a flight of stairs. So, with much regret, I tied the laces. *Big* mistake. I became the Lace Pariah.

I believed that wearing Nike trainers would make me cool. Then, I realised I was just advertising them. For *free*! Nike should have been paying *me* to wear them! Now, I think of fashion as the ultimate mode of conformity.

Genuine individuality is so heavily discouraged from day one that, by the time we're teenagers, it's taboo. I can't really blame the girls in my school for singling me out as a freak. How can I, when society preaches that conformity is the only way? It's pretty much impossible to expect impressionable teenagers to react positively to difference when mainstream values obsessively promote a religious adherence to prejudicial norms. How can we expect our youth to embrace diversity when the world around them is so archly, so aggressively, against it? Kids are hardly likely to accept a wobbly classmate when any deviation from the ubiquitous, tall, skinny, unshaky and Photoshopped ideal is derided as a failure of mammoth proportions.

Which brings me to that summit of human endeavour – the Celebrity Mag. Every time I pick up one of these priceless artefacts at my hairdressers, I feel like I need to go home and take a shower. The obsession with celebrity means we are constantly induced to compare ourselves to others who are deemed sexier, wealthier, skinnier, more tanned, less wrinkled than the rest of us. Reading celebrity magazines is like eating poo. Don't do it: it's bad for your health.

Their sole purpose is to make you feel bad about your life because you're not rich and famous. According to them, the pinnacle of human existence is shopping, partying and injecting rat poison into your already scarily smooth forehead. Because the ability to change facial expressions is Not Good, apparently.

The feted few in their glossy pages may be mocked for having errant hair or a weird underarm bulge but, ultimately, they are worshipped as shining examples for us all, carefully selected carrots dangling in front of our faces. These rags may seem like harmless diversions that sate our desire for a bit of gossip but they're not, they are spoon-feeding us the values that consumerism depends on, values that will rot your brain, body and soul.

Celebrities are used to embody the goals we're all supposed to adopt. Except, most of them don't seem terribly happy, judging by the parade of meltdowns, addictions, eating disorders, overdoses, break-ups, rehab-stints and cosmetic surgery stories that fuel the constant media frenzy. Michael Jackson, Amy Winehouse and Whitney Houston all had beauty, wealth, and fame but that didn't seem to translate into happiness. In fact, these 'desirable attributes' seemed to bring them huge challenges and problems, instead of inner well-being. I'm not suggesting that we all cry our eyes out for poor old Kate Moss but it's probably harder to disregard these superficial ideals as bollocks, the closer you resemble them.

When I was a kid, I envied a girl called Amanda. She was blonde and beautiful and able-bodied. Her parents looked like comic book heroes. I wished I could be her or, at least, more like her. Amanda died at sixteen from a rare illness. As I sat at her funeral, I felt hot with shame, and I promised myself that I would try never to be that shallow again.

Don't get me wrong, I think beauty will always be celebrated by humans. And I understand why. It's lovely to look at someone beautiful and it always will be. The problem lies in our cultural obsession with it, our pursuit of it, our deification of it. Beauty is a gift like a great voice or amazingly agile feet, or the ability to paint or write or run fast. Some people may be perceived to have it, others not. It shouldn't be seen as the ultimate possession and it's no indicator of someone's happiness, confidence or self worth – it is just one of many attributes that can give joy and shouldn't be placed above any other. And like other gifts, it can bring its own set of challenges and prejudices.

Here's a thought. Maybe, as a culture, we should cherish different ideals such as love, compassion and empathy, and repeatedly shove *those* down the throats of the next generation with monumental force. Who's in?

Our bodies give us life and we should thank them every day instead of obsessively comparing ourselves to troubled stars and semi-starved supermodels draped in luxury brands. We are screwing up ourselves by our worship of brands. Prada and Gucci and Armani are meaningless permutations of letters. They are empty vessels designed to enslave people economically and psychologically by masquerading as glossy and desirable symbols of success.

Advertisers used to promote products by saying stuff like 'this chair is strong' or 'this coat will keep you warm'. The trouble with that approach was that people stopped buying products once they had them. And this was seen as a major problem by the retailers and manufacturers. Which is why advertising execs came up with the ingenious idea of attaching aspirational traits such as success, attractiveness, power, and popularity to their products. All they had to do then was create enough dissatisfaction in people by incessant advertising so that they'd fall for this bullshit. Bingo! They've been laughing all the way to the bank ever since as the rest of us pile up debts and insecurities trying to keep up with the Joneses. Brilliant or what?

Politicians also benefit from the erosion of our innate confidence. I bet that anyone who's up to their eyeballs in credit card debt will be far less likely to cast a keen eye over the actions of those in power or kick up much of a fuss about anything. Fusses are hard enough to kick up normally, let alone when you're knee-deep in financial crap. I think it's safe to say that those in power would much rather rule a bunch of meek, paranoid, unhappy consumers, than a confident citizenry who possess such a level of self-worth that they expect a decent standard of living and general well-being. Because we all know how much trouble *they* are.

It's inescapable – we live in a world where what's seen as successful, fashionable or beautiful is heavily shaped by a power base with their own morally dubious agenda. This aspirational culture and body fascism promotes worship of 'perfection' and fear of anything else. Which is exactly what it's designed to do.

To be honest, sometimes I've felt nervous around other 'disabled' people. It may sound crazy, but the fact that I'm wobbly doesn't mean I haven't been affected by all this cultural nonsense, or that I instinctively always know the perfect way to respond. Especially when you factor in that I never felt 'disabled'.

I remember sharing a taxi when I was sixteen with a girl in a wheelchair. I asked her what her name was and she spent the next two minutes trying to tell me with a lot of head rolling and arm waving. I sat beside her, squirming with nervous embarrassment at the huge effort I'd made her expend. I debated whether to chip in and tell her it wasn't that important or just keep staring at her with this stupid grin fixed rigidly across my face. In the end, I just sat there like an idiot until she eventually got her name out, and then made sure I didn't ask her anything else. It was the first time I'd been in that situation. I know that if I'd grown up with kids who took longer to speak, I'd have been totally relaxed and able to communicate with her without feeling like a complete muppet.

More recently, I was confronted by another form of my own prejudice. I was doing a run of shows at a London theatre and received a message to the effect that an audience member called Jess, who had Tourettes Syndrome (another charming label), had booked tickets for the first show. The very show that was being recorded for DVD. On hearing the news, I chose to be mature in my response and promptly freaked out. What should I do? Would it ruin the show? How would I handle it? How the hell would the audience handle it? Given that the show was called *What The **** Is Normal?!* I knew there was no way I could ask Jess to come on another night.

I decided to postpone the filming and wrote to Jess to find out more about her. An email turned up the next day saying that she rarely went to live events but that she really wanted to see my show. She also said that she'd been to the same theatre the previous year and had had a horrible experience when other audience members complained about her vocal tics. At the interval, she'd been asked to sit in the sound booth, and spent the second half of the show feeling upset and humiliated.

I was deeply touched by the honesty of her reply and a huge wave of shame crashed over me. I felt so shallow for reacting with fear to her. My show was supposed to be about celebrating human diversity and here I was, fearing her difference. I suddenly felt proud that Jess had chosen to come to my show despite having been discriminated against the year before. It was brave of her to want to come back to the theatre again, to feel that she had an equal right to be there. Now I didn't care if she spoke up during the show. It didn't matter. All that mattered was for everyone in that theatre to feel welcome and included. That was much more important.

I wrote back to her and offered to introduce her at the beginning so that the audience would understand if she made certain sounds. Jess agreed that it would be a good idea to do this. A few nights later, when I walked out onstage, the applause died down and I heard someone say 'Biscuit… biscuit… biscuit.' In contrast to what I'd imagined her tic-words to be, Jess was the purveyor of possibly the sweetest one ever. I introduced her to the audience, assuring them that, though she might say 'biscuit' a lot, she didn't actually want one. Once I'd mentioned Jess, the audience relaxed. The show went really well, and the softly spoken 'biscuits' and 'hedgehogs' provided an occasional soundtrack and were a delightfully interesting bonus. (I'm just sorry that 'Harry Potter rape' – I'm not making that up – never got a look-in.)

I met Jess after the show and was greeted by one of the most eloquent people I've ever talked to. Her vocal and physical tics were pretty prominent but they quickly faded into the background and became normal. We're friends now and she is utterly brilliant and brave in a way that I have never had to be. Because of her, I am no longer nervous about audience members with Tourette's attending shows – and even DVD recordings: bring it on, I say! And I can't say 'biscuit' now without hearing her voice.

It's a shame that much of the media have emphatically refused, for a very long time, to represent diversity, because they play a crucial role in shaping cultural attitudes. They could play a vital part in normalising difference. But, instead of accurately portraying the huge range of human variety, they deliberately choose to depict an extremely narrow slice of humanity. This carefully selected segment just happens to contain perky young girls with sky-pointing nipples and men with strong chins, shapely forearms, and perfect teeth. Yes, TV nowadays is so terrified of physical imperfection that it's easier to spot a politician telling the unvarnished truth than it is to spy a dreaded wrinkle.

It's rare that a female presenter over forty is allowed to grace our screens. Because we can't have women thinking it's normal to age, can we? These atrophying horrors must be hidden from view to ensure that the viewing public continue to pursue youth and beauty at any cost. And if a harmless crease can't even make it on to the box, what chance for any sod with a syndrome or a palsy or a disorder? Telly is for physical 'perfection'. Except, of course, when it isn't. On the rare occasion that disability does make an appearance, it's usually X-rated inspiro-porn, a pity-fest designed to pull your heartstrings to shreds, or a Man-With-A-Testicle-On-His-Face freak show. The one thing these freakies definitely ain't portrayed as is 'normal' members of society with talents and flaws and hopes like the rest of us. Because that would mean that difference might be perceived as a natural part of life. Hell, viewers might even begin to accept their own imperfections. And, for our superficial culture, that would spell total disaster.

Just after leaving *Grange Hill*, I attended an Equity conference on diversity in TV casting, with Lisa. We sat for hours in a big hall listening to speakers bang on about how important it was for TV to have more disabled characters. All around us, producers, directors and writers nodded earnestly in agreement. The conference closed with a speech from a producer of *EastEnders*. She ended by saying 'diversity on our screens is important but we must be careful not to turn *EastEnders* into a freak show'. Lisa and I picked our jaws up off the floor.

Early on in my stand-up career, I began to see just how reluctant television is to allow someone wobbly to appear as a comedian. My high-powered and slightly Rottweiler-like agent was trying hard to get me on to a BBC stand-up show but the producers were having none of it. They agreed that I had the right credentials for the show, but were worried that the sight of me would send viewers at home into anaphylactic shock or something.

It turns out that I am allowed to go on TV to speak about 'serious' issues because that reflects my 'serious' condition. But comedy shows are largely out of bounds because cerebral palsy clearly is No Laughing Matter.

It seems the UK panel shows have decided that I must be kept far, far away from their jovial sets, even though I've been recommended to them by various 'big' names. I'm told they're concerned that I'll 'make the audience nervous.' Jimmy Carr tried for months to get me on *8 Out Of 10 Cats* and failed.

Jimmy is not the only comic to have stuck his neck out for me over the years. I've also been given amazing support by a list of incredibly talented people who've all helped me in crucial ways – Russell Brand, Steve Coogan, Ricky Gervais, Michael Barrymore, Lee Mack, Jonathan Ross, Johnny Vegas, Frank Skinner, Jeremy Hardy, Richard Herring, Stewart Lee and Adam Hills. It's true that the comedy industry is a tough world for any performer to break into. But, if you're wobbly, it seems to be a tad more difficult. I'll spare you the gory details but I've been dropped from a major award nomination list due to the head judge's contention that I was just a novelty act (despite not having seen my show), I was hoiked out of Lee Mack's sitcom pilot because an executive thought my appearance in *Extras* fulfilled the palsy-on-screen quota for that decade, and I've been dropped from BBC radio shows because of my 'funny voice'.

I could go on but I'm sure you get the picture by now... I am very scary. ROOOAAAR-AAAARRRGGGGHHHHHH! But only to the industry folk, not to comedians who want to work with me or the public who come to see my live shows. Work that out.

I don't take these experiences personally. I think they stem from a wider fear of difference. However, I think that fear is largely unfounded because, rather than being repelled by difference, our natural reaction is to be intrigued by it. The Paralympics was a ratings success. It showed that there is a huge interest in seeing more diversity, more difference, on our tellies. When I switch on the box and see someone 'different', I'm more likely to stay on the channel because it's unusual. It grabs my attention.

Funnily enough, the telly-folk in other countries are far less concerned about unleashing me on the public. In Ireland and Australia I've been invited on the top comedy shows without a hint of knicker-twisting. I couldn't get my head around how chilled out they were. When my Aussie PR lady told me that the most popular panel show in the country wanted me as a guest, I had to double-check whether they knew about my palsied brain. 'Yeah, but they think you're hilarious,' was the unexpected answer. And that was that.

I should point out that I do get offered some comedy work on TV in this country. One of the funniest things that has happened to me was receiving an invitation, a few years back, to play a role in a one-off BBC4 comedy. I eagerly opened the script and read the following description of my character:

CLAIRE IS SEVERELY DISABLED.
SHE IS INCAPABLE OF ANY SPEECH,
MOVEMENT OR EXPRESSION.

Well, I was, of course, flattered they had thought of me. After all, it's not every day I'm offered a major part in a TV show. After some consideration, I penned this reply:

```
Dear -----------
Many thanks for offering me the part of
CLAIRE.
Unfortunately, I do not feel I have the
skill to bring off such a complex and
demanding role successfully. I also fear
that a week's rehearsal would not give
me enough time to inhabit such a well-
crafted portrayal of disability in the
twenty-first century.
May I suggest casting a shoe or a carrot
instead?
Yours sincerely,
Francesca
```

The media do not often embrace difference or deal with it openly. They prefer instead to project an air-brushed reality that serves corporate interests. Perhaps as a result, many of us still don't know how to respond to disability. I think the key issue is that disability is fundamentally at odds with our consumer culture – a culture that sells us conformity, fear of difference and of ourselves, at every opportunity. We're not taught to accept our own so-called imperfections so how the hell can we deal with anyone else's?

I was shocked when I realised the reason why so many people in the West were deeply unhappy with themselves despite having so much. It's not that we're all weak and depressive mopes with a natural disposition for self-loathing and myopic obsession. It's not a random, unfortunate part of being alive. No. The truth is, our society is *designed* to make us feel this way.

Misery might add up to big bucks for the few, but it doesn't equal good mental health for the rest of us. Depression, eating disorders and poor body image have been steadily increasing in the West over recent decades. Studies show that citizens in English-speaking countries – all of whom have comprehensively embraced consumerism – are twice as likely to suffer from mental illness than in mainland Europe. Amazingly, America, the world's richest country and the prime exporter of aspirational culture, has the highest mental illness rates in the world.

I remember sitting in the living room as I neared my thirties, and feeling slightly sick at the fact that most of the misery and depression and dissatisfaction that people across the world have felt and are feeling, is precisely cultivated and encouraged. Of all the wonderful systems that we could have created, why is this the dominant one?

The image of a giant Unhappiness Machine came into my mind – a machine designed to pump out millions of dissatisfied consumers, who buy tons of pointless junk produced by millions of impoverished slaves. A mechanism that's been carefully engineered to strip away the layers of our youthful self-belief and reduce us to a gaggle of anxious gibbering wrecks.

We're not born with these boulder-like burdens of self-doubt. Toddlers don't cry because their bums look big in Pampers. Young kids don't care whether they're 'beautiful' or if their shoes carry the right logo. They don't let that superfluous shit fuck up their lives. It shouldn't be so damn hard for kids to keep that innate self-confidence as they grow into adults. Those of us who are fortunate enough not to be confronted by war, poverty and hunger every day should be walking around in amazement at being alive, at the wonders of this beautiful planet we live on, at the billions of natural 'miracles' it took for us to be here.

But the Normal Trap awaits us when we grow older. It is meticulously fashioned and brilliantly invisible. At the heart of it is the lie that we will all be better, happier, more satisfied, more 'normal', if we obediently fuel the never-ending fire of consumerism. Our entire economic system is based on a minority consuming more and more junk that is produced by an exploited majority. Not only is this ceaseless consumerism predicated on human suffering and environmental devastation, it also leads to an unfulfilling and empty existence for those who consume, with little sense of contributing anything of value, of substance, of meaning.

I grew up thinking that other people felt sorry for me and that if medics had their way, people like me wouldn't exist. Society might favour able-bodied babies, but it is massively guilty of disabling those healthy babies once they are old enough to imbibe the toxic values of materialism.

From a young age, we are told to be obedient, not to question 'authorities', and to strive to be 'normal'. By the time we leave the education system and venture out into the world, our self-confidence is as robust as a wet sock. Our youthful exuberance has been expertly disabled, and most of us emerge with a perspective that's been reduced to the size of a pinhead. Then we're 'free' to spend inordinate amounts of time worrying about trivial rubbish for the rest of our lives while an elite few cash in on our unhappiness.

Ker-ching!

CHAPTER THIRTEEN

****

Choosing to accept yourself is a political act. An act of liberation. Never stop fighting for it.

All we need to be happy is love, fulfilling work, self-acceptance, and freedom from fear. That's it. It ain't rocket science. Once you realise these goals are the only ones worth pursuing, life is a lot easier. I like to think of it as training yourself to be a ninja who can deftly avoid the torrent of shit that is routinely sprayed at us from multiple angles. With stunning accuracy.

I truly believe that a world of happy, confident people would be a lovely place to live, so to pursue happiness is not a selfish act. In fact, you can look at it as an altruistic action because you're saving the world from one more self-obsessed mope. And people will be far less likely to want to dominate and oppress others if they're busy gorging themselves on the nourishing fruits of inner peace. Hell, they might even want to empower others to do so too, which can only be a good thing, right?

When I stepped away from the Unhappiness Machine, I immediately felt my priorities change. Here's the incredible thing. None of my physical capabilities changed or improved but my new attitude towards them meant that I no longer saw them as a problem. The simplest of acts – thinking differently – had huge and tangible effects, effects I never would have imagined. I stopped hating my walk and started feeling intensely grateful that I could walk at all. When my writing flew off the page in crazy shapes, I marvelled at the originality and vitality of the hand that refused to be contained. The brow-furrowed scrutiny that my birthday card greetings always elicited from its readers no longer made me shrink. Instead, they filled me with joy. I was learning a startling lesson. Slowly, I began to see the wonderful paths that open up when you accept yourself. I began to see this wild body of mine as something beautiful, something to be proud of. A body that was never boring but always exciting and unique. A body that would teach me things for which I'd be utterly grateful. It had been a long and bumpy road but I was finally enjoying being me. And I didn't want to change a thing.

By accepting myself and focusing on what I had, all that time and energy I was wasting was freed up to think about *others*. Instead of myself! This new, outward focus made me even happier. New passions appeared. It was like some incredible cycle that kept on churning out more and more happiness. (If I'd paid more attention in maths, I could have illustrated this point with some kind of flow-chart.)

I used to worry about the way my knees moved when I walked. Now, I love my knees and worry about other stuff. Stuff that really matters. Like the huge inequalities in the world. And the way we are systematically destroying our environment. And how we're allowing hard-won freedoms to be chipped away by governments *we've* elected (or not). And how we can evolve a system that values genuine democracy, peace and sustainability above GDP. Who gives a toss about knees?

Bodies are next to impossible to change but how we choose to live on this planet isn't. It may be bloody difficult but creating a society and an environment that is better for everyone is always possible, and far worthier of our sustained attention than the thigh gap. All of us have the potential to make a difference, especially when we work together, if we only stop letting others make us feel so ridiculously disempowered.

I remember thinking, 'Why the fuck didn't anyone tell me about this "accepting yourself" schtick earlier? It would have saved so much heartache and shit!' I can't understand why we aren't told this as kids on the first day of school. Instead, society does its best to hide this from us by distracting us with shiny decoys. A lot. It doesn't want anyone to know that we can discover happiness all on our own. Because then we'd stop chasing empty goals, start thinking for ourselves, ask uncomfortable questions, look around, and – shudder! – demand better.

Funnily enough, the more 'beautiful' and 'successful' my friends have been, the less secure they've been. Without exception, they have been riddled with self-doubt and an obsessive desire to maintain their looks at any cost. It seems that if you are close to embodying the 'aspirations' of our time, you're more likely to feel obliged to adopt them wholeheartedly. In fact, beauty can be a disability that makes it more difficult to cultivate healthy goals in yourself. Perhaps doctors could come up with some ugly consonant-ridden moniker for that condition. Like 'Superficial Poison Syndrome'.

On the other hand, the happiest people I've met have not had much money or power or status. And, perhaps surprisingly, many of them have been light years away from society's stupid and unrealistic expectations. I have several mates with 'severe' CP (I prefer 'über-wobbly'), who fall over regularly or take an age to get a sentence out. But they tend to be happier than pretty much anyone else I've met. My friend Nathan Doidge is one of them.

When I first got to know Nath, I was immediately struck by his attitude to falling over (which happened a lot). He didn't care and wasn't at all embarrassed. It was normal to him, yet I'd grown up in a world where falling over was the ultimate embarrassment. Because of this, I'd always tried desperately not to lose what little balance I had. If an adult falls over, it's an event of biblical proportions ('Oh, the humanity', etc.). But here was Nath falling over on a daily basis and he didn't view it as a failure or a negative. It was just a part of his life. I fricking loved his attitude towards such a social taboo. It was so empowering and beautiful and rebellious. He made me re-evaluate my feelings on the matter and I concluded this: sod society's stupid expectations, falling over is nothing to be ashamed of. To me, his fearlessness is the definition of confidence if ever there was one. Oh, and he's now a qualified solo pilot so he is officially the coolest dude I've ever met.

Inspired by my *Top Gun* pal, Nath, I thought I'd share eight more reasons why being wobbly *rocks*. I realise you've more chance of personally witnessing Victoria Beckham tucking into a cheeseburger than of reading a mainstream (or even left-field) account that champions the mega-positives of having a palsied cerebrum, but I'm going to give it a crack:

1. As bizarre as it might sound, I think my old palsy has actually made me a happier person. Ha ha ha! Mad, I know – but bear with me. My 'disability' appears not to have caused the massive amounts of suffering that our medical folk would have us think. On the contrary. As you've seen, my wobbliness meant I never had a hope in hell of fitting in with the norm so, after those years of twisting my knickers into a very complex knot, I was forced to decide between crumbling under society's ludicrous expectations or rejecting them as a truckload of steaming rhino plop. The rhino plop was chucked, thankfully.

2. It's highly unlikely that I'd have been confronted with the preceding choice before my twentieth birthday,

had I not been a touch palsied. Chances are that I'd have bumbled around until my forties, trying my damnedest to be normal, until I spied some crow's feet around my eyes and freaked out like any good citizen ought to. So I'm glad that this shit was sorted out a lot earlier because it means I get an extra twenty-odd years enjoying all the perks that come with self-acceptance. And that is bloody brilliant.

Opening my eyes to this 'normal' blarney has had such a profoundly positive effect on my whole life that I thank my wobbles every day. Profusely. Honestly! Gimme the keys to happiness over perfect hand–eye coordination any day.

3. My relationship with my parents has been extra close. When you still need your parents to cut your food up for you as you embark upon your teenage years, you're less likely to exchange the usual half-dozen grunts a day with them. In fact, the physical help they gave me over my life until I finally moved out guaranteed that the tight bond between us was pretty inevitable. And, being a person for whom hugs are as important as food and air, I wouldn't change this intimacy for the world.

In terms of parents, I hit the jackpot. If you're wondering why there isn't more of my mum in this book, it's because she's so full of love and support – how many ways can you say that your ma is blooming wonderful before your reader needs a bucket? I actually like hanging out with my parents – they are that cool. How abnormal is that? My folks, with a little help from Dylan, are the reason I've enjoyed most of my waking hours. When I think of all the parents I could have had, I break into a sweat of relief.

I think kids who weren't so lucky are far more likely to suffer as adults. Not being loved enough creates the toughest kinds of disabilities – they might be invisible, but they're a lot harder to deal with than just being a bit wobbly.

4. My brother is the best brother you could hope for. (And he's mine – ha ha haaaa!) Which makes me very, very, lucky. Because of my wobbliness, he has accompanied me on numerous work trips all over the world, as my official Walking Stick. This means we've had tons of amazing and exotic experiences together and have spent shedloads of time talking about and exploring every issue under the sun. It's kind of our favourite thing to do. I wouldn't have had the excuse to drag him around with me but for the need to keep vertical so I'm bloody glad that staying upright is so tricky for me. We are the best of friends and he is the most delightful walking stick a girl could wish for.

5. I wish I could say that I try really hard not to let my disability get in the way of me doing things. Instead,

I'm utterly grateful that it does. Bring it on. The more stuff it stops me doing, the more time I have to read, watch *Breaking Bad* and sleep.

I love not being able to wash up, cook, iron and spring-clean. I feel so lucky that I have a viable excuse not to do those boring, tedious jobs that punctuate most people's lives. I have disabled friends who are so proud that they refuse to ask for help and would rather toil away at some mundane task for hours, gaining great satisfaction finally from doing it all on their own. I wish I had that pride but it buggered off long ago, sadly. Probably while I was sleeping.

Just to be crystal clear, if you ever find yourself meeting me and wondering whether to offer me help, the unequivocal answer you will receive is 'yes'. I am delighted to accept whatever it is you'd like to do for me.

6. Nothing is worth queuing for, in my opinion. A few years ago, I noticed something odd. I would suddenly become more wobbly when I approached the check-in queue at the airport. Just enough for the nice airline person to beckon me over to the special desk and check me in straight away. At first, I suffered innumerable pangs of guilt for sidestepping the long lines of tired people desperate to get started on their holiday, but now I can't wait to wobble it up and zip on through to Pret A Manger. I'm sure this makes me a bad person and I apologise for it.

7. If I hadn't been wobbly, I wouldn't have become a comedian. Since I consider – no, *know*! – this to be the best job in the world, I am rather happy that my damaged brain led me down this path. I would not have known the brilliant joy that goes with making people laugh and (hopefully) think a bit too. Not to mention the no-early-mornings and the getting-paid-to-talk bits. Thanks again, Dad.

It's a wonderful feeling when you discover what you're meant to do in life. I still remember standing backstage at the Open Mic Award at the Edinburgh Festival 2000. I had entered the New Act competition along with a thousand other hopefuls. Somehow, I made it to the final. My gig had gone well despite the nerves making my body jiggle more wildly than ever, it seemed.

The ten finalists waited backstage impatiently as the judges, who included Michael Barrymore, Harry Hill, and Henry Normal, were deliberating on who should win. A young Jimmy Carr stood beside me dressed in an immaculate suit, and sporting a slick hairdo with not a strand out of place.

'You had the best gig. You've won this, Francesca,' he said to me, matter-of-factly.

'Don't be silly!' I said, as my hands gripped the sides of the plastic chair I was sitting on. There was no way I was going to win this and I was fine with that. I was just happy to have been the only woman to make it to the final. That was enough of an achievement for me. I stared at the floor. It was nearly a year to the day since I'd done my first ever gig and here I was, at the Edinburgh Festival! In a major comedy final! I couldn't quite believe it. For a moment, I wondered if I was dreaming.

Chris Addison, who was hosting the show, bounded back on to the stage. We all looked at each other with heightened stares. This was it – he was about to announce the winner. The bottom of the plastic chair dug into my fingers but I couldn't stop gripping it.

'Ladies and gentleman, the judges have made their decision…' Chris sounded like he was in another world, somewhere far away from us, remote and untouchable. His pause was long. I closed my eyes and tried to root myself in the solid ground beneath my feet.

'The winner of the Open Mic Award 2000 is… Francesca Martinez!' The applause broke out, slowly at first, then louder and louder, building to a deafening crescendo, punctuated with whoops and cheers. I opened my eyes. He said my name, I thought. Why has he said my name?

'I told you,' said Jimmy. One of the organisers, Richard, offered me his arm.

'Come on. You've won! Time to get back onstage!' I took Richard's arm and stood up. He started to move towards the red velvet curtain and, with a surge of effort, my legs started to bounce around like the limbs of a marionette. Before I knew it, the thick drape was pulled aside and I was onstage, still holding on to Richard's arm for dear life. The audience grew louder in their response and all I could see were bright lights and hundreds of smiling faces. I could feel the intensity of energy in the theatre as it flowed into my feet and streaked through me like lightning.

'Francesca has won two thousand pounds and trips to perform at the Melbourne and Montreal Comedy Festivals! Is there anything you want to say?' Chris pointed the microphone at me and the room slowly quietened. I looked at Chris who was beaming warmly. I could see the judges smiling at me from the side of the stage. I would later find out that they had voted unanimously for me but a concern had been voiced that my subject material was 'limited'. Apparently, Michael Barrymore had challenged this by observing that I was just speaking about my life, the same as any other comic. I was so grateful that he'd pointed this out because that's exactly how I see it. Often people label you as an 'issue' comic if you talk about your disability or sexuality or gender. Unless you're a white bloke, of course. Then you're just talking about life. But we're all talking about our lives and views and experiences. That's what comics do.

I looked at the audience and my eyes fell on Raoul, then my mum, then Anthony Andrews and, finally, on my dad, who looked as if he was about to spontaneously combust with happiness. My mind was not in the right state to produce sentences or words but I knew I couldn't just stand there, in front of all these people, like a gawping, slightly sweaty, jellied idiot.

'Er… I can't believe this as you can clearly see! Thanks so much for giving me this award…' I looked at my dad.

'I just want to say a huge thanks to Dad who's over there…' I tried to point at him with my free hand but merely indicated most of the audience.

'My pointing's shit but he's here, I promise!' The room laughed.

'He always believed I could be a comic and he's the reason I'm here. I love you, Dad.' My voice strained with emotion and I decided that verbal communication was no longer an option. It would not be appropriate for the winner of a comedy award to shake like a leaf *and* start blubbering and gibbering like a sappy pillock. This wasn't the bloody Oscars. Or an episode of *Little House on the Prairie*.

I tried to keep the drops from running down my face and smiled down at Dad. He smiled back, battling to hold back the tears in his eyes too.

8. I wouldn't have met my Kevin but for the wobbles. After my experiences with Dylan, an interesting pattern emerged. I had quite the knack for attracting

arseholes, apparently. Indeed, you could say I was something of an arsehole magnet. There'd been the odd nice guy but they turned out to be a very rare breed. Arseholes, on the other hand, were two-a-fucking-penny. If there was one in the vicinity, well, I'd expertly sniff 'em out – before opening my heart to them without even a cursory check.

At the age of twenty-seven, I'd had my fill of them and decided that maybe those nuns had been on to something after all. I prepared myself for a life of singlehood. I reasoned that my rather elaborate notions of romance probably only existed in the realms of heady and magical imagination and were not attainable in real life. Occasionally I would indulge in a secret literary outpouring at the laptop but I put passwords on each document to make sure that my desire for love remained hidden.

In April 2006, I went to Dublin to do a show for my friend, Caroline Casey. I'd met Caroline years before when she'd booked me to perform at her charity's – The Kanchi Foundation – annual conference. We'd hit it off right away and both shared the view that society should focus on what disabled people can do and not on what they can't. I'd done various shows for her charity over the years and, in this latest performance, I joked about my ideal man being a poor Irish poet. Afterwards, Caroline asked me if this was true and I said yes. Rather too emphatically. It was a deeply held desire of mine to find a dreamy man with a soft-lilting accent, windblown hair, ginger-flecked stubble, and a propensity for reciting inordinately tender lines of heartache, love and woe at random intervals during the day and night. And who lived in a cottage on some desolate moor in a place that was battered by ceaseless winds but kept warm by a roaring fire. With bracken outside. I wasn't too sure what bracken looked like but I figured it had to be important. Caroline's eyes widened.

'I know a guy you should meet!' She smiled mischievously.

'Is he a poet?' I asked, trying not to sound overly nutty.

'No, but he's Irish and he's not rich,' she answered, looking at me closely to see my reaction.

'Hmm, well, two out of three ain't bad,' I concluded.

It's a shame he wasn't a poet – but I am, so, if the necessity arose, he could always read my ramblings out loud. And, although he mightn't be dirt-poor, hopefully we could still create a life where the supernatural force of our love rendered superfluous the need for material possessions (apart, that is, from books).

I went home to London and got on with life, and the thought of this tantalising man slowly faded away like a drawing in the sand. A few months later, in July, Raoul and I returned to Dublin to stay

with Caroline and Fergal, for a few days of fun.
They announced that they were going to throw a
party that weekend so we could meet some of their
friends. Caroline said that their mystery friend
was abroad, unfortunately, so no matchmaking
would take place on this occasion. This was a lie.
In fact they were throwing the party with the sole
aim of bringing this bloke and me together, but
they thought it best not to tell me (or him) so I
wouldn't feel pressurised. It was pure, rampant
deception. Clearly, they did not know of my super
unflusterability when it came to dealing with the
opposite sex. Or how deftly I employed coughs and
nervous laughter to devastatingly seductive effect.

On reflection, I appreciate my friends' complete
lack of faith in my ability to handle anything
approaching a potentially romantic situation with
either grace or charm. They made the right call. I
am very grateful to have been spared those tense
moments of anticipation. There was no chance of
my even considering a bungled attempt at a surprise
poem. And this could only be a good thing.

So, it was with utter ignorance that I greeted
Caroline and Fergal's friends that night of the
fifteenth of July 2006, throwing myself into the dual
delights of conversation and a mouth-watering
spread of grub. It was a cloudless and balmy night
and I sat outside in the garden, chatting. A while
later, I glanced over at the table of food and spotted

a man intensely surveying the salads on offer. He had short light brown hair and stubble that was dotted with orange highlights, and he wore a tan blazer with jeans. I could just about make out two green eyes. Well, I thought, that guy is definitely the cutest one here. And, with that important observation, I went back to devouring my plate of cheese.

At about a quarter to midnight, Raoul approached me. Unbeknown to me, my friends had let him in on the secret and asked him to drag me away from the group I was with so that they could carry out their evil plan. They were clearly frustrated that the party had been in full swing for six hours without the appearance of Cupid, so employed Raoul to whisk me over to the action. Reluctantly, I left my gang and walked over with Raoul to Fergal, who was standing near the sliding doors that led to the kitchen.

'Chess, I want you to meet my good friend, Kevin. We grew up together. He's an actor too!' Fergal placed a hand on Kevin's shoulder. I noticed that Kevin was the cute salad guy.

'Hi, Kevin.' I stuck my hand out. He smiled at me. A smile so full of warmth and poetry that I forgot what day it was.

'Hi, Francesca,' he said, shaking my hand. Wow. What a voice. And what an accent. That was a voice I'd like to wake up to every morning.

Seven hours later, we were still sitting beside each other on the sofa beneath two blankets. We had talked and laughed about everything and nothing. It had been the easiest conversation I'd ever had. As I listened to the sounds of the sleeping house around me, I felt my neck tingle. I looked over at Kevin's beautiful eyes and his startlingly familiar face, which sang with beauty and kindness and passion and intelligence and humour. I know this man, I thought. I know him better than anyone I've ever met.

We parted at 7.30 a.m. with a hug that lingered in the hazy morning light.

'Drop me an email, then,' said Kevin as he pulled away slowly.

'I will.' I smiled at him, not wanting his arms to let go.

'Are you sure you don't want me to write my address down for you?' His green eyes looked into mine.

'No. I have a good memory. You have to when your handwriting is as messy as mine!' His face was still delightfully close and I noticed the fine lines around his eyes when he smiled.

'Okay. I won't take it as a brush-off then.' His mouth closed lightly and I wondered whether I should kiss his lips. They looked like they were made to be kissed.

'Don't!' I said, after a moment's struggle to recall the English language.

He smiled at me. I opened the front door, and he slipped out into the sunlit Dublin street. I watched him until he disappeared.

We emailed each other every day for a month. I felt like I was in a Jane Austen novel, excitedly receiving letters from my dashing suitor. Slowly we discovered the details of each other's lives. He loved acting and theatre and nature and travelling and reading and Paris and wine and books and science and maths (yikes!) and art and food. He thought life was an adventure and should be approached with an open and fearless heart. Above all, he lived by his own rules, which made my stomach jump with excitement. I'd not met a man since Dylan who was so passionate about remaining free from the binding chains of adulthood and pursuing happiness and creativity above all else. Sadly, he did not live in a cottage on a moor but I thought I might, with time, be able to overlook that shortcoming.

Astoundingly for me, I remained calm and poised throughout all of this, nonchalantly telling my parents that I had met a nice Irish man. And that was about the extent of my communication on the matter. For reasons that remain unknown to me, I was spared the usual fireworks that had always accompanied the appearance of a possible love interest. Instead, I felt an unfamiliar serenity about the whole situation. I savoured the thought of Kevin in my mind, every night, letting his face into my dreams, but I didn't worry about the outcome. At all. And I never even thought about opening Microsoft Word to compose any kind of verse – a sign, I think, that I'd undergone at least a minimal process of maturation.

In late August, Kevin flew to London. Two days later, he was sitting on my sofa. It was four in the morning and we had talked for about twelve hours straight. I'd tried hard to spot any traits of the arsehole in him but had failed. Spectacularly. He seemed pretty much perfect. A slight feeling of suspicion grew inside me. Surely a man this wonderful can't be single? He's gorgeous and interesting and *very* funny and kind and has the kind of brain that I want to run around in. So, *why* on Earth is he sitting on *my* sofa when he is this bloody perfect? Suddenly my mind tuned back into his voice and, if any more sealing of the deal needed to be done, that did it. He may not be a poet, I thought, but everything that emerges from his mouth sounds like pure heaven. I decided that his mouth must be a place of sheer wonder to house such a voice, and decided that it warranted closer inspection. I fixed my eyes on his.

'Anyway, I want you to kiss me.' The words floated in front of his face for a moment like bright neon lights.

'Oh, sorry!' He reached over and touched my blushing cheek. And I knew, as his soft lips touched mine, that I loved him. And would always do so.

Thankfully, I had the self-awareness not to tell him this on our second date. I'm not that stupid! No. I have actually learnt about taking it slow with a guy and not being too forward. So, with this newfound skill, I managed to wait a whole *two* weeks before I dropped that bombshell. Mature or what? In my defence, we'd gone to France for a romantic trip along the Loire, which made it virtually impossible for me to suppress my increasingly powerful feelings. France is not a good place to go to if you already have trouble trying to repress waves of intense passion. Perhaps the north of Finland would have been a better choice in this respect. Somewhere, at least, that would encourage me to bury those feelings and appear cold and aloof. But, here I was with a beautiful Irishman, surrounded by the most amorous culture in the world. Spending my days visiting dreamy châteaux bathed in golden sunlight, driving alongside the Loire, which surged with wild tides, and eating food that made your heart melt. Impressively, I kept my feelings quiet for five hot and sultry days. *Five* days. But, on the sixth night, I found myself restlessly awake in a hotel room, unable to sleep because of the passion that rang through me like a loud bell. If I don't say something, I thought, my chest will explode with emotion. And I don't think that would be a very pretty sight.

'Kevin?' I said, turning towards him in the dark.

'Yes?' he answered. I could make out the silhouette of his face. He was looking at me.

'I think I love you a bit.' I hoped the slightly ambiguous phrasing would soften the impact of my declaration a tad. And maybe cushion the blow of a rebuttal. (Naïve doesn't come close to it.) He was silent. The curtains ruffled gently in the warm night breeze.

'I think I love you too,' I heard Kevin say, softly. The words rained down on me like tiny drops of joy. And have continued to do so for the last eight years and counting.

CHAPTER FOURTEEN

****

I wrote this book because I discovered that ideas – which are invisible and abstract and untouchable – are the most powerful thing we have. Ideas can free us or enslave us. None of us have any real power other than the power to choose what to think. But what we think can change the whole world and our experience of it. I find that truth incredibly beautiful, because any one of us has the ability to free ourselves by adopting new ideas – whoever we are, wherever we are, and whenever we like. It would have been selfish to keep the ideas that liberated me all to myself. So, I've written them down in the hope that they will have an impact on others. Because all of us could do with a bit of life-changing stuff now and again.

The biggest lesson I learnt from Dylan was that our lives aren't defined by what we look like, or how our bodies work, or how wealthy we are, or what we own – no matter how much we're told they are – no matter how much we're made to feel they are. I know this because the defining factors in my life have been the love I received as a child and the way I chose to view myself and the world – as a kid, and then as an adult. I don't think I'm particularly unique and I'm willing to bet that those two factors play the biggest roles in shaping each one of us.

It's important that we understand what really creates suffering in the world. It's not physical or intellectual differences that we should be worrying about, but emotional neglect and unhealthy aspiration. That's what causes real damage, and that's what we should be using our minds to eradicate. Not difference. You can have the most able body in the world, piles of money in the bank, and oodles of beauty and talent – but if you're not given enough love and support early on, life will be a constant struggle. So, we should be trying to create a world that values and encourages love and compassion and diversity above all else. A world in which all parents, no matter what their economic backgrounds, have the necessary support to enable them to spend enough time showering their kid with love, without having to worry about paying the bills, losing their home, or being exploited. Kids don't need to be physically or intellectually 'perfect' – or have shiny toys or fashionable clothes – to be happy, they just need to feel cherished. If you can make your child feel indestructible, chances are they'll be more likely to deal with what life throws at them – however their body works. That's how to reduce suffering. Build a society around the things that people really need to be happy. And it's pretty much the same for all of us – no matter what body we inhabit. We need to be *loved*. Enough to make us able to love ourselves. It's that simple.

It feels odd at first, to try to love yourself, when you've spent so long doing the opposite. You feel like a bit of a dick looking in the mirror and saying, 'I like you.' Especially if you've been brought up in England. Being English means that anything in the 'loving yourself' zone feels entirely unnatural and wrong. The English are not programmed to *like* – let alone love – themselves. But if you can resist the urge to cringe with revulsion, it's worth a try.

Whatever body we're born into and whatever we look like, we all face a similar journey – to find self-acceptance and peace before we fade back into the universe. Which is why not caring about what others think of you or how you measure up to someone else's questionable ideals is the ultimate act of liberation.

I watched my Yaya become a recluse in the last years of her life because she lost what she considered her defining feature – her beauty. Once a vivacious goddess, she was now a little old lady with a curved back, saggy tummy and liver-spotted hands. Her face was still beautiful but age had taken away the person that she felt she was. It was sad to see her confined to her chair for hours, lapping up the poo juice of Spanish satellite TV, refusing to go out because she was ashamed of her appearance. I begged her to venture out with me.

'Come on, Yaya. Come to the park,' I'd say, taking her hands in mine.

'No, Chessie. I look awful. I no want people to see me

like this. What they think of me?' she replied, gazing into my eyes like a scared child.

'Maybe people will just think you're an eighty-year-old woman, which you are. You should be proud of yourself! Don't worry about what they think. Who cares?' I stared back at her, trying to charge her up with strength.

'I care. I no like the way I look,' she said ruefully, slumping back down in the chair that was now moulded to her shape.

'I'm wobbly. People stare at me. I don't care!' I smiled at her, still holding her warm tanned hands that I loved. Yaya tried to smile back but her eyes were sad.

'I no the same as you. I can't change.' She looked off into the distance and I knew she was just beyond my reach.

Three years later, Yaya was admitted to hospital. I visited her every afternoon. She seemed to look smaller in the hospital bed with each passing day. Her arms and legs were thin brown sticks under the blanket and her head was nearly lost on the huge pillows that propped her up. She stopped talking and our visits then consisted of long hugs and handholding and arm stroking and hair fluffing and back rubbing and face touching. I realised that this was the way I'd always communicated with my grandma, through touch.

Each time I saw her, I was struck by her body. It was such an old person's body. Her limbs were mostly bare and I couldn't help fixating on them. I hadn't been confronted with the realities of what an eighty-three-year-old woman looks like before. I saw how she had been shaped, without pity, by the rough hands of time. Her legs had bruises on them as well as an intricate maze of blue veins, and her arms and legs had too much skin hanging off their bony frames. Her mass of curls, once lush and brown, were white and tired, and her neck looked scrawny and too delicate to hold up her head. That'll be me one day, I thought. If I'm lucky enough to live that long. I could see how life had worn away her once ox-like strength and rendered her into this fragile being. She seemed to be in mourning for her youthful self but all I could feel was an overwhelming love for the failing body that had housed my beloved Yaya for so long.

As the weeks passed, I felt a growing appreciation towards her body for keeping her alive for all this time, for allowing my grandma to exist in this world. I realised that the tired shell she inhabited told the story of her life. I saw a beauty in it that I did not expect to see. A beauty that had grown out of love and pain and struggle and time. Through this old lady's body, I saw the process of life with my own eyes and it took away my fear. I wanted to appreciate my youth and health but to also understand that they were temporary. Above all, I saw that there is an intrinsic beauty in all stages of life, but that we have been taught to cherish only our youth and to fear our ageing. But I knew that I didn't want to dread growing old, because being old would be proof that I was still alive. And, while I am alive, I want to live without fear of myself, fear of my changing body, fear of time. I wish I could have made Yaya realise how beautiful she was. How I loved her body just because it was hers. How she shouldn't have been ashamed of herself. I wanted to scream at someone for robbing her of the ability to enjoy the last few years, for filling her head with vacuous lies. But there was nobody there.

On the fifth of January 2010, I walked into a funeral parlour with my mum. A wooden coffin rested by the wall with its lid open. We walked over with slow steps, keeping our eyes on the floor as we moved. We came to a stop by the coffin. I shut my eyes for a second, grateful to be holding my mum's arm. I raised my head tentatively and my eyes found Yaya, eyes closed, lying in front of me. I breathed in sharply. I had not seen her dead before. Her face was at peace. My eyes searched over her silent being. This was a body I was so used to touching, but I couldn't touch her any more. The pain wound its way around my heart like a serpent.

'I love you, Yaya,' I said quietly. I looked at her face again. I loved that face. I would never see it again. As my eyes cradled her for one last time, I saw the young girl she had once been, the blushing bride, the flirty housewife, the passionate woman, full of smiles and tempers and tears, the greying beauty who was afraid to leave the house. And here she was, at the end of her journey. Her body, so faithful to her and us, had finally given up. My heart pounded in my chest and, beneath the crushing grief, I felt a bolt of gratitude for life and love pulse through me.

Thanks for using some of your precious time on Earth to read this book. I really appreciate it. If our paths don't cross, I hope you have a great life.

Oh, and if you hate your job, chuck it in. Because life's way too short to waste time doing something you don't believe in.

A few years ago, I had a dream. It had such an impact on me that I wanted to share it with you. So what did I do? I wrote a poem.

One night
when dark had draped its cloak
around my heavy limbs
Like
Thick
Dark
Inky
Smoke
and silence had climbed
into my ear
waiting like a curled-up child
I had a dream.

I lay like dry leaves on the ground
old and grey
my pale lips
fading away
into nothing.
I knew I was about to die.
I was about to die.

I pushed open my eyes
And looked at the sky
for one last time.
I saw the sun
burning

churning
in space
Its fiery hands
warming my face.
I would never see it rise
explode to life in my eyes
again.
Or see it tumble down the sky
and into bed
its dusky head
laying down
on horizon's soft pillow.

The rain would never play
upon my cheek
and soak
the petals of my flesh
Alive and fresh
Like baby's toes.

I would never go hunting as a child
Through the wild
forest of table legs
and adult feet
complete
with the spears
and fears
of my
imagination.

Or leave my sleep
and discover
the first morning of a summer holiday
which tasted like
strawberries and, well,
sweet, sweet caramel.
The days stretching out before me
Winding like
A lazy
hazy
river
waiting for me to jump
straight in.

My dad would never pick me up
and spin me round
turning the ground
into a kaleidoscope
while I choked
with laughter
and after
begged for more.

My cheeks would not be painted blush
by my teenage crush
who stole my words
and my heart
with just one smile.

My lover's voice would not
pour over me like butterflies
fluttering down to my belly
and those eyes
those eyes of green
That I dived into
The first time I saw them.

I would never get lost
in my grandma's bosom
gasping for air
but only finding her perfume
which tickled my nose
like a scented breeze
and made me sneeze.

And I remembered
the hours, days, years
I worried about
my eyes, my nose, my ears
my teeth, my feet, my toes
my clothes,
my shoes,
And who's
my friend
and who was not
And what
Will I do?
Where will I go

live, work, grow?
I don't know.

I wished I could
get down on my hands and knees
and search
for all that time I frittered away
Like scattering leaves.
Gone for ever
And more precious
Than all the gold
in the earth.

Tears lined up like soldiers
behind my eyes
Waiting to fall
to their death
off the cliff
of my chin
as I begin
to mourn
the time I wasted.

I feel the gentle sounds of
sleep calling me.
I look to the sky,
and try to take the blue
with me
wherever I am going.

I remember we are made of stars
From all the corners of the universe
My weary frame has galaxies within
each atom
and that makes me smile.

I see the universe all at once
still
huge
eternal
Black.
And in that moment
I thank everything
for being alive.
I didn't have to be
But I was alive.
And for a short time
this rock in space was mine.

As my eyes start to close
All my words float away
And I wish
I yearn
I beg
I pray
for one more day.
Just
one
more
beautiful
day.

ACKNOWLEDGEMENTS

* * * *

Huge thanks to those who helped me write all these words down. Especially to the following amazing people for their incredible friendship, support and much-appreciated feedback: Mya Pope-Weidemann, Caitlin Walsh, Jen Brister, Bronwyn Boyle, David Jordan, Jenny Landreth, Mark Thomas, Jean Simon, Rochelle Gadd, Katie Barlow, Jeremy Hardy, Steve Coogan, Jonathan Ross, Jo Brand and Russell Brand. Special thanks my editor, Kate Moore, for her frankly insane levels of passion and enthusiasm, and to Emma Freud for making it all happen (I owe you a kidney, Emma). Many thanks also to the Arts Council UK who funded the 2012 tour of my show, which was the inspiration for this book. Millions more thanks to my mum, dad and my best bud, Raoul, for their unwavering love and advice – I owe you each two of my kidneys (maths never was my strong point). Finally, thanks to Kevin for reading every word more times than one could fairly expect, giving me awesome notes, and being such a beautiful sight to wake up to each, er, afternoon.